THE REAL WAR ON WOMEN

Time's Up for Radical Feminism and the Democrats' Liberal, Progressive, Socialist Agenda

By Jennifer Kerns

All-American Media LLC
ISBN: 979-8-218-07664-1

ALL-AMERICAN

New York City | Oklahoma City
All-American Media LLC
AllAmericanMedia.com

TheRealWarOnWomen.com

Dedication

To my family & friends

To everyone who's ever given me the job of being your voice & representation in the media, the experience has been the dream job of a lifetime

TABLE OF CONTENTS

PREFACE/INTRODUCTION

CHAPTERS

PREFACE

I first heard the phrase "war on women" in 2013 when I was involved with a focus group in the battleground state of Colorado. The term had already been around for a while. In 1989 a radical feminist named Andrea Dworkin penned the term in a book introduction, and in 1991 it was picked up by feminist Susan Faludi in her famous tome, *Backlash.* The die was cast: Republican Party policies harm women.

It's a catchy slogan – albeit an erroneous one – that liberals have continued to use throughout the decades, from Code Pink attacks in 2004 on President George W. Bush, to then-Supreme-Court-nominee Brett Kavanaugh in 2018 as he was forced to refresh his memory on matters such as "Timmy and Squee" and "beer."

The narrative has become sort of an urban legend, winding its way through every midterm election season, wiggling into the media vernacular, and landing atop every Presidential debate stage.

I became determined to fact-check whether there truly was a "war on women" and if so, had Republicans perpetrated it?

What I found was truly shocking.

The war on women exists, alright. However, it's the polar opposite of what Democrats have been telling you.

Every policy position pushed by Democrats today has harmed women. On a range of topics from "defunding the police" – which has increased violent, sexual and criminal assaults on women, particularly minority women – to Democrat-led lockdowns that forced 2 Million women to run for the emergency exits of their careers, leading to the largest exodus of women from the workforce since the feminist movement began – women were undoubtedly harmed. Today, young girls continue to be harmed as Title IX is tossed far afield and our highest-ranking leaders refuse to answer even the most basic question about what the biological definition of a "woman" is. The worst part? Feminists have stood idly and turned a blind eye as their most liberal friends passed policies and hurled executive orders that harmed women at every turn.

In the wake of the U.S. Supreme Court's *Dobbs* decision to overturn *Roe v. Wade*, I knew that Democrats would once again set out to convince women that the *only* issue that matters in American politics today is the issue of "choice." However, as I waded through issue after issue it became clear to me that Democrats and their feminist friends today don't give women much of a choice on much of anything. I will prove the case in this book.

It my goal to set the record straight once and for all and to expose The *Real* War on Women. When I served as a writer/researcher for a popular U.S. Presidential Debate for FOX News, I was aware that the questions I researched would undergo intense media scrutiny. Likewise, I have painstakingly laid out the case for *The Real War on Women* in a well-researched, nearly 300-page book with more than 74,000 words and 280 endnotes which I welcome fact checkers to challenge.

Lastly, I wrote this book because my girlfriends who drop their kids off at school share with me that they are bullied in the car drop-off line by the adult version of "Mean Girls" standing around in their puffer vests, sipping from their YETI tumblers. If my girlfriends dared to say they liked Trump or any Republican, for that matter, they were immediately dressed down in front of everyone. They put out an S.O.S. They needed solid backup in the form of facts and figures. A handbook, of sorts, on all of the issues.

This book is my love letter to them.

It is my hope that this books finds itself on the dashboard of every mom in the school drop-off line, under the arm of every dad who is fighting for his kids at the school board meeting, and on the desk of every politician from the West Coast to Washington, D.C.

Thank you for reading.

Jennifer Kerns

THE *REAL* WAR ON WOMEN: GOVERNMENT LOCKDOWNS

No one has claimed to be a better friend to working women than feminists.

From fighting for equal pay to advocating for women in the workforce, the Second Wave of Feminism in the 1960s and 1970s prided itself on its solidarity with the sisterhood.

However, that promise of solidarity was broken when feminists stood idly by during the COVID-19 pandemic as Democrat officials ordered deeply intrusive government lockdowns and enacted policies which had a debilitating effect on millions of American women in the workplace.

How It Began

At the very beginning of the pandemic, we were all scared. No one knew quite what to expect.

Unsure about the virus and its ultimate impact, most reasonable Americans were willing to pause their lives for two weeks to "stop the spread" and "flatten the curve" in the early months of 2020.

However, it wasn't long before Democrat leaders from Los Angeles to New York City decided to "never waste a crisis" and take extraordinary advantage of the moment by enacting wide-ranging lockdowns from coast to coast.

What was ultimately asked of Americans — and of women, specifically — went far beyond any patriotic duty. In fact, it was downright abusive.

White House Daily Briefings: Must-See TV

In the early days of the pandemic, Republicans were actually the first to protect Americans from COVID-19. President Trump stopped all incoming flights from China in late January 2020 and subsequently stopped the flow of inbound flights from other at-risk countries. These quick actions are credited with saving countless lives.

Not yet understanding just how serious a pandemic could be, Democrats chided Trump on these early decisions, even called him "racist" for making such moves. They suggested it was an overblown reaction.

Meantime, Democrats were spotted out and about with no masks, virtually shrugging off this new thing called the "coronavirus." In mid-March, Speaker of the House Nancy Pelosi was caught by a local TV station strolling the streets of San Francisco, maskless, encouraging constituents to get out and enjoy the Lunar New Year celebrations. *You were racist if you didn't,* she insinuated. Her staff, also maskless and not bothering to socially distance, nodded in approval.

Senator Joe Biden, a mere presidential contender at the time, also held a rally on March 9, 2020 in which he appeared on-stage, maskless, with other maskless guests including Senator Kamala Harris, Senator Cory Booker and Michigan Governor Gretchen Whitmer. None of them socially-distanced and in fact, they all hugged, touched, shook hands, and talked closely, right into one another's mouths. The crowd of hundreds, maybe thousands, of loyal Democrat Party supporters were also maskless and also not socially distanced at the televised event.

Just six days later, New York City would shut down and come to a complete standstill. It turned out that the Democrats were wrong, and President Trump was right. The coronavirus was, in fact, a serious public health issue that was being appropriately handled by the Trump White House.

Trump took to the TV airwaves, updating the American people with play-by-play and day-by-day updates that we haven't seen outside of wartime footing. The daily briefings rivaled the "Stormin' Norman" Schwarzkopf briefings of the 1992 Gulf War.

The daily White House "Coronavirus Task Force" briefings became must-see TV. One top TV executive shared with me that Trump's daily coronavirus briefings made ratings soar. More specifically, the ratings with women went through the roof.

As women make 80% of the decisions on healthcare in the U.S., naturally women were tuned in like never before.[1] The nation was hanging on the president's every word. Trump's daytime television appeal was becoming a phenomenon with which "Days of Our Lives" nor "The View" could compete.

In effect, Trump was *winning the women's vote.*

Trump had stepped on the third rail of liberal politics: thou shall not become more popular with women than Democrats.

I believe it was at this precise time when Democrats realized that Trump was skunking them — in a presidential election year, no less. Democrats wanted a piece of the action. They wanted to seize upon the fear.

Almost in concert, Democrats donned their masks and went to work enacting the political trick they knew had worked so well for overbearing, authoritarian leaders so many times in history: *fear sells.*

Soon, liberal governors from Andrew Cuomo to Gavin Newsom were holding similar daily briefings as were liberal mayors Eric Garcetti and Bill DeBlasio. If Trump was going to get free network TV airtime then by God, they were, too.

Democrat governors — from New Jersey Governor Phil Murphy, to New York Governor Andrew Cuomo, to California Governor Gavin Newsom, to Michigan Governor Gretchen Whitmer — appeared in rolling press conferences, which were carried live on TV. One by one, each Democrat governor summarily enacted lockdowns then extended them week after week, then month after month.

It's hard to fathom, but less than a half-dozen Democrats were able to obliterate small businesses, destroy an entire national restaurant industry and disrupt the largest regional economies in America. They nearly destroyed America's economy as well.

The economic devastation created by Democrat-led lockdowns has our economy still reeling more than two years later which thus far according to Harvard University has cost our country at least $16 trillion.[2]

Sadly, no one paid a higher price during the pandemic than women.

Women in the Workplace

One of the places women were hurt most by Democrat lockdowns was the workplace.

Jobs reports from the U.S. Department of Labor show that a stunning 2 million women dropped out of the workforce during the COVID-19 crisis.

Women faced an inordinate amount of challenges. Pre-pandemic, 79% of women already made their household healthcare decisions, 77% reported they were the ones who ushered children to doctor's appointments and were the primary helpers with homework.[3] Those duties naturally escalated to new heights during the COVID-19 crisis.

Democrat-run states made life needlessly difficult for working women.

The proof is in the numbers.

During the early months of the pandemic, the majority of working women were able to do their jobs remotely just like millions of other Americans. However, in September 2020 something changed.

The bottom fell out of the labor force, and it all had to do with women.

In September 2020, nearly 1 million women dropped out of the workforce (865,000 women, to be exact.) The timing just so happened to coincide with the two largest cities in America — New York and Los Angeles — preventing millions of their children from going back to school.

Faced with a decision to either go back to work or stay home and ensure their children were educated, mothers self-selected out of the workforce.

How can one be so sure? The timing of data speaks volumes.

The first exodus of American women from the workforce occurred in September 2020. The second mass exit happened in January 2021. It just so happened to be around the time that the second half of the school year was scheduled to begin. In Democrat-led cities, parents found themselves having to make another difficult choice: with schools still closed, who would stay home with the children?

The result: Another 1 million moms left the workforce.

President-elect Joe Biden had a direct impact on this.

After being inaugurated that month, in January of 2021, Biden recommended that schools in some of America's largest cities remain closed for his "First 100 Days," even though America was already nearly a full year into the COVID-19 crisis.

He asked for a 100-day pause.

As a result, the largest school districts in the nation — run by Democrats, who were no doubt funded by Democrat-run teachers' unions, who were now supported by the incoming president himself — again made the devastating decision to keep schools shuttered.

At no other time in American history did women ever exit a room so fast. Think about it: In a short period of just six months, 2 million women left the American workforce. It is the largest exodus of women from the workforce since the feminist movement began 50 years ago and in fact, the largest exit ever recorded in U.S. history.

One would think this would set off alarm bells among advocates of working women.

Oddly, the news got nary a look from feminists who for decades based their very existence on the importance of women's participation in the workforce.

For decades, feminists and their Democrat Party allies preached that women's mere existence in the workplace made a difference. Former First Lady Michelle Obama once said, "No country can ever truly flourish if it stifles the potential of its women and deprives itself of the contributions of half its citizens."

However, under the thumb of Democrat-led lockdowns, women were most definitely being squeezed out of the workforce.

Feminists who once claimed to care about women in the workforce turned a deaf ear to the sisterhood because they perceived there was a "greater good" being pushed during the pandemic — universal basic income, pandemic unemployment assistance checks, and talk of universal free childcare[4] — all outweighed the plights facing individual women and their tough choices.

Instead feminists sat idly by, clapping for their liberal heroes and serving as enablers to Democratic overlords like Cuomo, Newsom, New York Mayor Bill DeBlasio and Los Angeles Mayor Eric Garcetti who were all instituting lockdown policies that were having disastrous effects on women.

It's ironic, really, as the feminist movement so often complains about the effects of Republican Party's policies on women. As with so many other issues explored in this book, the exact opposite turned out to be true.

Democrats were the ones who did the damage.

Attack on Women Small Business Owners

For some reason during the pandemic, liberals decided without a shred of evidence that small businesses were the greatest threat to America.

Naturally, liberals don't understand business or business owners in general so it's understandable how they missed the mark. (One doesn't have to travel back in history terribly far to remember President Obama's infamous remark to business owners, "You didn't build that.")

Perhaps it's their old Marxist way of thinking that leads them to equate "business" with white male power.

Perhaps it's just that Democrats fail to realize what it takes to make a business work.

Whatever the case, despite fancying themselves champions of women, Democrats failed to realize the incredibly significant role that women play in running American businesses in modern times.

So it happened that lockdowns continued to be outright hostile to American businesses — nearly half of which are owned by the very women that liberals claim they support.

Here's the proof, by the numbers:

In 2019 B.C. (what I call, "Before COVID"), women owned more than 11.6 million businesses in the United States and employed almost 9 million people according to American Express OPEN's report titled, "The State of Women-Owned Businesses."[5]

Women represented 39% of all privately-run businesses.

According to National Association of Women-Owned Business (NAWBO), women-owned businesses generated a whopping $1.7 trillion in sales each year before the pandemic.

Liberal politicians seem to have missed the correlation that with women well-integrated into the business world in the year 2020, draconian lockdowns and emergency executive orders that harmed the business community would be direct hits to women.

In this instance, Democrats delivered the knockout punch.

Yelp[6] reported that 800 American businesses closed, per day, from mid-March through September 2020. With nearly half of businesses owned by women, women therefore took a nearly equal hit as male business owners. This happened in the most populous cities, where Democrats were in charge of lockdown policies.

Sadly, Yelp reported that of the American businesses that closed, more than 60 percent of the closures were permanent. With a nearly equal number of these businesses owned by women, that meant crushed dreams and lifelong savings drained for women.

Despite the fact that liberals and feminists often promote the importance of women's equity in business ownership, their policies had the diametrically opposite effect on women.

The truth is that Democrat attacks on businesses were an attack on women business owners. Their policies caused a giant step backward for women's equity in business ownership, and their sisters in the feminist movement didn't raise a single red flag about it. It is a dismal record that both the Democrat Party and the feminist movement should be forced to carry around with them, not just into the 2022 midterms and the 2024 presidential elections, but long after the COVID-19 pandemic has left us.

Attack on Women of Color

Feminists will never admit it, but the Democrat Party's monstrous lockdowns hurt women of color as well.

More than 5.4 million businesses in America pre-COVID were majority-owned by women of color, according to the National Association of Women Business Owners.[7]

As of 2019, those minority-women-owned firms employed 2.1 million people and generated $361 billion in annual revenue according to American Express.

The year prior to the pandemic, 64% of new women-owned businesses were started by women of color.

Latina female-owned businesses had grown more than 87%.

In fact, women started more than 1,800 net new businesses per day in the year prior to the pandemic.

The National Bureau of Economic Research reported that in just the first few months of the pandemic, the number of African-American business owners plummeted from 1.1 million to 640,000 — a 41 percent drop.

"Latinx" business activity fell by 32 percent.

Immigrant businesses overall experienced a 36 percent drop in business.

Female business owners experienced a 25 percent drop in business activities.

Yet the big boys such as Costco, WalMart, Target, and others were allowed to remain open in liberal states.

As liberal officials kept many small businesses shuttered, WalMart clocked a stunning $141 billion in revenue. The Brookings Institute reported that from October 2020 to October 2021, WalMart earned an extra $1.8 billion in profit — a 56 percent gain — mostly due to COVID-era shopping.

Amazon also clocked record sales. While small businesses were squashed in liberal cities such as New York and Los Angeles, Amazon set astounding records.

For all their lip service loathing "when the rich get richer," liberal politicians presided over one of the fastest accelerations of wealth for some of the richest families in America.

The Brookings Institute reported that Jeff Bezos and the WalMart heirs grew $116 billion richer during the pandemic.[8]

There is nothing wrong with the free market, of course — consumers make the ultimate buying choice — but when liberal politicians socially engineer the selection of choices from the outset, it is no longer the free market at work.

Once again, liberal politicians went against the very class of people they claim to protect.

Sadly, as of August 2020, two out of three minority-owned businesses (66%) expressed concern about having to close permanently according to a report by the U.S. Chamber of Commerce and MetLife.[9]

As for feminists, they didn't critique a single Democrat politician for the overbearing lockdowns. As liberal leaders from New York to Los Angeles created an extremely uneven playing field, they crushed the dreams of women small business owners and women of color, and feminists didn't say a word.

Attack on Women-Owned Restaurants & Female Restaurant Workers

Women didn't just own businesses in 2020, they happened to owned businesses that were greatly affected by liberal lockdowns — restaurants, in particular.

Anyone with a television during the pandemic witnessed that restaurants were particularly targeted by Democrat city and state officials and arguably, they suffered more than any other businesses during the lockdowns.

In cities like New York and Los Angeles, restaurant owners became public enemy #1.

In New York City, restaurants were allowed only to provide takeout and delivery. In California, even outdoor patios were closed even though Dr. Anthony Fauci himself had once said that coronavirus could survive no more than a few minutes in areas of direct sunlight and 80-degree temperatures.

DeBlasio and Garcetti sent their goon squads to check on whether restaurants were requiring staff and customers to wear masks. If they weren't, they were written up.

The Democrat-led harassment of restaurant operators is even more shocking when you consider that the National Restaurant Association reported that more than 50 percent of restaurants in America have women either as full owners or co-owners.

The National Restaurant Association also reported that 45 percent of restaurant managers are women, an average higher than other industries in which women only account for 38 percent of management positions.

The Bureau of Labor Statistics also reported that 70 percent of waitstaff are females and that women held 56 percent of jobs overall in the restaurant industry (compared with 47 percent of jobs in the broader U.S. economy).

The National Restaurant Association also reported that 65 percent of women have worked in a restaurant at some point during their career.

That didn't stop liberal politicians from harassing them.

The full negative impact on these female owners, managers and restaurant workers remains to be fully seen. The National Restaurant Association stated in March 2021 that even they didn't know exactly "how many women-owned or operated restaurants had to close in the last year" because the numbers were so overwhelming, it was difficult to place a precise number on it. It appears that the closures were so numerous. they had just plum given up keeping track.

The National Restaurant Association released a report on August 31, 2021 alerting the industry that they believed women would be instrumental in restaurants' recovery (as women often are after a disaster)[10] yet they cautioned that many challenges still awaited the industry. Tantamount among these challenges were the threats of food inflation, fuel prices (for trucks that deliver the food), and staffing shortages[11] — all additional challenges have also been created by President Biden and liberals in Congress.

In other words, a veritable mess if you're one of the female restaurant owners or co-owners of 50 percent of restaurants in America[12] who are attempting to recover from a disastrous year.

How any female business owner could vote for a Democrat after their party's disastrous path of destruction through women-owned businesses and women's places in the workforce is beyond comprehension.

The "Fourth Shift" for Women: Homeschooling the Children

At the same time Democrats were attacking women's rights to work, they were also — ironically — offloading more work onto women.

After shutting down businesses and choking off their cities, Democrat leaders foisted upon American moms the monumental task of homeschooling their kids and serving as tutors and proxies for schoolwork and screen time.

This phenomenon of the additional workload of caring for the children has often been labeled the "Fourth Shift" — work that women do in addition to their jobs, including the care and feeding of their families and their extracurricular activities in their communities.

In the case of the lockdowns, an extra workload was caused by Democrats and their draconian lockdowns in liberal cities and states, yet once again nary a peep was heard from feminists as women even in the most progressive cities fell backwards to an era that feminists once used to hate — the 1950s where women stayed at home, cared for the kids, and tended to the homefront.

For years, feminists have complained that women do most of the housework, despite having an almost equal representation in the workforce.

Feminists have previously called for radical ideas including that women should be unionized and paid for their chores at home. Can you imagine what the pay would have been for professional mothers, lawyers and engineers who suddenly became teachers in the midst of the pandemic?

The fact that Democrat politicians and their feminist friends didn't appear to take into account the impact of school closures on career women shows once again that they don't really care about the advances of women. They only cared about power and control.

The Damage to Minority Moms

Democrats don't appear to have cared about women of color, either, as the burden on parents in school districts with minority students was even worse.

In predominantly minority districts such as the Los Angeles Unified School District, school doors were closed for more than a year.[13] When school districts in wealthier, white, neighboring areas re-opened but their schools did not, desperate LAUSD parents tried all sorts of protests — including a Zoom blackout[14] in the Spring of 2021, to no avail.

By comparison, wealthier areas such as Pasadena and the Kardashians' enclave of Calabasas reopened their schools, while minority children and parents were stuck in the ghettos of the garish LAUSD system held captive by the inept policies of their Democrat leaders and the selfishness of the liberal-led teachers' unions in those districts.

Liberals were of little help.

The Los Angeles Times reported that the best thing to do if your child was locked out of an LAUSD school was to quit your job and "file for unemployment."[15]

Think about that.

As a working mother and a woman of color in a state representing the world's fifth-largest economy and which claims to care about women, unemployment was your only good option under the trifecta of Governor Newsom, Mayor Garcetti and liberal teachers' unions.

Disgraceful.

The disadvantages of year-long school closures to minority children and the disruption to their working parents during those 18 months cannot be understated, just as the additional work for mothers everywhere may never be able to be fully measured.

Women's Mental Health Crisis during Democrat Lockdowns

So much of the Democrat Party's and feminists' tropes today preach of the need to take care of women in society. From universal healthcare to proposals for more government-funded mental health programs, one would think that liberals were the only heroes looking out for women's health.

Yet, an interesting thing happened specifically after Democrat-led lockdowns were extended for additional weeks, then months, throughout the COVID-19 pandemic.

Women in America had a mental health crisis.

To be sure, women are more emotional creatures (present and accounted for here) and thereby suffered the most anxiety in the earliest days of the pandemic. A University of Chicago Medicine report showed in the first few weeks of the pandemic, women suffered from things like "food insecurity," domestic disturbances and other health-related socioeconomic risks (HSRS).

However, upon lockdowns being extended predominantly in liberal-led, blue cities and blue states week after week then month after month, women's mental health began to spiral.

A stunning 83% of women reported an increase in depression during those months[16] compared to just 36% of men.

Overall, 57% of women reported that their mental health generally had declined specifically throughout the lockdowns, compared to just 37% of men.[17]

An entire year after the pandemic first started, *Atlantic Health* reported that women were seriously struggling. With one in 10 women having no choice but to quit a job, the taxation on mental health had affected women's health, career, sleep and appetite.[18]

Yet feminists did not question their party on the factors that led to this mental health crisis, even as it was becoming clear that their policies were having a direct, specific, increasingly negative effect on women's mental health.

Churches Shuttered

I believe part of the reason many women began to feel depressed, anxious and hopeless is that Democrat government officials also choked off women's support systems.

The onset of job losses, telecommuting and homeschooling caused women to lose touch with other human beings who once helped them stay grounded and sane.

With churches closed, women lost their spiritual connections outside of the home.

According to Pew Research, more than one-third of Americans (31%) attended church on a regular basis prior to the COVID-19 pandemic. Of those church-going Americans, women tended to "lean in" to their faith.

Prior to the pandemic and the Democrat lockdowns, 7 out of 10 Christian women stated that their faith was "very important in their lives" compared to 62% of men.[19]

According to Pew Research, Christian woman also attended church services in higher percentages than men (though in Mormon churches, the gender ratio was about the same.)

Prior to the pandemic, 74% of Christian women also prayed privately and participated in devotionals, compared to 60% of Christian men and just 49% of Catholic men.

It is clear that women relied upon their faith in their daily lives.

Yet liberal leaders such as California Governor Newsom were particularly hard on churches, shuttering them in the earliest days of the pandemic and not relenting until over a year later. (A year later!)

Think Californians don't go to church? Think again. Gallup reports that California's church-going population prior to the pandemic was 37%.[20] This means that over one-third of California's 40 million people were kept from praying and seeking spiritual support during these times.

Democrat orders to shut down churches and other religious institutions were, first and foremost, unconstitutional as they violated the First Amendment which states that government shall not infringe on a citizen's right to worship. Yet with their policies, Democrats alienated millions of women and separated them from spiritual outlets that supported their mental health.

However, perhaps even more grotesque was the fact that the Democrats' feminist counterparts — who rail against religion regularly — seemed to snicker, even as women were clearly paying the price.

Conclusion

The truth is, Democrat governors and mayors ordered lockdowns which hurt women of all walks of life, races and religions.

If feminists today were true to their stated beliefs, they would be doing what they did in January 2017 — marching in the streets and "screaming at the sky" about how cruel and sexist their leaders were, yet they continue to cover for their male counterparts in the Democrat

Party and serving as enablers of power-hungry-male misdeeds against all womankind.

The next time the media or someone on social media states it was the "pandemic" that cost Americans their jobs, be sure to share the finer point: the pain came mostly to women and it came directly from Democrat-forced lockdowns in Democrat-led cities and states, which led to the largest exit of women from the workforce ever recorded in American history.

HOMEWORK

> To help prevent lockdowns in the future, read my friend and colleague Cheryl K. Chumley's book, "Lockdown: The Socialist Plan to Take Away Your Freedom." In it, Cheryl details the extraordinary powers that Democrat leaders and government bureaucrats invoked in order to to keep Americans locked away in their homes. Even more alarming, she explains how the left today is using those same pandemic policies to attempt to gain even more control over Americans' lives.

REFERENCES:

[1] Women Make 80% of the Healthcare Decisions in America
https://news.ohsu.edu/2017/05/11/women-responsible-for-most-health-decisions-in-the-home

[2] COVID-19 Cost America $16 Trillion as of Fall 2021: Harvard University
https://news.harvard.edu/gazette/story/2020/11/what-might-covid-cost-the-u-s-experts-eye-16-trillion/

[3] 79% of Women Make Healthcare Decisions at Home, 77% Usher Children to Doctor Appointments
https://healthwaresystems.com/2020/01/22/women-as-healthcare-decision-makers/

[4] Brookings Institution: Government Should Offer Free Childcare

https://www.brookings.edu/essay/why-has-covid-19-been-especially-harmful-for-working-women/

[5] American Express OPEN's "The State of Women-Owned Businesses"
https://s1.q4cdn.com/692158879/files/doc_library/file/2019-state-of-women-owned-businesses-report.pdf

[6] Yelp's Report on Business Closures
https://www.yelpeconomicaverage.com/business-closures-update-sep-2020.html

[7] Women of color are majority owners of 5.4 million firms in the U.S.
https://www.nawbo.org/resources/women-business-owner-statistics

[8] Brookings Institute: WalMart and Amazon wealth soared during COVID
https://www.brookings.edu/blog/the-avenue/2020/12/22/amazon-and-walmart-have-raked-in-billions-in-additional-profits-during-the-pandemic-and-shared-almost-none-of-it-with-their-workers/

[9] U.S. Chamber of Commerce and MetLife Poll: Pandemic Hit Minority-Owned Small Businesses Disproportionately Hard
https://www.uschamber.com/press-release/coronavirus-pandemic-hits-minority-owned-small-businesses-disproportionately-hard-new

[10] Bureau of Labor Statistics – Women in the workplace in the restaurant industry
https://www.restaurant.org/articles/news/women-get-ready-to-kick-start-the-industry

[11] Even after surviving pandemic, now "Labor and food costs remain top challenges"
https://www.restaurant.org/association-releases-mid-year-soi

[12] More than 50% of restaurant owners or co-owners are female
https://www.rewardsnetwork.com/blog/state-women-food-industry-2017/

[13] Los Angeles Unified School District: Closed for a year, 49 percent of parents want kids back in schools
https://www.nbclosangeles.com/news/local/la-unified-school-district-reopens-all-schools-as-of-this-week-after-a-year-of-closures/2581931/

[14] LAUSD parents plan Zoom blackout protest
https://abc7.com/lausd-when-will-reopen-los-angeles-unified-school-district-zoom-blackout/10352147/

[15] L.A. Times: Kid still not in school? You may be eligible for unemployment
https://www.latimes.com/business/newsletter/2020-07-21/fall-school-closures-unemployment-benefits-child-care-business

[16] 83% of Women Severely Depressed after Pandemic, Lockdowns
https://axiawh.com/resources/covid-mental-health/

[17] University of Chicago Medicine Report on Women's Mental Health
https://www.uchicagomedicine.org/forefront/research-and-discoveries-articles/women-and-mental-health-in-the-pandemic-study

[18] Atlantic Health: Women's Mental Health Showed Serious Declines a Year after Pandemic Began
https://www.atlantichealth.org/about-us/stay-connected/news/content-central/2021/womens-mental-health.html

[19] Pew Research: 31% of Americans attend church; Women rely upon Church more than Men
https://www.pewresearch.org/fact-tank/2018/04/06/christian-women-in-the-u-s-are-more-religious-than-their-male-counterparts/

[20] 37% of Californians identify as Church-goers: 2013
https://news.gallup.com/poll/1690/religion.aspx

THE GREEN NEW DEAL IS A RAW DEAL FOR WOMEN

Since the day she took office, Congress member Alexandria Ocasio-Cortez has been pushing "The Green New Deal" — a $93-trillion-dollar boondoggle that professes to save the planet from doom and gloom while absolutely fleecing Americans' pockets.

For all of the ballyhoo over the Green New Deal, there has never actually been a "deal." The Green New Deal has never passed muster in the United States Congress; it's never received an up or down vote; it's never been agreed upon by both parties; and no president has signed it into law either by regular order nor executive order.

That's right, the Green New Deal does not actually exist.

For as little as we know about it, the landscape that the Green New Deal has the potential to cover is vast, and therefore it has the ability to creep into the daily lives of all Americans.

The worst part of the Green New Deal is that it specifically targets America's free markets, and it attacks the very capitalism which has helped elevate millions of women throughout American history.

Oddly enough, the Green New Deal also limits "choice" — the *one* thing liberals preach they care so much about. That such a draconian program has been dreamed up by a woman is particularly jarring; after all, feminism as long proclaimed to promote freedom of choice and autonomy from the government, yet the Green New Deal offers anything but either. It also stands to hurt women the most.

First Things First: Hypocrisy

First of all, if you ever want to know how serious Democrats truly believe a crisis is, look not at their speeches — instead, look at their actions.

Just like the COVID theatrics they perpetrated against the American people every day for the span of two years, Democrat Party leaders haven't been walking the walk on climate change prevention, either.

For all of her talk about the Green New Deal, AOC herself has not changed her living habits. That should tell you something regarding how much of an imminent crisis she actually thinks climate change is.

A review of the expenses for which AOC requested to be reimbursed while running for Congress gives us a glimpse inside the daily habits of AOC. It's shockingly instructive about the choices she makes on matters such as methods of transportation, travel arrangements and carbon emissions. AOC's own campaign finance paperwork shows that she most definitely did not follow her own advice about how Americans must change the way they live in order to "save the planet."

It turns out, just as she and her colleagues were lecturing Americans about having an addiction to fossil fuels, AOC dabbled in a bit of the petrol herself.

The hypocrisy began early in her campaign. In 2018, FOX News reported that AOC took 160 trips via Uber from April through June that year, amounting to roughly $4,000.[21] She took another 90 rides in a car service named Juno. That wouldn't be a problem for say, a Republican candidate, but AOC at the time was railing against what she considered the piggish use of fossil fuels. (She was also railing against Uber itself for its labor practices yet still giving them business — a hypocrisy we'll visit some other time).

According to *The New York Post*, AOC took Uber-style rideshare services more than 1,000 times throughout her campaign, amounting to approximately $30,000 in charges. Even worse? It wasn't as if she couldn't find transportation. The New York City subway system was just 138 feet away from the front door of her campaign office.[22]

You see, far-left politicians today are pushing ideas that are so radical and restrictive that they can't even live under the rules themselves. However, once they become politicians, they know they can live by a different set of rules.

The problem with the Green New Deal is that the rest of America will be forced to suffer under the policies and programs set forth by this group of climate fascists.

Radical, self-described socialist AOC warned in a speech that "the world is ending in 12 years," a famous trope from Al Gore's "An Inconvenient Truth" film tour where he suggested that the world would imminently end due to global warming. (Liberals later had to change the phrase "global warming" to "climate change" to better suit the cooler weather pattern around the globe. What a farce!)

After we failed to career to our deaths to the disappointment of Gore and others in the climate activism movement, AOC raised questions about the kind of lives she might ask Americans to *live* under her Green New Deal. She dared to suggest that every human being on planet earth is basically a liability and that Americans must ask themselves a "legitimate question: Is it OK still to have children?"

The fact that AOC would dare to ask fellow Americans to question their own families' existence and to forgo starting families, when she herself can't even forgo a ride to dinner or a campaign meeting tells us a lot about whom exactly is going to pay the ultimate price for the Green New Deal.

Make no mistake, the cost will be high for the average American but especially for women who wish to exercise their right to have a baby, start a household and ah yes, have to figure out how to pay for a nearly $100-trillion-dollar price tag for AOC's plan when 2 million of those women are still struggling to get out from under the massive economic damage that Democrat Party leaders caused women throughout the pandemic.

Green New Deal? More like a raw deal for women and for anyone who wants to drive a car, have a baby and live a life of freedom in America.

Even Bigger Hypocrisy

Even greater than AOC's own hypocrisy is the hypocrisy of her friends in Hollywood, media, the fashion industry and big government who talk the talk but don't walk the walk when it comes to saving the environment.

Sure, we've all seen the likes of Leonardo DiCaprio and former Secretary of State John Kerry jetting off to green summits. We've seen the private jets lined up on the runways at the Paris Climate Accord Summit. Just one private jet operating for one hour produces two tons of CO_2. In fact, the 1% elites of the world cause 50% of the world's aviation emissions.[23]

However, it goes far beyond Leo DiCaprio and the global elites.

Right here in America, whole industries are contributing to much bigger waste and pollution atrocities that AOC and her friends should care about, but they don't.

Hollywood

Liberal Hollywood is one of the biggest waste-filled industries on the planet. With its lavish movie sets, just one large movie production can leave behind "225 tons of scrap metal, nearly 50 tons of construction and set debris, and 72 tons of food waste," according to *The Los Angeles Times.*[24] That's a lot of craft service tables!

However, Hollywood's carbon footprint is just as big.

The Guardian newspaper reported that the average film production produces 500 tons of CO_2 emissions, which is the same as running 108 cars for a whole year.

That's just the "average" movie set. A film project with a budget of $50 million can produce at least 4,000 tons of CO_2. Films with even bigger budgets, well, you get the drift: the footprint is even greater. So much for our superheroes!

The Fashion Industry

The liberal-run fashion industry also has a dirty little secret. It is also secretly at odds with Mother Earth.

The fashion industry produces four percent (4%) of the world's pollution with a shocking 92 million tons of textile waste every year.[25] This means the equivalent of one garbage truck of textile waste is either placed in a landfill or incinerated every second. [26] Literally every second! While you were reading this sentence, four garbage trucks were filled with fashion waste.

Remember this the next time one of the glossy fashion magazines — which are ironically, printed on paper — lecture Americans about their consumption.

Starbucks

Liberal-run Starbucks is also one of the biggest offenders. The liberal company — which has lectured Americans on everything from labor practices to defunding the police — uses more than 8,000 paper cups per minute[27] — per minute! — which leads to more than 4 billion Starbucks cups per year.

Nearly 2 million trees are killed every year for those cups. According to the organization Clean Water Action, the cups aren't even really recyclable since they are technically lined with a sheer plastic coating. In fact, only four American cities actually allow Starbucks cups to be recycled.

Gaming

Even AOC's fun little video games are a huge problem for the planet. After AOC and Rep. Ilhan Omar made a surprise appearance playing the popular video game "Among Us," which was live-streamed on the social media platform Twitch, I delved into what this fun little hobby of AOC's is actually costing the environment.

In an article titled, "Next-Gen Gaming is an Environmental Nightmare," *WIRED Magazine* reports that U.S. gaming platforms "represent 34 terawatt-hours" of energy use per year[28] — that is more than Sen. Joe Manchin's entire state of West Virginia uses in power each year.

Even worse, the popular gaming consoles used by AOC and her friends reportedly produce the same carbon dioxide emissions as 5 million cars per year, and those emissions are on the rise as the popularity of gaming increases.

Even more piggish? Waste from discarded gaming consoles contributes to approximately 10% of the 4.7 million tons of e-waste generated every year, according to the United Nations' Global E-Waste Monitor.[29]

Oops. Saving the planet is hard!

It turns out even for AOC and her liberal friends, from Hollywood to high fashion to yep, even Starbucks, life would be nearly impossible living under her Green New Deal.

"Conserve"-atives Were the First Environmentalists

Before we go any further in the discussion on how to keep the planet beautiful and more importantly, livable, it's important to note that conservatives aren't anti-environmentalist. In fact, conservatives were the first to conserve energy and promote the importance of the conservation of our natural resources.

First and foremost, it is at the core of our name. "Conserve"-ative. True fiscal conservatives love not having to pay a penny more than needed for energy, utilities, and day-to-day living expenses. It's who we are. We are a penny-pinching bunch.

The conservative movement is littered (proverbially speaking, of course!) with prominent figures who were on-the-record for over the last century as conservationists.

President Theodore Roosevelt is the first and likely most well-known Republican environmentalist. A fan of nature his whole life, Teddy believed to his core that we must leave the world better than we found it and when he became President of the United States, he used his power and appointed the Public Lands Commission; issued several proclamations and orders aimed at irrigation and the protection of wildlife and parks; and he also founded the United States Forest Service.[30]

Yet "conserve-ation" didn't stop there.

According to a UC Berkeley Public Law Review Paper[31] conservative leader William F. Buckley, the founder of *National Review*, was an ardent conservationist. So was conservative U.S. Senator Barry Goldwater. They both took "vigorous public stands in favor of environmental protection."

Another conservative, California Governor-turned-President of the United States, Ronald Reagan, also dedicated his career to looking out for Mother Earth. According to UC Berkeley papers, Reagan himself oversaw California's pollution control agency and during his presidency "personally championed the international ozone agreement" of the 1980s and advocated for the protection of wildlife.

So, how did the left become so interested in the environment?

As with most policy issues championed by Republicans, they co-opted it.

I believe that as modern-day Democrats became hungry for more and more power, they realized that Socialist-based environmentalism was simply one more way to control people and yet one more tool to take down titans of industry in our capitalist society.

If you read the chapter in this book on Socialism, you'll see that Marxist-based ideology is all about killing major industries within capitalist societies and turning those industries into property of the government.

Seeing that environmentalism could help them control the public masses and transfer massive private wealth to government programs, Democrats hopped the turnstile, jumped aboard the climate change gravy train and never looked back.

The Green New Deal's Cost to America

Bloomberg News reported in 2019 that the Green New Deal will cost at least $93 trillion over ten years.[32] By those estimates, the Green New Deal will cost the average American family at least $65,000. By my count, that's $6,500 per year, per family, during a time when the cost of food, energy, and other goods are skyrocketing.

To make matters worse, this burdensome cost comes at a time when Americans are still digging out from under the economic calamities caused by the pandemic and specifically, strict Democrat-led lockdowns.

Sadly, all of this comes just one year after President Donald Trump delivered the best economic numbers in 20 years and the lowest unemployment numbers in American history, particularly for women.

As the Green New Deal has gotten its foot in the door of President Joe Biden's Infrastructure Investment and Jobs Act, there are real-world costs to consider.

The price tag now only *begins* at $93 million.

Biden's new infrastructure act alone costs $1.2 trillion, according to the House of Representatives. The act doesn't even scratch the surface on what liberals would like the Green New Deal to alter.

For starters, AOC and her friends want to "green" America's supply chain.

Bloomberg News reported in October 2021 that in order to get the supply chain to turn green it will take a lot of green — $100 trillion, to be exact.[33] That is, if there is any supply chain left after Biden and Transportation Secretary Pete Buttigieg are through with it. These two can't even get a treadmill delivered on time; they're going to improve the entire global supply chain? Not likely.

According to The Heritage Foundation,[34] the switch from traditional energy sources that Americans use in every day life to sources put forth by the Green New Deal would also cost a fortune.

The move away from clean coal, nuclear power and natural gas which millions of Americans use today, to Green-New-Deal-approved renewable energy sources would cost an additional $5 trillion. Someone's got to pay for that, and it would likely come out of the hides of energy producers and American businesses.

American families would also bear the burden. Under the Green New Deal, Americans' own household electricity would increase 12% to 14% according to an analysis by The Heritage Foundation.

It's a lot of green.

What we don't know may also hurt us when it comes to funding AOC's Green New Deal.

Even the left-leaning FactCheck.org states, "experts told us the Green New Deal is too vague to try to estimate its cost."[35]

Talk about alarming.

As if a nearly $100 trillion bill weren't enough, Americans could face the prospect of a much higher price tag. Most Americans understand that things in Washington, D.C. are often over-budget and rarely on schedule.

Even the left-wing CATO Institute estimates that for every $1 billion the federal government pledges to spend on a project (such as the Green New Deal, or sending a man to space), it usually ends up spending approximately $2 billion.[36] Given CATO's analysis, that means that the Green New Deal would actually cost more in the ballpark of $200 trillion. It's hard to believe that an American public already gasping at a $100 trillion price tag would go for a budget twice that.

Yet, it gets even worse when you consider that the Green New Deal is what one researcher would call a "mega project" — a public project so large that it tends to have even higher cost overruns.

For example, the launch of the Obama administration's healthcare.gov website for "Obamacare" had a price tag that grew from $464 million to $864 million, quickly. We all remember how it fell flat on its face on its launch date. And that was just a website!

In another example, CATO reports that the International Space Station had a "quadruple" cost overrun, from $17 billion to $74 billion.

In yet another example, Veterans Administration hospitals over the decades have had — you guessed it — massive cost overruns. Not incidentally, they've also had dismal performance records of caring for *actual* humans.

As further proof that the Green New Deal would likely have major cost overruns, one could look at the research of Danish researcher Bent Flyvbjerg, co-author of the book, *Megaprojects and Risk.*

According to the CATO Institute, the professor examined 258 "large transportation projects across 20 countries. He found that 90% went over budget." That's a mighty high number.

Under this logic, the Green New Deal — which AOC purports would completely re-engineer American society on everything from infrastructure to education, from healthcare to housing — would almost certainly fall into the category of gargantuan International-Space-Station-kind of cost overruns. By the experts' math, the Green New Deal would more accurately cost upwards of $400 trillion — nearly half a "quadrillion."

The cost to each American family, then, would be upwards of $250,000 to enact the Green New Deal — not $65,000 as initially estimated.

That, my friends, is a price tag that I believe very few Americans would support — especially women who are responsible for managing most household budgets.

From Diapers to Ziploc bags to SUVs: The Green New Deal is an Attack on the Everyday Lives for Women and Children

In addition to its staggering price tag, the Green New Deal would make everyday products which most Americans rely upon, disappear.

In fact, it takes direct aim at most of the products that American women use on a daily basis — especially moms.

Most people don't know it but diapers are made of petroleum, as are many other everyday products.

It takes approximately one cup of petroleum to create one diaper. Twenty-eight billion disposable diapers are used each year, which is a lot of product from an oil industry which liberals today despise.

According to AOC, American moms today should force themselves to wash poop-filled cloth diapers over the toilet like their great-grandmothers did. She wants to set women back 70 years. Imagine if a Republican male had made such a suggestion! ("What's next, being barefoot in the kitchen?" I can hear the Twitter chatter now!)

AOC's logic, of course, spills over to other everyday products: the Ziploc bags that many American moms use for their children's soccer games, the sippy cups that toddlers use and heck, even the SUVs that American women choose to cart the kids around to school and their various after-school activities. All of these everyday activities would come to a screeching halt if AOC's Green New Deal were ever to become a reality.

Yet that is her aim.

An attack on petroleum and the petroleum-derived products that are so prevalent in America today is an attack on the women who use them. If the companies are forced out of business, the products that women use will go right out the door with them.

It's ironic that when it comes to the "choice" of how to run their everyday lives, AOC doesn't want moms to have much of one.

Higher Gas Prices

We've already seen the price of gasoline skyrocket during the first two years of Biden's presidency.

It didn't happen because of the pandemic; in fact, during the pandemic gas prices were among the lowest of the last decade, because few people in America's largest cities were driving to work. (It is called "supply and demand" in economics school.)

The increase in gas prices came directly due to one of President Biden's earliest decisions to shut down a key energy source in America — the Keystone XL Pipeline — in large part due to pressure from his friends in the far-left, radical environmental wing of his party.

Under President Trump, the United States was not only producing plenty of oil and gas for ourselves — we actually had a surplus left over to sell to other at-risk countries and at a profit to ourselves, to boot. For example, under Trump we were able to sell energy to countries such as Poland in the dark of winter which helped them break their dependency upon Russian oil which had been not only bad for the North Atlantic country, geopolitically, but also bad for the rest of the world. When Russia and other authoritarian countries (Venezuela, etc.) sell oil, they fund their regimes.

There is no greater example of this than the Russian invasion of Ukraine. Whichever side you're on, the invasion was undoubtedly being funded by the 900,000 barrels of oil that Russia was selling to the world as countries could no longer get their oil from the United States of America. With American energy output being ground to a near halt, countries — especially those in Europe — had no choice but to purchase Russian oil.

In Biden's America, we are now faced with importing oil from foreign countries who don't like us — and that means spiked gas prices, longer wait times from tankers to the pump, and most ironic of all, potentially dangerous journeys that foreign tankers must travel across our precious oceans, something that should bother even the slightest environmentalist.

Meantime American states such as Oklahoma, Texas, and even some parts of California stand ready to provide energy to the world, but the barriers are too high with Biden-era permitting rules and environmental requirements. The irony is that American oil is reportedly 64% cleaner than the Russian oil that we are now forced to import.

Allowing American companies to fulfill the demand could greatly drive down the price of gas at the pumps for single moms, working moms, carpooling moms, and their families AND it could help the planet, too.

That is good, clean foreign policy and simple math that everyone should be able to get behind.

Job Losses

The job losses that experts estimate would take place under a Green New Deal is also jaw-dropping.

AOC and proponents of the Green New Deal admit that at least 6 million jobs would be lost — most likely in the oil, coal, and natural gas industries.

However, they don't include other jobs which economist Stephen Moore states will also be lost: those in the industries of manufacturing, transportation, and steel industries. Those jobs, he says, will likely go overseas to countries like China and India who will continue to pollute.

Other economies could also suffer. As jobs in the energy industry dry up, whole communities will as well.

It is estimated that Pennsylvania, which recently benefited from a natural gas boon, will lose more than 322,000 jobs if the Green New Deal goes into effect.[37] All of the industries that support the workers — the cafes where oil workers grab their morning breakfast and coffees, the real estate markets in the area, the property taxes that helped the schools — will all die on the vine. (This is in addition to the average family in Pennsylvania that will see their home energy costs go up more than $300 per month.) It will have a real impact on real people.

It's amazing to think that the Green New Deal which stands to wreck so many lives is all based off of a 14-page proposal by a young socialist who has presented zero evidence to convince Americans that this is actually worth doing. It's frightening to think that America has followed her this far down the path.

Uneven Playing Field

For all of its "saving the world" propaganda, the Green New Deal actually has very little bearing on, well,… the world.

The Green New Deal would *only* affect America's energy consumption and carbon output. It would have no bearing on the rest of the world.

The Green New Deal doesn't hold the world's biggest polluters — China & India[38] — accountable.

China is reportedly the largest polluter in the world, yet there is nothing in the Green New Deal to stem the tide of that country's output. According to the International Energy Agency, carbon emissions in the People's Republic of China increased 80% between 2005 to 2019, while emissions in America dropped by over 15 percent during the same time period.

China has repeatedly been the world's largest annual emitter of greenhouse gases since 2006 with a rate that is increasing every year, according to the U.S. Embassy.

The State Department also reports that the industrial mecca of Beijing is pumping into the air the world's highest levels of mercury, a harmful toxin that can affect people's brains.[39]

Although President Xi Jinping has committed to "carbon neutrality" by 2060, the State Department suggests that — much like AOC's — Xi's plan has been very light on details.

India does not fare much better.

China's and India's fossil fuel use has increased by 600% and 700%, respectively, since 1980.

They're not looking to slow down any time soon.

Between the two nations, China and India had 284 new coal plants in development as of January 2021.[40] Of the 20 most polluting cities on the planet, 15 are cities in India. Air quality in India's capital city of Delhi became so bad in November 2021 that government officials orders schools closed, power plants were shut down and businesses were ordered to keep half of their employees at home.

None of these tangible facts are being addressed in the Green New Deal.

AOC seeks to punish only American companies.

And that's just unfair.

Even though a Pew Research Poll in June 2020 showed that Republican woman favor more measures to help the environment than GOP men, I know one thing about America's women voters: "fairness" is important to us. If the rules of the game are fair, American women tend to support a policy. However, if the rules aren't fair, then women voters (especially independent/swing voters) don't want to have anything to do with it.

How do I know? I've focus-grouped women voters on climate change and other issues over the past two decades, and what I've seen and heard from them from the other side of the two-way mirror confirms their fair-mindedness. Sometimes, "fairness" matters to female swing voters more than the facts.

If the playing field isn't even, then all bets are off.

When it comes to the Green New Deal giving the world's two largest offenders of pollution a free pass while placing all of the financial burdens on Americans and their families, America's women will take a hard pass at that.

American moms are acutely aware that their children are already behind other countries in other areas such as education. They're not about to give additional advantages to the children of other nations while Americans foot the bill for vast social programs that don't hold others to account.

Besides, It's Been Tried Before: Solyndra

As the ideas in the Green New Deal continue to be debated, it's a shame that we have no reference point to which we can compare a government takeover of green programs.

Oh but wait, we do.

There is probably no better example than the government-subsidized Solyndra solar panel company to illustrate just how poorly the Green New Deal would play out.

In 2009, the Obama administration touted its darling in the "clean energy" industry and set out to make Solyndra a shining (no pun intended) example of how America could help cultivate alternate sources of energy.

What happened next was a colossal failure.

The White House threw their support behind the company, as did Wall Street. Through President Barack Obama's stimulus plan to get the economy going again in 2009, Solyndra had hit pay dirt.

However, the company quickly began to falter as its technology could not keep up with traditional energy sources and could not compete with cheaper solar panels being sold by (shock!) China.

Solyndra ended up filing for bankruptcy in September 2011, and it was later discovered that the company's executives had "misled federal officials to obtain $535 million in government-backed loans" (wait for it...) "with the help of the Obama White House."[41]

As a result, the U.S. government got soaked. Investors did too, to the tune of $198 million.

It's precisely what will happen if the Green New Deal is allowed to go forward.

The only difference is that Solyndra was merely *one* company, in *one* town, in just *one* industry. AOC's Green New Deal would create a million little Solyndras, a million little scams.

It appears that Democrats have also learned lessons on how to pay for it. Instead of the government footing the bill for these experimental energy solutions like Solyndra, AOC would have the American people pay for it instead.

Bait and Switch

Perhaps the worst part of AOC's Green New Deal push is that it most likely isn't about saving the planet at all.

The Washington Post reports that AOC's former chief of staff Saikat Chakrabarti was recently caught suggesting, "The interesting thing about the Green New Deal is it wasn't originally a climate thing at all… we really think of it as a how-do-you-change-the-entire-economy thing."

If her former chief of staff's statement is correct about AOC's true sentiment, and I believe it is, then the Green New Deal has more to do with instituting Socialism than greening the universe.

It's even more grotesque when you consider that the so-called "climate thing" carries a $93 trillion price tag. If the Green New Deal isn't about the planet and is more about restructuring the economy as AOC's adviser says it is, then that would equate to the largest government-ordered transfer of funds from the American people to the government, thereby the largest bait-and-switch fraud of the century.

Snow Job

There's something else that stinks in Queens.

For all of the discussion, debate and cost comparisons over it, the Green New Deal does not actually exist.

But don't take my word for it.

Even the liberal publication *The Atlantic* reports, "The Green New Deal Does Not, Strictly Speaking, Exist."[42]

The so-called biggest climate change policy of our lifetime has never been voted into law; in fact, it is not written down anywhere outside of a 14-page "resolution" that AOC introduced along with Senator Ed Markey in 2019.

Sure, some components of her Green New Deal were cobbled into Bernie Sanders' platform when he ran for president in 2020 and as I mentioned, some of it made its way into Biden's infrastructure plan. Other than that, however, *The Atlantic* goes so far as to say, "The idea has reshaped global climate policy, but is far less concrete than its supporters have been led to believe."

That's because it is a total snow job.

The Atlantic suggests that for all of the "histrionics" on social media about the Green New Deal, there isn't a lot of there "there."

To my knowledge, the Green New Deal has never been released as a policy "white paper" nor has it been submitted to the greatest scientists in the world for peer review, which is what scientists do when they want feedback, fact-checks, and constructive critiques to show that their work can stand rigorous review. That fact alone shows that the concept is riddled with flaws.

The Atlantic is also spot on when it reports that even as President Biden's "Build Back Better" infrastructure deal was being debated, the Green New Deal sat atop its shoulder cheering it on. Yet still, the Green

New Deal itself as a standalone concept has never so much as passed muster in the U.S. Senate.[43] It is too radical to stand on its own two feet.

The fact that the Green New Deal doesn't really exist on paper separates it from other gargantuan policy proposals pushed by liberals in the past.

The Affordable Healthcare for America Act — otherwise known as Obamacare — was 1,990 pages in its final form. It included a whopping 234,812 words.[44] Its pages were discussed ad nauseam on Sunday morning talk shows and a "white paper" of sorts was circulated far and wide within days of Obama's 2008 election victory. The language for Obamacare listed concrete tenets of the plan, its costs, and more — just ask Speaker Nancy Pelosi who finally read the bill (you know, after she passed it!) Whether you agreed with instituting government-run healthcare or not, one thing was certain: unlike the Green New Deal, Obamacare was an official bill, with official bill language, it moved through the floors of Congress where it was vigorously debated, and the American public knew what it was about.

GOP Leader Kevin McCarthy's American Tax Cuts and Jobs Act[45] was significantly shorter at approximately 200 pages, but its bill language was also clear. It was presented as a congressional revenue act, with specifics on tax cuts for families and reduction of taxes for businesses. Unlike the Green New Deal, the American Tax Cuts and Jobs Act's benefits were laid bare for all to review.

Even President Franklin Delano Roosevelt's New Deal[46] in the 1940s existed in printed form, which were generated by typewriter; in fact, the New Deal took the form of numerous congressional bills which all winded their way through Congress and were passed one by one then signed into law. FDR's New Deal included the congressional repeal of Prohibition; the passage of the Tennessee Valley Authority Act; the National Industrial Recovery Act to allow unionization; the Glass-Steagall Act to impact banking; the New Deal and the Second New Deal, to name a few. The point is unlike AOC's Green New Deal of today, FDR's New Deal was detailed, scrutinized and had enough support from Congress to pass it and for the president to sign it into law.

The fact that the Green New Deal has not advanced through Congress in the nearly four years that AOC introduced it is concerning.

Most alarming is that the Green New Deal's financial components have never been scored the Congressional Budget Office.

I believe it is all by design.

If the Green New Deal's parameters are never fully written down on paper, AOC and her left-wing radical activists can continue to move the goalposts — just as liberals did on matters such as COVID-19.

AOC has moved the goalposts before. She previously inserted language into her informal "resolution" things like "affordable and safe housing, and protections for workers' right to unionize." These things that have nothing to do with how hot the earth gets if the temperature goes up by one degree.

If that isn't a snow job the size of Mount Kilimanjaro, I don't know what is.

Make no mistake, whether the Green New Deal exists on paper or not, the quest for zero carbon emissions worldwide is just as elusive as other liberal policies which have gone before it. "Zero COVID," anyone?

Follow the Money

Lastly, when you're not sure what to believe in politics just remember the age-old saying, "Follow the money."

To understand what is truly going on with the Green New Deal, one must remember that Democrats perennially look for ways to neutralize their political opponents in Washington, D.C.

Historically, Republicans have been closely allied with the oil and gas industry. They've supported exploration and drilling. They've also benefitted throughout the decades from the lobbying spent on behalf of those oil and gas companies.[47] Most leaders in the oil and gas industry are Republican ideologues, from southern states, and they mostly back

Republican candidates much like their extended cousins in the tobacco industry did for decades.

Like "Big Oil," the Democrat-coined "Big Tobacco" cared a lot about limiting taxes on their products, limiting government intervention and letting the free market dictate. Powerful lobbying groups such as Altria Group, Philip Morris International and Reynolds Group prominently backed Republicans who agreed with those tenets.

Just as Democrats ran the Republican-allied tobacco industry nearly out of business[48] they have designs on doing the same to the oil and gas industry today. I've long held this theory, but now Biden administration officials aren't even attempting to hide it.

Biden's recent nominee to a key post at the Treasury Department was caught on video suggesting of oil companies, "We want them to go bankrupt."[49] Saule Omarova, who once identified as a young Socialist while studying in Russia, suggested a war on fossil fuels by utilizing the American government and the very banking system she would oversee to bankrupt companies.

Talk about picking winners and losers.

I believe that Democrats are so vengeful against the oil and gas industry mostly because they couldn't compete with the hundreds of millions of dollars that the oil and gas industry was forced to spend to defend itself over the last decade.

In 2020 alone, "oilies" spent $112 million in lobbying. That is a pretty penny with which Democrats had to contend. As a reaction, I believe Democrats have determined they must "bankrupt" these oil businesses and put them out of business — forever — so they don't have to fight them in Washington, D.C. anymore. Just like the tobacco companies.

I also believe that Democrats' love of everything electric — electric cars, electric energy, and more — is derived from the very government control that their leaders have over the electric grid itself.

Think about it.

When Democrats control government, they control the electric power grid. When they can control the electric grid, they can control how much you use energy, and when.

Just look at the recent climate edicts from California Governor Gavin Newsom. He recently asked Californians to forgo using electricity in their homes between the hours of 4pm to 8pm every day, in order to conserve electricity. If Californians don't? They'll face power outages.

Therefore, it wasn't really a "choice." It was an order.

You know where else they control the power grid like this? North Korea.

Famous satellite imagery shows the stark difference at night between North Korea[50] and South Korea, with the former being almost entirely dark at night. It's partially due to North Korea's inability to keep up with the modern world over the last five decades; but, make no mistake, it's all about authoritarian control.

Yes, I believe the real reason Democrats are rushing to get everyone off of fossil fuels and other traditional forms of energy is that they want to control the supply of the energy you will be limited to use on a daily basis.

As soon as Americans understand that this is more about money, political power and control than it is saving the environment, the better they'll be able to fend off this impending attack on your wallet and your American way of life.

Conclusion

The Green New Deal seeks to control every American's way of life as she knows it today, from which diapers moms purchase to which SUVs in which they choose to drive their kids to sports activities. Radical liberals like Rep. Alexandria Ocasio-Cortez want to rob women of their "choice" in virtually everything from how to heat your family's home in the winter, to when you turn your lights on in your home. Robbing American women of the ability to choose how to live their lives freely is wrong. Even worse, AOC and her powerful friends in Hollywood, fashion and big government are hypocrites who don't follow their own rules as they spend millions of dollars on lifestyles, travel and industries that destroy the planet according to their own definitions. This is America, and you are a free person. Buy what you want, drive the car that you want yourself and your children to be safe and comfortable in, be green if you choose, but don't let anyone tell you how to live your day-to-day life.

HOMEWORK

➤ Read the book, "The Moral Case for Fossil Fuels" by Alex Epstein. In it, Epstein addresses the argument that fossil fuels are destroying our planet and our lives. He points out that human life, especially for the underserved in our society, has actually *improved* thanks to the advances of fossil fuels — especially fracking, which is far less invasive to Mother Earth. The book is full of examples you can share with the climate change warriors ironically idling their engines in the carpool drop-off line.

➤ Also sign up for free "Energy Talking Points" to be delivered right to you from Epstein. He provides powerful points about the energy crisis, why fossil fuels actually make the world a better place, and debunks radical environmentalists' arguments. Sign up at: EnergyTalkingPoints.com

REFERENCES:

[21] Socialist "It" Candidates Rips Uber, then Rides Uber
https://www.investors.com/politics/editorials/socialist-candidate-ocasio-cortez-uber/

[22] Gas-Guzzling Car Rides Expose AOC's Hypocrisy amid Green New Deal Pledge
https://nypost.com/2019/03/02/gas-guzzling-car-rides-expose-aocs-hypocrisy-amid-green-new-deal-pledge/

[23] Gas-Guzzling Car Rides Expose AOC's Hypocrisy amid Green New Deal Pledge

https://nypost.com/2019/03/02/gas-guzzling-car-rides-expose-aocs-hypocrisy-amid-green-new-deal-pledge/

24 Hollywood's Waste
https://www.latimes.com/business/la-fi-ct-onlocation-20140731-story.html

25 Fashion Industry Waste: 92 Million Tons of Textile Waste, per Second
https://www.fashionrevolution.org/waste-is-it-really-in-fashion/

26 Ellen MacArthur Foundation: Fashion Industry Waste
https://ellenmacarthurfoundation.org/a-new-textiles-economy

27 Clean Water Action: 8,000 Starbucks Cups Are Used per Minute
https://www.cleanwateraction.org/features/starbucks-and-our-plastic-pollution-problem

28 WIRED: Next-Gen Gaming is the Environment's Worst Nightmare
https://www.wired.com/story/xbox-playstation-cloud-gaming-environment-nightmare/

29 How Much Waste Gaming Produces
https://www.dw.com/en/can-video-games-inspire-climate-action/a-57357630

30 U.S. Parks Service: Teddy Roosevelt and Conservation
https://www.nps.gov/thro/learn/historyculture/theodore-roosevelt-and-conservation.htm

31 UC Berkeley Public Law Review Papers: "The Conservative as Environmentalist: From Goldwater and the Early Reagan to the 21st Century"
https://papers.ssrn.com/sol3/papers.cfm?abstract_id=2919633#

32 Bloomberg: Green New Deal Will Cost $93 Trillion
https://www.bloomberg.com/news/articles/2021-07-21/greening-energy-to-fight-climate-threat-may-cost-92-trillion

[33] Bloomberg: For Supply Chain to Turn Green, It'll Take $100 Trillion
https://www.bloomberg.com/news/newsletters/2021-10-28/supply-chain-latest-shifting-to-green-will-cost-100-trillion

[34] Heritage Foundation: It's Not Just about Cost: The Green New Deal is Bad Environmental Policy, Too
https://www.heritage.org/environment/commentary/its-not-just-about-cost-the-green-new-deal-bad-environmental-policy-too

[35] FactCheck.org: Green New Deal Is Too Vague to Try to Estimate Its Cost
https://www.factcheck.org/2019/03/how-much-will-the-green-new-deal-cost/

[36] CATO Institute: Federal Government Cost Overruns
https://www.cato.org/sites/cato.org/files/pubs/pdf/tbb-72.pdf

[37] Costs of Green New Deal Would Be Devastating
https://www.foxnews.com/politics/conservative-group-estimates-devastating-green-new-deal-would-drive-up-energy-costs-kill-jobs

[38] World's Most Polluted Cities
https://www.iqair.com/world-most-polluted-cities

[39] U.S. Embassy: "China's Air Pollution Harms Its Citizens and the World"
https://ge.usembassy.gov/chinas-air-pollution-harms-its-citizens-and-the-world/

[40] China and India Had Nearly 300 New Coal Plants in the Works as of January 2021
https://energytalkingpoints.com/1-in-5-myth/#fn-3

[41] Remembering Solyndra
https://www.forbes.com/sites/adamandrzejewski/2021/04/12/remembering-solyndra--how-many-570m-green-energy-failures-are-hidden-inside-bidens-instructure-proposal/?sh=2b67a63e2672

[42] The Green New Deal Does Not, Strictly Speaking, Exist – The Atlantic
https://www.theatlantic.com/science/archive/2021/07/the-green-new-deal-doesnt-exist/619424/

[43] Mike Bloomberg: Green New Deal Has "Zero Chance" of Passing
https://www.cnbc.com/2019/03/05/mike-bloomberg-says-green-new-deal-stands-no-chance.html

[44] By Comparison: Obamacare Bill: 1,990 pages and more than 200,000 words
https://computationallegalstudies.com/2009/11/08/facts-about-the-length-of-h-r-3962/

[45] American Tax Cuts and Jobs Act
https://www.republicanleader.gov/mccarthy-tax-cuts-and-jobs-act/

[46] FDR's New Deal
https://www.history.com/topics/great-depression/new-deal

[47] How Much Money Oil & Gas Companies Spent on Lobbying in 2020
https://www.americanprogress.org/article/oil-lobbyists-use-rigged-system-hamstring-bidens-climate-agenda/

[48] Similarities to The War on the Tobacco Industry
https://www.eenews.net/articles/lawmakers-study-big-tobacco-perjury-before-big-oil-showdown-2/

[49] Biden Treasury Nominee Saule Omarova on Oil Companies: "We Want Them to Go Bankrupt"
https://nypost.com/2021/11/11/biden-treasury-pick-saule-omarova-wants-fuel-companies-to-go-bankrupt/

[50] North Korea at Night: Satellite Imagery
https://www.dailymail.co.uk/sciencetech/article-2725415/Nasa-satellite-images-North-Korea-secretive-space.html

#TimesUp for #MeToo Hypocrites

Over the last few years, feminists have lectured Americans about the importance of "Believing All Women." The slogan was coined after Dr. Christine Blasey Ford accused Supreme Court justice nominee Bret Kavanaugh of sexually groping her[51] more than 35 years ago at a rowdy high school party.

The nation was riveted day after day as a future Supreme Court Associate Justice was dragged through the mud on national TV.

America hadn't seen anything quite like it since "the high-tech lynching" of another conservative Supreme Court nominee, Clarence Thomas.

During a key moment, despite Ford presenting zero evidence of her allegations one of the vocal senators on the Senate Judiciary Committee, Maisy Hirono, said of Ford, "I believe her."[52]

Those three little words set off a mantra that became the new feminist trope.

The female founders of Bumble placed a full-page ad in *The New York Times* that simply read, "Believe women."[53]

Glossy magazines from Elle to Vogue to Glamour kept the narrative going in the pages of their publications.

MSNBC hosts such as Joy Reid pushed guests (including myself) to answer whether they #BelieveAllWomen, regardless of any evidence of any wrongdoing.

Since that time in the Fall of 2018, liberal feminists have aggressively chided Americans that they must #BelieveAllWomen — regardless of the facts.

However, four years down the line it is a mantra that the #BelieveAllWomen camp themselves have not been able to live up to, as feminists hypocritically stood by Democrat Party politicians and liberal media figures who were accused of far worse things than liking "beer" with "Timmy" and "Squee."

Over the last year especially, we have witnessed the downfall of some of the biggest champions of the #MeToo and #TimesUp movements, one of which ended in disgrace with the resignation of embattled New York Governor Andrew Cuomo.

The downfall proved that the very liberal feminist organizations which say they support women, often don't police their own.

Yet conservative outlets do.

How do I know?

I've been in the trenches and experienced it firsthand.

In June of 2015, I received a phone call from FOX News Channel. It was the Vice President of Recruitment for FOX News. She was the right-hand executive to the longtime chairman of FOX News, Roger Ailes.

Bridget Boyle asked if I was available to come to New York City. She asked if I had seen that FOX News had just been chosen to air the first presidential debate of the 2016 election season. I said that indeed, I had.

To be clear, the first presidential debate had initially been granted to Salem Media Group, where it would be broadcast live and moderated by nationally-syndicated talk show host Hugh Hewitt. Boyle quickly told me in her warp-speed New York City tempo — a trademark of everyone at FOX News, I later learned — that Ailes had protested strongly, arguing that presidential debates were visual events that needed the FOX News Channel in order to do it justice. The presidential commission acquiesced, and the first presidential debate was granted to FOX News.

That's where I came in, said the FOX News recruiter.

Three hosts had been chosen to moderate the debate: Chris Wallace, Bret Baier and Megyn Kelly. Kelly, she said, was a legal maven but could use a political attaché' of sorts who knew politics backward and forward. Boyle said that I could be of service as someone who knew my way around the political issues having been a political communicator.

Over the next week I shuttled back and forth to New York City, interviewing with top brass at FOX News — everyone from Boyle, to executive Suzanne Scott (who is now the first female President of FOX Corporation overall), to then-executive producer Tom Lowell (now the Senior Vice President of Programming), to finally the host and white-hot star of FOX News primetime at the time, Megyn Kelly.

Megyn was absolutely, stunningly, gorgeous even as she sat at her desk with her fresh face free of makeup and her hair pinned back neatly behind her ears. She wore a slim pair of jeans and slim flip-flops.

All appearances aside and my awe of FOX News aside, as I sat at Megyn's desk I knew what the stakes were. It was one of those surreal career moments for any girl coming up in television, especially political television, at the start of what would ultimately become the most memorable Presidential election cycle in American history. We got right down to business.

We discussed the 17 candidates who were running in the GOP primary — the largest presidential primary field in American history — and Megyn asked my assessment of the strengths/weaknesses of each candidate.

A lot of the conversation kept coming back to Donald J. Trump since he was the newest and of course most vocal candidate in the race.

Trump had declared his candidacy just a few blocks away two weeks prior, calling criminal illegal immigrants from Mexico "rapists" and suggesting that Mexico was "not sending us their best." He turned out to be right, by the way, the countries to our south still aren't sending their best[54] but at the time the comments drew outrage and Trump was off to the races. Literally.

Megyn said that a piece I had written for *TheBlaze* or maybe *The Washington Times* had caught FOX News's attention.

Actually two pieces.

My first piece was a glowing analysis of Trump, an in-depth fact check on Trump's comments about illegal immigrants. Digging in deep to FBI crime reports, I concluded that Trump wasn't wrong about Mexico not sending us their best and brightest. According to an FBI crime report, a majority of the criminals on the most-wanted list in Los Angeles were illegal immigrants. In that piece, I opined that even if it was an unpopular and uncomfortable opinion, Trump had been right.

The other piece I had written was a more critical piece about Trump, an expose' of sorts on Trump's political donations dating back to the early 1980s. I reported that Trump actually gave heavily to Democrats, not Republicans — that is, until he thought about running for office as a Republican sometime around 2012. I pointed out that despite Trump's claim that he had to give these donations as part of "doing business in New York City" to get projects approved, Trump's donations to Democrats actually ranged far outside of New York City and oftentimes, went to Republican enemies such as the Democratic Congressional Campaign Committee (DCCC) in critical election years. In fact, Trump had given to the DCCC "building fund" which literally helped Democrats build campaign headquarters in districts where they were viciously fighting Republicans.

"*See*," Megyn said, "Even as a conservative, you're willing to investigate and report the results of something you might not want to write. You're independent-minded… that's how I think, too. I like that."

And just like that, my fate was sealed.

I was then invited to sit in the control room where the production team sat for *"The Kelly File,"* Megyn's hit show on FOX News Channel that aired at 10p.m. I sat in the dark control room with audio and bright lights whirring all around me, as the show began in "3... 2... 1..." and I couldn't help feeling that my own life was about to change "bigly," as Trump would say.

The Question Heard 'Round the World

I landed the gig at FOX News, headed to New York City, and right away we began circling the 17 GOP candidates' careers like hawks. *What was their voting record? How had they voted on certain issues, such as abortion, gay marriage, taxes, spending? Did any of them say anything publicly that was contradictory to their voting record?* Those are the kinds of things you look for when deciding what to ask at a debate.

Occasionally, we were given notes from above (meaning: Roger Ailes) with instructions to dig further into someone's record on an issue. I remember then-Wisconsin Governor Scott Walker, then-Texas Governor Rick Perry, Sen. Marco Rubio, former Florida Governor Jeb Bush, and then-businessman Donald Trump were the five candidates that had the most interest at the time. Specifically, word was that Ailes had a sort of love/hate relationship with Trump. After all, they were both huge figures in highly competitive New York City.

Having suitcased in from Washington, D.C. I was holed up in a short-term, sort of corporate housing hotel called The Phillips Club just around the corner from FOX. I spent most of my days at FOX News world headquarters — what my friends and I affectionately still refer to as "the mothership." There was a Washington, D.C. bureau of FOX News, but New York at that time was where all of the action happened.

By day, I helped produce segments a few times per week for "The Kelly File" which at the time was the #1 primetime show in America, often competing with FOX News' other hit show "The O'Reilly Factor" for nightly ratings. Most of my other hours were spent poring over research and staring at the 17 respective binders I was compiling on each of the candidates. (No Mitt Romney "binders" jokes, please.)

Virtually no one from my life outside of the building was allowed to know where I was or what I was doing. FOX News had specifically asked me not to mention my role to any of my political friends, especially individuals at presidential campaigns that might attempt to sway me. Only my family and a few non-political girlfriends knew where I was. Later, when it was reported that then-CNN Contributor Donna Brazile had leaked debate questions to Hillary Clinton's presidential team, I shook my head. Nothing of the sort would have been allowed at FOX.

All the while I was falling in love with New York City. What little spare time I had, I would go to a Yankees game or to the top of the Empire State Building. Touristy stuff, to be sure, but I was soaking it all in. I enjoyed getting lost in a city of millions of people, and I smiled anytime I passed someone on the street and heard them talking about the presidential race.

Every once in a while, I would spot Sean Hannity in the makeup room (he was super kind), and later at FOX I would see Laura Ingraham in the hallway at what I now deduce was her interviewing for her current role on "The Ingraham Angle." Both had been supportive of my prior campaigns in politics, on both traditional marriage (the Prop. 8 campaign in California) and Second Amendment rights (the Colorado recalls), though I brought up neither to them. After all, I was there to work not to promote my own political career. Nonetheless, amid such serious work it was fun to have these light reprieves of "star sightings."

Finally, after weeks and weeks and mountains of research, the moment arrived to hone in on Trump.

I had already written about his past donations to Democrats, and everyone knew he was a bit brash when talking about immigration or President Barack Obama's birthplace. But what, exactly, was going to be "The $64 million question" on Trump?

One day, it became glaringly clear.

"Megyn," I said as I called Megyn Kelly on the phone. "I think there's something you need to see."

I had been doing deep dives into Trump's time hosting "The Apprentice" at NBC, watching hours and hours of old footage and combing through tons of entertainment industry articles, because that's what Trump had been at the time — not only a businessman, but an entertainer.

In the entertainment industry articles, in particular, I kept coming across suggestions that he had made inappropriate comments to women on the set, and it's something I dove into further to see if there was any "there" there.

I emailed Megyn several things that kept cropping up regarding Trump's treatment of women. One was a video clip of Trump saying to a female contestant (his subordinate on the show), that he wanted her to "get down on her knees" and beg him to pick her, and then a follow-up comment he made to that same female contestant that he bet she'd look beautiful on her knees. It was the kind of stuff that would pass in Hollywood, to be sure. But a presidential campaign, not so much. After all, Sen. Gary Hart dropped his presidential bid after a photo emerged of former church secretary Jessica Hahn sitting on his lap.

"Is there video of this?" Megyn wrote back to me.

"Yes," I said. "I've got links to everything."

I remember feeling somewhat badly at the time about that line of questioning for Trump — whom I was a big fan of at the time and still am. In full disclosure, I had told all of my superiors early on that he was in my top-three favorites, if not my favorite, among the 17 candidates. But, there's a point to all of this.

Ultimately as an independent-minded journalist who was fond of Trump, I followed the information where it led us and that was toward the question regarding women. The point is, I don't think that liberal journalists would have done the same if it had been the other way around.

In fact, I know liberal journalists don't.

Throughout 2020, then-candidate Joe Biden had worse allegations against him in 2020 and no one brought it up at *any* of the presidential debates.

In the end, Megyn got raked over the coals for daring to ask such a bold question. Left-leaning outlets and feminist leaders everywhere should have applauded. Instead, they focused solely on slamming Trump.

Feminists and liberal journalists missed the point of the whole exercise.

Nonetheless, everyone ended up winning: FOX News won in the ratings. The event won the title of "the most-watched Presidential debate in American history." At the time it was the most-watched TV event of all time outside of a Super Bowl. It had even beaten the ratings of the series finale of M*A*S*H in the 1980s, which I vividly remember sneaking out of my bedroom and down the hall to watch against my parents' wishes; so, to be even a small part of something that was even in the same sentence as M*A*S*H was a big deal for me. Indeed, the ratings boon for FOX News was "yuge" and continued for three straight years, with no other network even coming close to catching up with them.

As for Megyn, she went on to land a $70 Million contract with NBC.

As for Trump, it didn't hurt him one bit. By boldly addressing the question head on and in the humorous way as only Trump could do, he shot to the top of the pack of 17 GOP candidates in the Cleveland arena that night and never looked back. The rest is (presidential) history.

Fifteen months later, it turned out just as I thought it would. A taped conservation between Trump and "Access Hollywood" entertainment reporter Billy Bush arose. Just as predicted, that "locker room talk" didn't hurt his election chances because the question — *our* question — had already been asked and answered. America was fully prepared. American voters knew they weren't electing a virginal choir boy, and they were okay with it. They weren't looking for one anyway.

Trump was elected exactly 30 days later.

The Women's March

The Democrat Party and their supporters in the feminist movement took our Presidential debate question and went to the extreme with it, taking out on Trump any anger they had for men over the course of their lifetimes — every bad boss they ever had, any construction worker who had ever whistled at them on the sidewalk, you name it.

Shortly after Trump's election, talk began to spread of an impending "Women's March" set to take place on the heels of his inauguration.

I was in Washington, D.C. for Trump's inauguration on another assignment for FOX News and FOX Business. We covered two of the most beautiful things about American politics — the peaceful transfer of power and a beautiful evening of Inaugural balls.

However, the sparkle of the evening departed quickly the next day when upon waking, I heard the most awful screeching and chanting and banging of drums.

The Women's March had rolled into town.

We were warned by security that the crowd was growing bigger by the moment, and becoming more heated. I stopped by a room to pick up a FOX laptop that another producer had asked me to take back to New York City, and I helped our team get safely to their cars.

I couldn't help but notice that the temperature in nation's capital was beginning to rise — and anyone who's been to D.C. on a frigid morning in January knows I'm certainly not referring to the weather.

As protestors walked en masse to get to the Women's March blocks away, I remember being shocked that women were screaming all sorts of vulgarities: screaming the p-word and carrying signs which contained intimate details of their own sex lives — which surprised me, as many of them had their young daughters in tow.

The protesters' signs were vulgar, showing women's female body parts in graphic detail and suggestions about what would happen if they grabbed the new president by *his* genitalia.

There were also many, many signs about one of the most violent acts in life — taking a baby's life through abortion. I scratched my head at what that had to do with Trump because I knew from the deep research I had done on him as a candidate that he had been pro-choice for most of his life. Prohibiting abortion wasn't a huge priority for him at the time, so these women using that as a battle cry struck me as odd.

Then I saw their pre-printed signs, courtesy of Planned Parenthood's political arm, and it all started making sense. This was bigger than even Trump.

As the morning wore on, I was stuck by how these women screeched like banshees heading to a slaughter — only, I saw instead that this would be the attempted proverbial slaughter of President Trump.

I hurried to gather my suitcase so that I myself could get out of town as my colleagues had just done. Worried, I immediately flipped my FOX employee badge around. I remembered that during the final weeks of the 2016 election, FOX News Human Resources had sent alerts to all employees to not visibly wear our badges on subways, on the streets, or in public places due to threats of violence that FOX had received or that its security intelligence teams had picked up from, you know, the "tolerant" left.

Security definitely remained on my mind as the irate crowd began to build in numbers. Then, I smelled the worst smell which could only be described as burning rubber. I smelled smoke. I turned around and there was a limousine on fire in front of our hotel. An actual limousine! "Get back, get back! It could explode!" A security guard began clearing people from the area. Was it safe to go back inside the hotel and grab my bag? Was this part of The Women's March? As I quickly packed up and hopped a train back to New York City, I wasn't sure that I wanted to know much more about these "nasty women."

The New York City Women's March

As I returned to New York, I noticed that the city had just had its own version of the Washington, D.C. Women's March. In fact, there was an entire chapter in New York.

They, too, wanted "equality" and to drive out what they called hate speech by President Trump.

They did well for a while, keeping questions about Trump's treatment of women in the news cycle for three years (yawn). The national group even affected women's turnout in a major way on behalf of Democrats who won the 2018 midterms with "record turnout" of women voters.

However, it wasn't too long before The Women's March was exposed for having some hate speech of their own.

As it turned out, the New York City Women's March was founded and led by women who had a deep affinity for the Nation of Islam and a big fan of its founder Louis Farrakhan, who has made numerous anti-Semitic (anti-Jewish) remarks over the years.[55]

Farrakhan has blamed Jewish people for everything from the slave trade in America, to controlling the U.S. Congress, to knowing about the 9/11 attacks before they happened.

In one of his rants toward Jews in Chicago on Saviors Day in 1996, Farrakhan called the Jewish religion "the synagogue of Satan" and accused Jews of sucking people's blood.

As The Women's March luck would have it, Tamika Mallory, one of the original co-founders of the New York City Women's March, not only attended at least one Farrakhan event but the Tweeted that Farrakhan was the "GOAT," meaning the Greatest of All Time.

Yet it wasn't just her affiliation with the Nation of Islam leader that raised eyebrows. Mallory herself had also called Jews the "mother and father of Apartheid," referring to their supposed oppression of Palestinians (despite the fact that Palestine has declared a lasting war on Israel, not the other way around). She also publicly supported Farrakhan's extreme remarks when he stated, "…Jews are my enemy."

Reports have since emerged that some of this anti-Semitism by Mallory was known during the formation of the New York City Women's March.[56] However, as it so often seems to happen in the feminist movement, they looked the other way in the striving of their more important goal: taking down a Republican.

Despite her hateful rhetoric and disgraceful exit from The Women's March[57] Mallory was still invited to speak at the Democratic National Committee meeting in August 2020 for the Democratic Black Caucus meeting.

Where was the media? Silent.

Another leader in the Women's March movement who kept showing up like a bad penny was Linda Sarsour, a self-proclaimed "Palestinian-Muslim-American Activist" who is also on-the-record as having made anti-Jewish statements.[58]

Like Mallory, Sarsour also has an affiliation with Farrakhan.

She has also praised Arab terrorists who killed Jewish students, and she Tweeted her approval of the "intifada" — a violent campaign that killed 12,000 Jewish people at the hands of Palestinian terrorists.

I don't know about you, but any movement that claims to be for "equality" and "standing up" for others yet has a track record of hate speech against a particular group of people, has an inherently hypocritical problem that should invalidate much of its work.

Yet the media still said nothing.

In yet another similarity to the co-founder of the Women's March, Sarsour unbelievably — even after being exposed as a vicious anti-Semite — was also invited to speak at the Democratic National Committee convention in August 2020.

Then-presidential candidate Joe Biden said nothing.

As he was literally about to become the nominee, Biden's team brushed off the presence of Sarsour suggesting that she wasn't a keynote speaker and the she was simply speaking at a "Muslim Delegates and Allies Assembly" meeting. Yet, the fact that she spoke at the DNC Convention *at all* speak volumes.

The fact that these hate-filled, anti-Jewish women were not only tolerated by the Democrat Party but embraced by it, tells you everything you need to know about today's Democrat Party, the presidential candidate who benefited from it all, and the feminists who enabled them all.

TIME'S UP

The Women's March isn't the only feminist group that has faced problems.

Shortly after The Women's March appeared on the scene, Michelle Obama's former Chief of Staff Tina Tchen got together with some of her liberal colleagues and decided to form their own group — a more politically-connected, high-powered (not to mention highly-paid) version of The Women's March.

With Tchen's experience in the Obama administration, these ladies would become the real feminist power brokers around Washington, D.C. long after the confetti and the pink knit hats were picked up off of the steps of the U.S. Capitol.

The TIME'S UP organization was born.

Tchen and her fellow executives began to do what they knew how to do best — fundraise — and by February 2018, they had already raised $20 million for their legal fund and millions more for their other organizations, TIME'S UP Foundation and TIME'S UP Now, the lobbying arm of the movement.[59] It's safe to say most of their monied efforts went to favor Democrats and to fight Republicans.

Tchen and her colleagues made the rounds to speak about the TIME'S UP movement, including landing numerous national TV interviews and glossy magazine covers. They also held panel discussions, 'lots of panel discussions, to gripe about Trump.

Curious what the other side was saying given my involvement in the Presidential debate and the ultimate women's question, I attended one such panel during *The Wall Street Journal*'s Festival of Ideas, I believe it was called, during which Tchen hosted actress Sara Jessica Parker for a talk about the women's movement.

During the lecture, Tchen talked about how powerful men — mostly Republicans — had abused their positions of power. There was talk of Supreme Court Associate Justice Bret Kavanaugh and President Trump, but literally zero references regarding many liberal men in media who were falling from their pedestals. In disgust, I quietly got up, threw away my glass of wine and uttered, "Hacks" under my breath after Tchen assuredly made clear it was big, bad Republican monsters who had been making life difficult for women.

It turns out, it was actually Tchen and her colleagues at the TIME'S UP organization who were the ones making life difficult for women.

There were rumblings about New York Governor Andrew Cuomo's treatment of women in his office. Eventually, female accusers began to come forward one after another with detailed stories regarding alleged sexual harassment they'd suffered at his hands.

One accuser, Lindsay Boylan, shared a detailed account of Cuomo's alleged serial harassment. More women began to come forward.

Yet Cuomo managed to stay in office for months after these accusations came out.

Now we know why.

According to news reports which came out in the final days of Cuomo's reign, the co-founders of TIME'S UP had been shamelessly aiding Governor Cuomo in his defense and at times, aggressively going after his female accusers.

TIME'S UP CEO Tchen was reportedly so in the tank for Cuomo that she commanded TIME'S UP staff to "stand down"[60] after staffers expressed interest in putting out a public statement of support for Lindsay Boylan in her sexual harassment claims against the governor.

Tchen's fellow executive at TIME'S UP, Roberta Kaplan, had also been involved in helping smear Cuomo's alleged victim by advising Cuomo staff on how to handle the sexual harassment allegations. (The TIME'S UP executive also had not disclosed that she had represented Cuomo's top aide, Melissa DeRosa, in the New York attorney general's inquiry into the matter.)

Think about that for a moment. The time was, *literally*, up for Governor Cuomo yet the two founders of the women's organization that was *supposed* to protect women in the workplace and fight for them ended up doing the very thing they accused Republicans of: ignoring then even worse, obstructing and smearing their accusers.

As Cuomo exited office, time was finally up for these women, too. Both TIME'S UP executives stepped down from their posts in shame, copping to what they had done.

Their movement lasted barely three years — but there is no doubt that these hypocritical feminists had an impact on one of the most important midterm elections of our lifetimes, the 2018 midterms. If only the American public knew what they were really up to.

Lean In

TIME'S UP executives weren't the only ones who covered for Governor Andrew Cuomo and in fact went out of the way to smear his alleged sexual harassment victims.

Meta's (formerly Facebook's) Chief Operating Officer Sheryl Sandberg has made a fortune off of her image as a champion of women, as an executive who has encouraged women to *"Lean In"* at the workplace or get left behind. Sandberg, like Time's Up's Tchen and Kaplan, went everywhere on the lecture circuit for a few years.

According to the New York attorney general's report, it turns out that a Meta communications executive who had previously served as a communications aide to Cuomo, reportedly helped draft or at the very least reviewed a statement that — just like the TIME'S UP statements — smeared Boylan and other female accusers who dared to come forward against the Democrat governor. [61] The Meta executive's involvement in the matter clearly appears to be far outside the purview of her job at the social media giant.

There's never been a public announcement stating that the staffer was ever disciplined or suspended (or even fired, as a conservative would have been) for smearing an alleged victim of sexual harassment. In fact, I think it's safe to presume that she hasn't.

Perhaps in all of her lectures, Sandberg meant that feminists should "Lean In" when there's a dissenter against the Democrat Party whose voice needs to be snuffed out. That appears to be what was done in the case of Cuomo and his many alleged feminist enablers, even at the oh-so-liberated Meta. So much for believing all women, right?

Keith Ellison

The left's #MeToo movement and #BelieveAll Women mantra also failed a woman in a state not too far from Trump's New York.

In 2018, then-Congressman Keith Ellison of Minnesota was accused by his former girlfriend, Karen Monahan, of physical and emotional abuse.[62]

Ellison, who was running to be the state's attorney general at the time, was accused of violently beating his girlfriend including throwing her onto a bed and dragging her by her hair — all in front of her young son.

Despite vivid details from Monahan about the alleged abuse, feminists and the Democrat Party largely let Ellison skate because he had already the Democratic nomination and was facing a tough race for attorney general. They didn't want Democrats to lose the office only to turn it over to Republicans for the first time in 40 years.

Perhaps even more unbelievable, at the time the allegations came out Ellison also happened to be the Deputy Chair of the Democratic National Committee — the #2 in command. Let that sink in for a moment. They were not frivolous allegations, they were quite detailed in nature, and Monahan appeared to be a serious individual who never changed her story. Yet no one in the Democratic National Committee asked Ellison to step down from that post, either.

It speaks volumes about what — and whom — Democrats and their feminist enablers are willing to sacrifice in order to reach higher and higher political office.

Clearly, they're willing to sacrifice women.

Somewhere along the way, Democrats knew that they couldn't afford to lose Keith Ellison in such a high position of power in such a key electoral state.

Sure enough, they were right.

Just over two years after he narrowly escaped losing his race, in May 2020 in the wake of the George Floyd incident in Minnesota the state's attorney general — now Keith Ellison — announced that he would take the high-profile case away from the Minneapolis District Attorney (where the case would normally land) and instead personally get to the bottom of whether Officer Derek Chauvin was criminally liable for the murder of George Floyd.

The allegations of Ellison's violent abuse of a woman just two years prior to the Floyd incident didn't seem to matter. Like so many other Democrat men, Ellison was just another useful vehicle to get progressives where they wanted to go. Ultimately, they set their eyes on a murder verdict for a police officer and set off the beginning of a national movement to defund the police.

Conclusion

The truth is the liberal, feminist, #MeToo, #BelieveAllWomen and #TimesUp movements have been filled with incredible amounts of hypocrisy — so much so, it ought to invalidate today's feminist movement entirely.

You notice that there was no "Women's March" protest against President Joe Biden at his inauguration, even though Biden himself faced an incredibly serious and detailed allegation of sexual assault against a young female staffer in the basement of the U.S. Capitol when he was a U.S. Senator. Adding insult to injury, Biden and his senior staff allegedly subsequently harassed the young woman out of a job when she came forward to report the alleged event to her supervisor.

Unlike the FOX News debate team, no liberal Presidential debate moderator ever asked then-presidential candidate Joe Biden if the allegations were true. It never came up *once* at a Presidential debate.

In fact, the silence was deafening as virtually every Democrat turned a blind eye to the allegations against Biden. Liberals threw their #BelieveAllWomen mantra right out the window to protect Biden and to ensure that he would be elected, since he championed all of the other things they care about like free abortions, universal child care, universal healthcare, free healthcare for illegal immigrants and more.

Feminists turn a blind eye because they know their chosen men will deliver on so many other progressive promises for the movement. In doing so, they fail to #BelieveAllWomen and ultimately become unbelievable themselves.

The next time feminists and Democrat Party leaders lecture you about the treatment of women, understand this: they don't genuinely mean it. They *only* mean it when the person being accused just happens to be a Republican standing in the way of their precious progressive policies.

HOMEWORK
➢ If you want to see how un-serious liberals are about policing their own, watch the "60 Minutes" interview with Tara Reade — the

female staffer who accused her former boss, then-Senator Joe Biden, of sexually assaulting her while on the job. Notice the absence of feminist heroes on the left such as Sen. Mazie Hirono, who paved the path for the "Believe All Women" mantra during the Supreme Court confirmation hearings of Bret Kavanaugh. Last we checked, Hirono has still made no comment stating support for Reade, nor calling for more information the alleged sexual assault. Watch the Tara Reade interview in full here on YouTube: https://www.youtube.com/watch?v=OOti0PJlJ7A

REFERENCES:

[51] Christine Blasey Ford vs. Brett Kavanaugh
https://time.com/5415027/christine-blasey-ford-testimony/

[52] Maisy Hirono on Christine Blasey Ford: "I Believe Her"
https://www.nytimes.com/2018/09/25/us/politics/mazie-hirono-kavanaugh-senate.html

[53] #BelieveAllWomen
https://www.newsweek.com/dating-app-bumble-believe-women-ad-new-york-times-kavanaugh-hearing-1144540

[54] Murder Suspect in Las Vegas Stabbing Was Here Illegally from Guatemala
https://nypost.com/2022/10/07/las-vegas-stabbing-spree-suspect-yoni-barrios-in-us-illegally-has-criminal-record-report/m

[55] Nation of Islam's Louis Farrakhan's Outrageous Comments
https://www.splcenter.org/fighting-hate/extremist-files/individual/louis-farrakhan

[56] Initial meeting of The Women's March included anti-Semitic remarks
https://www.tabletmag.com/sections/news/articles/is-the-womens-march-melting-down

[57] NY Post: The Women's March still has an anti-Semitic problem

https://nypost.com/2019/09/21/the-womens-march-still-has-an-anti-semitism-problem/

[58] Women's March founder Linda Sarsour's anti-Semitism
https://www.commentary.org/christine-rosen/linda-sarsour-bernie-sanders-anti-semitism/

[59] TIME'S UP Raises Its First $20 Million
https://www.forbes.com/sites/natalierobehmed/2018/02/06/with-20-million-raised-times-up-seeks-equity-and-safety-in-the-workplace/?sh=3a6e5288103c

[60] TimesUp CEO told staff to "stand down" on statement of support for victims of Governor Cuomo's alleged sexual harassment
https://www.nytimes.com/2021/08/26/business/times-up-tina-tchen.html

[61] Meta Exec Helped Cuomo Smear Sexual Harassment Accuser: Attorney General
https://nypost.com/2021/08/04/Meta-exec-helped-cuomo-smear-sex-harassment-accuser-ag/

[62] Keith Ellison Is Reeling after Abuse Allegations
https://www.politico.com/story/2018/10/27/keith-ellison-abuse-allegations-minnesota-ag-2018-943086

DEFUND THE POLICE or DEFEND WOMEN: THE REAL ISSUE OF "CHOICE"

Nearly two years ago, the nation erupted in protests in the wake of the George Floyd incident in Minneapolis after an officer's use of force was caught on a video that soon went viral.

Cities burned, stores were looted, and Black Lives Matter protestors demanded the defunding of police.

While 2020 was the year that the movement went mainstream, what most Americans don't know is that the "defund the police" movement started long before the George Floyd incident. By the time that Floyd refused to get into the back of a squad car outside Cup Foods, the movement was already afoot. It's important that Americans know the full stories behind the figures who preceded Floyd.

Eric Garner

Criticism of police officers and their "use of force" began in July 2014 over Eric Garner's death in New York City, when Garner was arrested for selling single cigarettes — an act which is illegal in New York City because it flouts the otherwise high cost of a full pack of tobacco products. The police had given Garner warnings previously, and when they returned to arrest him a scuffled ensued and he ultimately died.

Even though Garner was visibly overweight — clocking in at 395 pounds at the time of his death — and he had asthma, diabetes and heart disease as contributing factors, the New York City Medical Examiner ruled that a police chokehold triggered the events that led to his death.[63]

Soon, the New York City Police Department became public enemy number one in minority communities. Under pressure, the department discontinued chokeholds for all individuals, and Garner's family ultimately became $6.9 million richer with a settlement with both New York City and the hospital that had treated Garner.

The multi-million-dollar settlement was heard 'round the country, and "I Can't Breathe" became the new slogan for anti-police protestors and progressives. It was the beginning battle cry... the preamble, if you will, to the movement to defund the police.

The Whole Truth about Breonna Taylor

In March 2020, just over two months before the Floyd incident, another high-profile death emerged when police arrived at Breonna Taylor's apartment in Louisville, Kentucky to serve a search warrant related to Breonna's ex-boyfriend. As police entered the apartment, they were reportedly fired upon by Taylor's new boyfriend at the time, Kenneth Walker. [64] Officers reportedly returned fire, accidentally striking Breonna in the crossfire and causing her death.

Liberals and feminists alike held Breonna up as a rare female victim of police shootings.

However, it turns out that Breonna may not have the angel she was portrayed to be in the overall matter. Her ex-boyfriend testified in a sworn affidavit that she had helped his drug gang "handle their money" and that she had also managed his personal money for him as a known drug dealer. [65]

Police also asserted that Breonna's apartment address — the location for which the warrant was obtained and where she was shot — had in fact been used in the mailing of illegal drugs. In fact, they had been tracking packages to her address for a period of time prior to the incident.

But that's not all.

In 2016, Breonna Taylor had another odd brush with the law — a man turned up dead in a rental car in her name.[66] It was no car accident. The man had been shot 8 times.

Bet you never heard that on the mainstream news.

Breonna was never arrested for the murder of the man found dead in her rental car, and she claimed that her drug dealer ex-boyfriend Glover used the car on occasion. It certainly does raise questions about the criminal conduct happening all around her and specifically, in property that was rented in her name and paid for by her.

Liberals, feminists and the glossy magazines who've repeatedly held Breonna up on a pedestal never happen to mention these other facts about her. Perhaps they simply don't know or didn't care to do the research because it didn't fit their narrative.

To be sure, no one deserves to be accidentally shot by law enforcement, but the point is Breonna Taylor appears to be far from the innocent choir girl that liberals, Black Lives Matter organizers and feminists have portrayed her to be.

George Floyd

The same can be said of George Floyd.

In May 2020, a man in Minneapolis named George Floyd reportedly attempted to pass off a counterfeit $20 bill at a Cup Foods store then shoplifted and stumbled out onto the sidewalk, his body reportedly already pulsating with toxic amounts of the illegal drug fentanyl. Police arrived to question him about the shoplifting incident after the store called the police, and the rest of course has since been seen on videotape as Officer Derek Chauvin placed his knee on Floyd's neck and didn't relent.

Even though the medical examiner testified that heart disease and fentanyl were contributing factors to his death — just as there were other contributing factors in Eric Garner's death before him — the officers were charged for his death.

What the mainstream media didn't report on were the nearly 25 years of crime that Floyd lived.

Between 1997 and 2005, Floyd served eight (8) jail terms on various charges including drug possession, theft, and trespassing. In one of these cases, in 1994, Floyd was convicted of possessing crack cocaine.[67]

According to The Associated Press, by August 2007 Floyd was "arrested and charged with aggravated robbery with a deadly weapon. Investigators said he and five other men barged into a woman's apartment, and Floyd pushed a pistol into her abdomen before searching for items to steal."[68]

Floyd pleaded guilty in 2009 and was sentenced to five years in prison. In total, Floyd had been arrested or charged with a crime 23 times in his life and police had stopped or arrested Floyd on 19 of those occasions according to police records, friends and family. https://www.washingtonpost.com/graphics/2020/national/george-floyd-america/policing/

While no one deserves to die in police custody, Floyd was certainly not the angel he was painted to be — literally — in graffiti that would soon pop up on the Cup Foods building.

In each of these cases, the subjects-turned-victims were not entirely innocent — far from it. However, that didn't matter. The narrative had been set, the die had been cast. According to police-hating activists, law enforcement was entirely the problem and therefore must be defunded.

Defunding the Police

At the epicenter of George Floyd's death, Minneapolis was the first city to announce it would consider defunding the police. Thirteen cities rushed to join them[69] and acquiesced to rioters as their cities were literally on fire during violent protests.

What happened next can make one's head spin.

Within just a few weeks of George Floyd's death:

New York City cut a stunning $1 billion from its NYPD budget.

Los Angeles approved a $150 million budget cut to police.

Washington, D.C. cut its police budget $22 million.

Austin, Texas — a liberal bastion in a very red state — followed suit, with its city council voting unanimously to cut $150 million from its police budget.

More cities followed suit.

Baltimore, Maryland cut its police budget $22 million.

Philadelphia, Pennsylvania cut $33 million from its police department.

Portland, Oregon stripped $16 million from its force.

Hartford, Connecticut cut $1 million.

Even Norman, Oklahoma — much like Austin, a liberal university town inside a deeply red state — the police budget was slashed by nearly $1 million.

The City of Atlanta looked into defunding its police budget to the tune of $73 million, although Mayor Keisha Lance Bottoms boasted that under her leadership the city had already defunded the police "for years" by diverting funds away from police and into community organizations that pledged to stop crime.

Last but not least, after months of debate Minneapolis — the city at the apex of it all — moved $1.1 million from its police budget to support "violence interrupters" such as community groups that city officials assured would stop violence in the city.

So, did it work?

What was the result of this cavalcade of defunding?

None of the cities experienced their intended positive outcomes after defunding their police or reallocating funds to non-police community groups.

Literally, none.

In fact, the explosion that would come next would place all Americans in the crosshairs of danger — and it might come as a surprise to the mainstream media that the biggest victims were people of color and women.

Deadly Results of Defunding the Police

Liberal politicians who promised that "Defunding the Police" would be the magic bullet that would solve unrest in their cities and that it would actually improve crime were either lying, delusional, or swept up in the moment of the George Floyd protests.

If I'm to give them the benefit of the doubt, my guess is that out-of-touch politicians actually believed that criminals would magically be relieved the police weren't on their backs anymore and suddenly choose not to commit crime.

Nothing could be further from the truth.

It turns out, crime spiked terribly[70] specifically in cities that defunded their police.

The New York Times reported, "Murder Spiked in 2020 in Cities across the U.S." It was the largest spike in homicides nationally in recorded history.[71]

More specifically, murders spiked nearly 33% in cities with over 1 million people according to the FBI's Uniform Crime Statistics Quarterly Report (the latest statistics available).[72] (Murder rates also jumped double digits in cities with under 1 million population.)

Ironically, women and people of color make up a strong demographic presence in these large cities, and they're the very citizens that progressives always claim to help the most. They include the more than 4 million women who live in New York City; more than 2 million women who live in Los Angeles; and the nearly 1.5 million women who reside in Chicago. People of color also represent approximately 40% of the population in those large cities.

Yet, feminist enablers of the Democrat Party haven't said a word about the women nor the women of color who have been increasingly, negatively, impacted by violent crime after "defunding" public safety in these cities:

Minneapolis

In Minneapolis, crime spiked a stunning 60% in 2020 — the very year the city defunded the police. Violent crime also spiked severely even as Minneapolis politicians were holding sit-ins, catering to violent mobs and pledging to strip police of their funding.

For women in Minneapolis, the news was even worse.

Rapes of women in Minneapolis rose 22% the year the city defunded the police.

Murders also spiked in Minneapolis after the defunding. From December 2020 to Spring 2021, murders rose nearly 50%.[73]

Total crime was also up 22%.

Property crime in Minneapolis after the defunding of police also rose 10%.

In January 2021, crimes involving "gunshots" spiked a stunning 250% over the previous year before the George Floyd incident and the defunding of police.

People of color fared equally as poorly as women in Minneapolis post-defund.

The north side of Minneapolis which has a large minority population experienced the greatest increase in crime after the defunding of police.[74] According to the Minneapolis Star-Tribune, "On the North Side, the Fifth Ward saw violent crime climb 36% over the five-year average, with homicides, robberies and aggravated assaults like shootings and stabbings going up. The neighboring Fourth Ward to the north saw similar increases."

Tragedy upon tragedy inflicted upon a city that had already been through so much.

Ironically, liberal politicians capitulated to violent mobs of liberals and pledged that defunding the police would help people of color yet, a year later statistics show it actually got more women and minorities injured, raped, shot and killed.

Los Angeles

The "City of Angels" is anything but angelic since its mayor defunded the police in 2020.

Murders rose 25% in Los Angeles in just the first half of 2021.

More than 600 people were struck by gunfire in just the first five months of 2021 as Los Angeles saw a spike of 50% in shooting victims.

In fact, the first half of 2021 was the deadliest first six months of any year in Los Angeles in more than 12 years. Month by month, crime was increasing by rates of 21% each month.[75]

Aggravated assaults also increased.

Since then, it has given virtually no signs of slowing down.

Ironically for a town that prides itself on strict gun laws, arrests for weapons charges skyrocketed to 83% which means that more, not fewer, guns flooded the L.A. streets.

In a laughable (if it weren't so serious) article in *Los Angeles Magazine* titled, "'Experts Are Trying to Figure Out What's Causing L.A.'s

Crime Wave," city officials suggested that trying to determine why crime was spiking was like trying to put together "a puzzle."

Allow us to hand you the puzzle pieces.

Even in the wake of the 1992 L.A. riots over the Rodney King verdicts, after the riots concluded crime began to slowly decline.

There was very little difference between the King incident and the Floyd incident, when you consider that both incidents were the police's fault, both instances were caught on tape by alert citizens, aired on broadcast and cable news, and both cities erupted in riots afterward.

However, there was ONE difference: L.A. didn't defund the police in the wake of the King riots. Once the riot died down, the city went back to its normal state, people went back to work and got on with their lives. Even King was able to get on with his, receiving a huge settlement from the city of L.A. and even asking the public for calm in his famous plea, "Can't we all get along?"

The difference between 1992 and 2020 is the fatal misstep by Los Angeles Mayor Eric Garcetti to follow the same knee jerk reaction as other cities, capitulating to violent crowds and stupidly pulling the plug on police funding.

Then again, what do you expect from a guy whose dad lost O.J. Simpson.

Atlanta

In Atlanta. where Mayor Bottoms claimed to have been more "thoughtful" about defunding the police by shuffling funding around to other entities, 2020 actually turned out to be "the most violent year on record" for her city.

The number of murders in the newly-defunded Atlanta were the highest they've been in 20 years, up a shocking 62% according to FBI crime statistics.

Violent crimes went up as well. Across the state of Georgia, violent crime rose 23% and assaults rose 33%. In Atlanta, the figures were even higher.

The crime has been so bad in Atlanta, that the residents of the Buckhead area formed an effort to secede from the city.[76]

By August 2021 — just one year after the defund movement began — Atlanta had already reached the grim total of 100 murders in the city. The prior year, it had taken them until mid-October 2020 to reach that number.

"Thoughtful," Mayor Bottoms?

Hardly.

Austin

In Austin, Texas murders spiked a catastrophic 200% after the city defunded its police.[77]

Austin experienced not only a terrible crime wave in 2020 immediately after defunding, but the trail of destruction continued for more than a year.

Last summer was particularly deadly for Austinites.

In July 2021 — only a year after the defunding — Austin residents were victims to more murders in *just one month* than the entire year of 2020. By the end of Summer last year, Austin had already reached 60 homicides for the year. The last time the murder rate was that high in Austin was in 1984.[78]

Other crimes have spiked in Austin.

Aggravated assaults increased 36%.

Car thefts also increased roughly 77%, though car theft was already on the rise prior to the city's defunding of police. (Perhaps another reason they shouldn't have defunded in the first place.)

This is a terrible record for a city that hosts the world-class University of Texas. The university has nearly 50,000 students, including a high rate of National Honor Society scholars, and 56% of its students being female. Surely these parents of these young, bright women sent their daughters off to this college town with reasonable expectations of safety.

Unfortunately, that expectation is not so reasonable in the Democrat-run, post-Floyd era of policing in Austin.

Washington, D.C.

By the end of 2020 — not even six months after Washington, D.C. defunded the police — the murder rate rose to the highest it had been in 16 years.[79]

By 2021, the figure wasn't any better as homicides outpaced 2020 and soared 46%.[80]

Car theft spiked 50%.

Violent crime also rose 20%, along with gun violence.

In Washington, D.C. the chance of being the victim of a violent crime — such as murder, assault, robbery or rape — was 1 in 95. That is a dismal statistic in the once-walkable town where hundreds of thousands of women reside, including half of whom are women of color and tens of thousands of young female students who attend college in the capital city.

Odd, isn't it, that female Mayor Muriel Bowser — once awarded as the Boys and Girls Club of Greater Washington's first "FEARLESS WOMAN" Award[81] — would want to defund the police and instill fear in lives of so many young women and women of color in D.C. by placing them in the crosshairs of criminals.

So much for fearless feminism.

REFUNDING THE POLICE — Too Little, Too Late

Lo and behold, one year after the "defund the police" movement was successful in getting liberal mayors to scale back police in their towns, *The New York Times* reported that crime spikes[82] have forced liberal mayors to reconsider[83] and to re-fund the police.

New York City

In the wake of devastating crime spikes, even one of the first defunders of police — leftist, Communist-loving, New York City Mayor Bill DeBlasio — opted to refund the police.

Despite pledging to cut a whopping $1 billion from the NYPD police budget, DeBlasio ended up cutting only about half that amount.

The mayor also authorized $92 million for a new precinct after previously killing the project in the Summer of 2020.

In what might be the biggest victory, liberal candidates in the New York City mayoral race turned away from further conversations about defunding the police, and in fact spoke of ways to improve public safety amid a crime wave. A shocking 93% of New York City registered Democrat voters said that crime was their #1 issue in the race.

Minneapolis

In Minneapolis, the city opted to restore $4.5 million to the police department in 2021, after defunding it by $6 million in the wake of the George Floyd riots. Out-of-control crime and early officer retirement were stated as reasons for the refunding.

Baltimore

Baltimore's Mayor once led the effort to defund the police by $22 million when he was a city council member. When he ran for mayor, he pledged to "reimagine the police."

Re-imagine he did.

After reviewing crime statistics, the Baltimore mayor decided to "reimagine" police funding to the tune of a $27-million increase.

Oakland

Following a rise in murders in Oakland, in 2021 city leaders restored more than $3 million of the $29 million they cut in 2020. Oakland's mayor also proposed an increase to the police budget by $24 million, which would make the proposed increases in 2021 slightly more than the amount that was cut in the wake of the 2020 George Floyd riots. What folly.

Los Angeles

Like the other cities facing crime spikes, Los Angeles Mayor Garcetti proposed a refund of $50 million in 2021, in an attempt to piece back together the Los Angeles Police Department after $150 million cuts in 2020.

Seattle

After enjoying their "summer of love," Seattle's city council came to (some of) their senses as well. They opted to only defund their police by 11%, rather than the 50% originally promised during the heated CHAZ/CHOP occupation in 2020.

Austin

In some scenarios, state legislatures are stepping in to save cities from themselves.

Republicans stepped in to stop the bleeding with Texas House Bill 1900, which penalizes any cities who choose to "defund the police" if city officials do not align their budgets with a proper police-to-citizens ratio.

Burlington, Vermont

The town that once had Socialist Bernie Sanders as its mayor has also now re-funded its police force and in quite a turnabout is now offering $10,000 signing bonuses for new police recruits.

Washington, D.C.

After defunding her city's police department to the tune of $22 million, Mayor Muriel Bowser has also done an about-face and agreed to refund the police $27 million — $5 million more than she took away in 2020.

Conclusion

When they proudly defunded the police, liberals often cited protection of minority communities; however, crime statistics show that they actually ended up hurting minority communities.

In a Gallup Poll not long after the death of George Floyd, a surprising 61% of Black Americans stated that they wanted more police officers — not fewer — in their communities.[84]

Newsweek reported that 81% of Black Americans either wanted more police in their communities or for the level to stay the same.[85] Black Americans cited the violence in their communities which occurred *after* the defunding of police as the reason.

Funny, if you watched mainstream media and pop culture, you would have thought that Black Americans were more concerned about police pulling their kids over and shooting them. Yet that's *not* what Black parents were concerned about. That was the lie peddled by reality stars and media hosts. The truth is that Black Americans, even in the wake of George Floyd, actually wanted police in their neighborhoods because for a year they got a glimpse of the world without them.

In the end, all of this "defunding" and "refunding" speaks to the foolishness of the liberal rush to defund the police in 2020. What a fool's errand it has been to see hard-working, upstanding police officers defamed and defunded — only to have cities drag their residents through violent crime waves, murders and rapes before realizing their mistakes and committing to fund the police again.

Imagine if these cities not defunded the police at all. They would have saved countless lives and traumatic experiences as men and women across America joined the ranks of violent crime victims.

Let this be a lesson in the disastrous effects of bowing to the demands of violent protestors and making important policy decisions in the "fog of war." Let this be a lesson the next time "mob rule" takes over and attempts to change the fabric of some of our greatest American institutions.

HOMEWORK

- ➢ Read Heather MacDonald's book, <u>"The War on Cops: How the New Attack on Law and Order Makes Everyone Less Safe."</u> One of my favorite guests to book when I worked at FOX, Heather is one of the best experts on policing in America. She investigated a phenomenon she termed the "Ferguson effect" which since 2014 has caused officers to back away from proactive policing out of fear of stoking racial riots, such as those that occurred in Ferguson, Missouri. That effect has continued well into 2022 more than two years after the George Floyd incident and the ensuing Black Lives Matter protests.
- ➢ Also read Heather's work at The Manhattan Institute. Her regular reports on policing as well as diversity and "woke" culture are worth the read: https://www.manhattan-institute.org/expert/heather-mac-donald

REFERENCES:

[63] New York City Medical Examiner's Findings in the Eric Garner Case
https://apnews.com/article/1903161fb60848a7851e68b25167f73b

[64] Reports: Breonna Taylor's Boyfriend Shot at Police First
https://www.dailymail.co.uk/news/article-8799423/Breonna-Taylor-cops-knocked-three-times-grand-jury-testimony-reveals.html

[65] Testimony: Breonna Taylor Had Been Handling Ex-Boyfriend Jamarcus Glover's Cash "Proceeds" from Drug Deals
https://www.wkyt.com/2020/08/26/warrants-issued-for-arrest-of-breonna-taylors-ex-boyfriend-amid-leaked-new-documents/

[66] Was a Dead Body Found in Breonna Taylor's Car in 2016? Yes.
https://heavy.com/news/breonna-taylor-rental-car/

[67] George Floyd 1994 Arrest for Possession of Crack Cocaine
https://en.wikipedia.org/wiki/George_Floyd

[68] The Associated Press: George Floyd Arrested and Charged with Aggravated Robbery with a Deadly Weapon after Shoving a Pistol into a Woman's Stomach, then Robbing Her
https://apnews.com/article/virus-outbreak-us-news-ap-top-news-hip-hop-and-rap-houston-a55d2662f200ead0da4fed9e923b60a7/gallery/57257393c7b148c7ac8a9a0de92a59d2

[69] Defunding of Police: By City
https://www.forbes.com/sites/jemimamcevoy/2020/08/13/at-least-13-cities-are-defunding-their-police-departments/?sh=14fca21d29e3

[70] Crime Increases as Police Defunded
https://nationalpolicesupportfund.com/what-happens-when-cities-defund-police-departments/

[71] NY Times: Murders Spiked in 2020 in Cities across the U.S., Largest Spike in Recorded History
https://www.nytimes.com/2021/09/27/us/fbi-murders-2020-cities.html

[72] Murder Rates Rise in Big Cities, FBI Uniform Crime Statistics Quarterly Report
https://www.wsj.com/articles/cities-reverse-defunding-the-police-amid-rising-crime-11622066307

[73] Rape and Other Violent Crimes Increase in Minneapolis after Defunding the Police

https://minnesota.cbslocal.com/2021/01/22/early-2021-minneapolis-crime-stats-show-250-increase-in-gunshot-victims/

[74] Minority Wards Hit Hardest by Crime Spikes in Minneapolis after Defunding
https://www.startribune.com/minneapolis-violent-crimes-soared-in-2020-amid-pandemic-protests/600019989/

[75] NBC Los Angeles: Violent Crime Outpaces Crime of Recent Years
https://www.nbclosangeles.com/news/local/2021-violent-crime-in-los-angeles-continues-lapd/2612701/

[76] Buckhead Residents Seek to Secede from Atlanta over Crime
https://www.washingtonpost.com/national/buckhead-secession-atlanta-crime/2021/05/29/30e25cce-be25-11eb-b26e-53663e6be6ff_story.html

[77] Violent Crimes Spike in Austin, Crime Growing More than Population Growth
https://www.kvue.com/article/news/local/austin-homicide-record-number-2021/269-e3c419af-9722-456f-9b5d-c044944e128d

[78] Murders in Austin, Texas Highest since 1984
https://www.kvue.com/article/news/local/austin-homicide-record-number-2021/269-e3c419af-9722-456f-9b5d-c044944e128d

[79] The Washington Post: Murder Rates in D.C. Rose to 16-Year High after Defunding of Police
https://www.washingtonpost.com/local/public-safety/homicides-rise-washington/2020/12/31/59dd659e-3953-11eb-bc68-96af0daae728_story.html

[80] D.C. Murders Soar another 46%
https://www.wusa9.com/article/news/crime/dc-homicide-rate-skyrocketing-2021/65-fad6f3f9-c527-49b5-b949-c8231373d265

[81] Mayor Muriel Bowser Awarded "Fearless Woman" Award, Despite Placing Other Women in Danger
https://bgcgw.org/fearless-women/

[82] FBI Crime Statistics Report for 2020
https://www.fbi.gov/news/pressrel/press-releases/fbi-releases-2020-crime-statistics

[83] Cities Reverse Defunding of Police Amid Rising Crime
https://www.wsj.com/articles/cities-reverse-defunding-the-police-amid-rising-crime-11622066307

[84] Gallup Poll: Black Americans Want Police to Keep Presence in Their Communities
https://news.gallup.com/poll/316571/black-americans-police-retain-local-presence.aspx

[85] Newsweek: 81% of Black Americans Want Either More Police or the Same Presence, Not Less
https://www.newsweek.com/81-black-americans-dont-want-less-police-presence-despite-protestssome-want-more-cops-poll-1523093

CRITICAL RACE THEORY, PARENTS, and FBI... Oh, My!

School board meetings across America today are abuzz with talk of Critical Race Theory (CRT).

It has parents asking, "What exactly is CRT?"

The more important question should be, "Where did it actually come from?"

It might surprise Americans that Critical Race Theory[86] was born out of the 1960s liberal Marxist movement, when radical liberals hated everything about America — her capitalism, her institutions, and to some extent, her people. They hated the "system." You know, just as they do today.

The early version of CRT in the 1960s was simply called, "Critical Theory."

In that era, the theory supported pitting workers against the Capitalist system, aka "sticking it to the man." Radical leftists asserted that if Capitalism was bad, then all of the products of industry that came out of that Capitalist system were bad, too. (To a large extent, feminists agreed with them — especially the "sticking it to the man" part.)

Most proponents of this 1960s version of Critical Theory were not just Marxists but also Socialists, much like "The Squad" and many in the Democrat Party today. They believed that the very systems of America, the very engines of industry, would be more fair if they were run by a Socialist state. They based this presumption on the theory that Socialism would equally share the gains of the system with everyone, which of course we know throughout the history of Socialism that has not been the case.

In the 1970s and 1980s as more in academia studied this theory, Critical Theory began to evolve and focus more on race. Specifically, it suggested that American systems of industry, justice and law had disadvantaged people of color especially. As a result of those discussions about color, Critical "Race" Theory was born.

The Founding Mother of CRT

One of the founders of Critical Race Theory — Kimberlé Williams Crenshaw[87] — has a background that is equally as radical as the social construct itself.

Crenshaw is a radical Black feminist whose career makes former President Barack Obama's and former First Lady Michelle Obama's college interests in radical politics and the Weather Underground look like Tiddlywinks.

She got steeped in the concepts of intersectionality and Marxist critical theory at Harvard Law School, and she overlayed the filter of race and gender onto what were already radical theories.

As a member of Harvard Law School she held the first-ever workshop on Critical Race Theory and the rest, as they say, is history.

To say that Crenshaw has been simply an "academic," as the left is suggesting today (no doubt in order to make her look less radical) would be a great mischaracterization of her career.

The founder of CRT is very astute in politics. She knows exactly what she is doing.

Many people aren't aware but in the 1980s, the founder of CRT was an adviser to feminist Anita Hill's "slick legal team" when Hill famously testified against Supreme Court nominee Clarence Thomas.[88] In her testimony, Hill alleged that Thomas had made sexual references to her, claimed he discussed films in which women were having sex with animals, and even allegedly once remarked that it looked like there was a "pubic hair" on his can of Coke (as if that would be attractive to a woman!). Hill had no evidence of these statements, not even an audio recording, despite that fact that she said it happened routinely. In fact, it was the 80s version of the Christine Blasey Ford's testimony during the Supreme Court confirmation hearings of Bret Kavanaugh in that Anita Hill claims she never intended to testify until she was outed in a "leaked" letter.

Hmm…sounds familiar, doesn't it?

Believe me when I often say that Democrats use the same page out of the playbook over and over again.

In the same way that many Americans believe that Blasey Ford and Anita Hill spun a yarn during heavily-watched Supreme Court confirmation hearings, there is evidence that Crenshaw may have done the same in her career.

In the 1980s, Crenshaw began to take her Critical Race Theory workshops on the road (likely funded by Harvard at that point). CRT began to be critiqued by other scholars as too based in theoretical talking points instead of legitimate legal arguments based on law. According to one report, in at least one of her workshops, Crenshaw is quoted as waving her hand at the criticism and suggesting that her Critical Race Theory arguments could be best described as, "Fake it till you make it."

That in and of itself is alarming, that the architect of such a radical theory gaining a foothold in America today, once stated that her own academic gobbledygook was "fake."

However, it does explain the radical Black feminist Crenshaw's core principles of CRT: her suggested that you can name your own reality and just keep talking until your opponent finally acquiesces. That describes the entire Black Lives Matter movement of 2020. In fact, it describes almost the entire liberal movement today.

In fact, in her CRT teachings Crenshaw and her colleagues instruct followers that if you cannot win an argument on the facts — especially in a court of law — that instead of presenting evidence, you should switch to tell a "narrative" (i.e., a story). Crenshaw instructs followers to tell a story in such a way that it will cause the other person to become so "empathetic" that the person you're arguing with will simply forget about the facts and give in to your point of view. She specifically suggests that lawyers should argue this way in our legal system today.

Sounds nuts, right?

The creator of CRT says that you can, in essence, make your own truth.

It explains a lot about CRT in our education system right now, as well as transgenderism, as well as what I call the "Oprahfication" of society today in which we have allowed people to share "their truth" as if it is the gospel. As in, "my truth," "your truth, "her truth" and "his truth," when in reality there can only be one truth: God's truth, which is THE truth.

While Crenshaw's teachings sound ludicrous and go against every tenant of our legal system today in which you are supposed to win by presenting the facts then have a jury or judge adjudicate those facts, it's not the first time that her tactics have worked.

According to at least one scholar, it explains how the O.J. Simpson verdict was reached. Throughout the trial and in closing arguments, Simpson's attorney Johnny Cochran appealed to the jury on the grounds that they should not judge the case based on its own legal merit and the multitudes of DNA evidence found at the scene, but instead on the grounds that Black Americans — and especially Black American men — have been living in a racist society and specifically, a racist criminal justice system. Never mind the fact that Simpson was a wealthy NFL player, with millions of dollars and a lifetime pension and probably had more in common with his white neighbors in Brentwood than the jury. Cochran's message to the downtown Los Angeles jury was that this verdict, in this trial, was the way to even the playing field.

Did Johnny Cochran follow Crenshaw in her teachings of CRT? I don't know, and we can't ask him since he's since passed away, but the Simpson verdict may have been the first, most relatable example of

CRT legal arguments winning in their goal to dismantle the American justice system.

Make no mistake, this is dangerous territory we have entered into. Although the intention might have initially been to level the playing field for Black Americans, this construct could be twisted very easily to cause advantages for bad players within the legal system whether it's a wealthy NFL football player or regular criminals out on our streets.

The Three Components of CRT

There are three main components to CRT and when a person understands these, one will see just how far this theory has infiltrated our American systems today:

- **America's Justice, Capitalist and Legal Systems Are Inherently Bad** — Unlike its Marxist precursor, CRT goes further than simply saying that Capitalism is bad. CRT suggests that even our justice system and legal systems are inherently *bad*. According to CRT, because those systems are unfair and have been racist in the past, they need to be destroyed.

  We have begun to see the beginnings of this destruction of the criminal justice system in America through the "defunding of police." By stripping the funding of those who work the front lines of the system, you begin to impact the system's ability to exist. That's just fine to proponents of CRT who believe that the system has been so racist, that it should no longer exist.

  The elimination of cash bail is another tool that CRT activists have used to chip away at the criminal justice system. By not requiring criminals to post any money in order to get out of jail, they escape the otherwise punitive parts of the justice system such as incarceration. To CRT theorists, the incarceration system has been so unjust, that it had it coming.

  CRT activists, then, should have issue with President Biden's co-sponsoring of the 1994 Crime Bill which actually incarcerated more Black American men than were enslaved in American history, but hey, let's not bother the theorists with these details.

CRT goes so far as to suggest that some can even use violence on systems that are unfair to them:

- Critical Race Theory and the politicians who were influenced by it, basically supported the theory during the Black Lives Matter protests and Antifa riots that you ought to let people rob and loot and burn things down because the American system had been racist in the past, therefore we should allow people to get their rage out on the system, burn down businesses, and assault upwards of 100,000 cops without punishing the perpetrators.

- There is a movie similar to this called, "The Purge" where citizens are allowed to go out for one night and do anything they want, break any laws they'd like, without ramifications. This is, in essence, what happened for more than 109 days in the Summer of 2020 when then-presidential candidate Joe Biden said nothing about the harm that rioters and protestors were causing to fellow man and our American systems. Biden and the Democrats sort of snickered, as if they believed America had it coming. Perhaps CRT really stands for "Critical Retribution Theory."

- **According to CRT, Dr. Martin Luther, King, Jr. Was Wrong; We Shouldn't Try to Be Color Blind** — CRT also critiques the idea of Dr. Martin Luther King, Jr.'s idea of a color blind society, which many Americans have tried to achieve since Dr. King's famous "I have a dream" speech in Washington DC and he asked us all to judge his children by the content of their character not the color of their skin. The proponents of CRT say that is not only impossible, but it suggests that we actually SHOULD judge people by the color of their skin. Alarmingly, they mean that Black Americans should now be superior to whites, Asians, Jews, Hispanics, Indian Americans and others in a new society. I don't believe that's what America wants at its core. Are we imperfect? Yes, but America is extraordinarily proud of its melting pot of different races, colors and creeds.

- **CRT Suggests if You Deem a System Bad, You Can Penalize the People within the System** — CRT initially taught that it's not that individuals necessarily are racist, it's the system that sucks. However, CRT goes diametrically against that today as it seeks to penalize the very individuals within the system who happen to be performing well. (Examples of these would be stockbrokers and hedge fund managers within the Capitalist system; individual police officers within the criminal justice system; Asians; and white people.)

We see this more frequently in university settings today, such as the University of California Los Angeles where a colleague of mine, Professor Gordon Klein, was asked to grade Black students more leniently than white students in the wake of the George Floyd riots. This request wouldn't necessarily help those Black students become better in their academics nor more prepared for the real world, but CRT activists said they needed leniency because of the grief from the George Floyd incident and the overall racism of the American justice system. Actions like that not only wouldn't have helped the Black students get to a better place in life, but it also would have penalized Asian American students and others who had scored high grades at the time and would be affected by any grading on a curve/leniency plan. However, CRT proponents simply didn't care — they were alright with other students being penalized, so long as Black students were given an advantage to make up for the ills of society that had pressed upon them and their ancestors. It was a textbook CRT drill.

Critics of CRT have found that this sort of differential treatment and penalizing of those who happen to excel in the current system could lead to anti-Asian and anti-Semitic sentiment. We saw this precise thing happen in New York City after the COVID-19 and the Black Lives Matter protests — Asian-Americans were ruthlessly attacked and Jews became the targets of anti-Semitic hate crimes. In case after case, Black Americans were seen kicking Asian-American grandmas to the ground, beating them mercilessly, and defaming Jewish property in what I believe were a result of Black Americans angry about those who had excelled in American system, a system in which they had been disproportionately disadvantaged. They were simply doing what today's CRT suggested they should do: tear down the *individuals* within the system they hated so much.

The problem is that CRT can lead to precisely this kind of violent reaction — a quest to tear others down in retribution against the "systems." If someone is successful inside the Capitalist system, then CRT views that person as inherently evil as well. In my view, this is a dangerous slippery slope and an incredibly dangerous movement.

Even in its less violent form, CRT's assertion that we should judge people differently and that people become more "supreme" than others to get revenge on the past — from academia to the justice system — goes against all of the tenants of America's forward-looking spirit. While America is not perfect, we've been a nation that strives to constantly improve — from the Emancipation Proclamation, to women's suffrage, to the Civil Rights movement, to the feminist movement.

That feminists would support CRT as they are doing today in support of their liberal, academic friends is a real head-scratcher. Clearly feminists have forgotten the tenets of their own movement, which called for "equality." Yet, their support of Critical Race Theory suggests that feminists are now okay with some individuals in society being treated more supremely than others and that, sadly, is harshly "unequal."

CRT, FBI and Parents…Oh, My!

The growing trend of CRT in schools is equally problematic, especially when one considers that CRT educators are pushing for African-American children to be "supreme" above white children.

Nothing could be more ridiculous than telling an 11-year-old today that they are responsible for something their great-great-great-great-great grandfather did 200 years ago.

Parents are right to be concerned about this encroaching curriculum, and they're right to protest schools who seek to teach it.

The New York Post reports that Megyn Kelly, former FOX News and NBC News host, yanked her son from his swanky Upper West Side school over a racist letter that circulated and landed on her desk. The letter accused white kids of being future "killer cops" (read: people who would allegedly grow up to kill Black people) and suggested that white students "gleefully soak in their whitewashed history."[89]

Make no mistake, this is all part of Critical Race Theory in our schools.

As parents across the country began to learn about the dangers of CRT, they began to question its teaching in schools. Concerned moms and dads began to show up at school board meetings.

However, as is the case with most radical liberals today, the school boards and the Biden administration made clear that they don't appreciate dissenting opinions.

By now, everyone has heard that the Biden administration communicated with the FBI about siccing the nation's federal law enforcement agency on parents.

What most didn't know at the time is that the request didn't initiate with Biden, it actually came from the National School Board Association — a liberal labor union that represents school board bureaucrats.[90]

You see, while "school teachers" and "school boards" sound like innocuous terms, these educator-activists are some of the most far-left, progressive ideologues of our time. That puts them directly at odds with most parents of young schoolchildren, who send their kids to school to learn about reading and arithmetic not to learn about radical, racist, social constructs.

The sad truth is the adults in school today aren't protecting your children — they are instead working hand-in-hand with the Biden administration, the creators of CRT curriculum, and others who wish to see these radical ideals forced upon America.

With their liberal, unionized, bureaucratic friends in the education establishment, these educator-activists (most of whom are women, by the way) are now peddlers of hate against all of our American systems. They've joined forces in order to bully us all — or as the founder of CRT says to *just keep talking until they run us out* of the school board meetings — or if the Biden administration has it way, until the parents are dragged away by the FBI kicking and screaming.

It sounds complex, but one must understand that the ultimate goal of these leftists in power is for all of our traditional American systems to collapse. They have learned that the only way it will happen is if Marxist-based CRT gains a foothold in America. These educators, politicians and social constructionists who teach history know exactly how it works in authoritarian, Marxist, socialist societies: If they can indoctrinate kids, then they can shape the next generation of adults. If the adults in the next generation are already comfortable with Marxist rule, then America is doomed.

CRT Creep in "Woke" Corporate America

Sadly, CRT isn't being contained to public schools nor higher education systems.

There are increasing reports of major Wall Street firms bringing in "Critical Race Theory" trainers to perform so-called diversity training.

One such example is American Express.

That's right, "American" Express.

American Express (AmEx) is one of the world's most successful capitalist companies. They earned a $2.3 billion profit in the last quarter alone by offering financial products to individuals and businesses.

Sadly, American Express has gone woke and in a bizarre, self-loathing way they are now attacking — wait for it — American capitalism.

The New York Post reports that American Express has forced employees to listen to socialist propaganda from none other than Khalil Muhammad — the great-grandson of the founder of the Nation of Islam.

During his presentation, Muhammad told employees that capitalism is based on "racist logics and forms of domination" — coincidentally, the *exact same things* that Critical Race Theory pushes. In other words, the great-grandson of the Nation of Islam told capitalists at one of the largest American financial companies that their "system" sucks.

Muhammad then proceeded to tell American Express employees that their company should begin to "price" customers based on the color of their skin.

That's right, people who have fought for racial equality are now telling companies to actually discriminate based on the color of people's skin.

It goes against everything that Dr. Martin Luther King, Jr. taught Americans.

It's difficult to know if American Express knew what his remarks would be in advance, or if the billion-dollar-company felt it had no choice but to acquiesce to social justice warriors in the aftermath of Black Lives Matter protests. My guess is that the company got shaken down in the way that Jesse Jackson and the Rainbow-PUSH Coalition reportedly did of major corporations in the 1980s and 1990s.[91] In fact, I bet all of the major companies are facing the same proposition.

After forcing its employees to sit through this racist dribble, American Express reportedly mandated employees to take part in radical Critical Race Theory trainings which reportedly required employees to identify themselves in a racial "hierarchy" to determine whether they are an "oppressor" or the "oppressed." The exercise no doubt was to make people feel that "empathy" and pain that CRT founding mother Crenshaw said we should force white people to feel.

This is happening all day long in corporations across America.

I know of at least one other Wall Street firm in New York City who subjected its employees to dozens of hours of online trainings and lectures from a social justice warrior who straight up told employees, "Each of you are racist." That so-called "expert" was seen the very next day on MSBNC discussing her support of — you guessed it — Critical Race Theory.

CRT proponents can speak their narrative all day long on Wall Street, but it doesn't change the fact that capitalism is still the best institution on the planet. Why? It has done more to raise up minorities and women out of poverty than any other system around the globe.

To suggest that America's leading financial institutions now have to capitulate to the socialist, Marxist proponents of Critical Race Theory shows just how far CRT has managed to worm its way into the American conversation, from elementary schools to the halls of Wall Street.

Conclusion

Critical Race Theory seeks to upend every American institution that has served us, such as capitalism and the American justice system.

However, the movement is so obsessed with race it becomes as race-focused as the individuals and institutions it criticizes.

It's puzzling why so many American feminists are adopting critical race theory when it absolutely puts women — especially white women, Asian women, Hispanic women, Indian American women, and mixed-race women — into positions now subordinate to some races of men.

Instead of striving for a more perfect society where ALL members of society are treated equally, CRT activists instead advocate for more racism. That is offensive to the numerous Civil Rights fights and feminist rights battles that were fought to advance America.

HOMEWORK

➤ As Americans, what can be done about this creeping curriculum? For starters, parents should continue protesting CRT at every turn in their kids' schools. If you don't have kids, maybe you have an American Express card. Start by cancelling your card and tell American Express the reason for your cancellation. If you think it won't matter to American Express, just remember that in November of 2016 more than 600,000 Americans pulled the plug on ESPN over the disrespectful, unpatriotic act of football players kneeling at games. It was the largest single-month "unsubscribe" of ESPN since its inception. Their profits tumbled, and NFL's ratings also hit their lowest point until NFL Commission Roger Goodell finally ruled that kneeling in protest would no longer be televised. American Express' phone number is (800) 528-4800, their mailing address is P.O. Box 981535, El Paso, TX 79998-1535, and their Twitter handle is @AskAmEx if you'd like to let them know how you feel.

➤ Also read Vivek Ramaswamy's book, "Woke, Inc.: Inside Corporate America's Social Justice Scam." In it, Ramaswamy suggests that woke, "Stakeholder capitalism" has taken over corporations and outlines how corporations can check their politics at the boardroom door.

REFERENCES:

[86] Critical Race Theory
https://www.britannica.com/topic/critical-race-theory

[87] The Mother of Critical Race Theory – Kimberle' Williams Crenshaw
https://www.vanityfair.com/news/2021/07/how-critical-race-theory-mastermind-kimberle-crenshaw-is-weathering-the-culture-wars

[88] Crenshaw Worked for Anita Hill
https://www.dailywire.com/news/6-pieces-evidence-anita-hill-was-lying-amanda-prestigiacomo

[89] NY Post: Parents Yank Children from Schools that Ask Kids to Apologize for Being White

https://nypost.com/2020/11/18/megyn-kelly-pulls-sons-from-woke-uws-school-over-anti-white-letter/

[90] National School Board Association Letter to Biden Administration Requesting the FBI https://nsba.org/-/media/NSBA/File/nsba-letter-to-president-biden-concerning-threats-to-public-schools-and-school-board-members-92921.pdf

[91] Jesse Jackson and the Rainbow-PUSH Coalition https://www.latimes.com/archives/la-xpm-2001-mar-13-mn-36957-story.html

SOCIALISM & 'THE SQUAD:' WHY THEY'RE BOTH BAD FOR WOMEN

Alexandria Ocasio-Cortez and "The Squad" have been advocating for socialism since the day they ran for office.

It's hard to believe they've made such progress in advancing socialism since they were elected a in the 2018 midterm elections.

The four original members of "The Squad" — which consists of AOC (R-New York), Ilhan Omar (D-Minnesota), Rashida Tlaib (D-Michigan) and Ayanna Presley (D-Massachusetts) — were reportedly inspired by Socialist Bernie Sanders' presidential run in 2016.

Since they were sworn into office, they have welcomed two other radicals into their Congressional clique: Democrat Representatives Jamaal Bowman of New York and Cori Bush of Missouri, who were swept into office in 2020 in the wake of the George Floyd riots and Black Lives Matter protests.

What a difference these six women have made in pushing their narrative so aggressively and so persuasively that I believe they've begun to significantly move the needle on Americans' acceptance of socialism.

Here's the proof: Polling shows that for the first time in American history, a majority of Democrats now believe that socialism is a more favorable system than capitalism.

In a FOX News poll last fall, nearly 60% of Democrat-registered voters had a positive view of socialism[92] compared to just 49% who felt positively about capitalism.

The numbers are a huge shift from where they were 18 months prior, when just 40% of Democrats had favorable views of socialism. That is a stunning 20-point shift toward a vastly different way of governing in America — one that was pushed by "The Squad" in unfettered mainstream media interviews during that same time period.

Even more unsettling? A majority of Generation Z (young adults born between 1997-2012) now have an unfavorable view of capitalism at 54%, while only 42% of them have a positive view of it.[93]

Before older generations pooh-pooh the Gen Z figures as just a bunch of "kids these days" or a small segment of the population, allow me to point out that Generation Z represents a whopping 72 million Americans.

Even more shocking?

Gen-Z'ers aren't the only ones beginning to view socialism as a good thing.

An *Axios*-Momentive poll taken last fall shows that adults aged 18-34 also have an increasingly negative view of capitalism. At the same time, they are increasingly viewing socialism more favorably.

In fact, less than half of American adults aged 18-34 held a positive view of capitalism (just 49%) nearly half of them (46%) actually viewed capitalism negatively. (Compare this to 2019, when the numbers were flipped: nearly 60% of adults viewed capitalism positively.)[94]

The news is even more discouraging among young Republicans.

Young Republicans have also come to view capitalism less favorably.

According to the Axios-Momentive poll, young Republicans who had a favorable view of capitalism fell from 81% in 2019, to just 66% in 2021. This is *not* an encouraging statistic for a Republican Party counting on the next generation of blue-blazer activists to carry the mantle of capitalism.

The polling shows just how far "The Squad" — along with Sanders and Elizabeth Warren — have brought socialism into mainstream conversation in America.

"The Squad's" socialist philosophies are especially ironic when you consider that the leader of their pack, AOC, was raised in Westchester County, New York — one of the wealthiest counties in America. The median home price in Westchester rings in at $870,000.

Her sister-in-arms, Rep. Omar, is also an odd proponent of socialism. Omar came to America when her *very* powerful family fled from war in Somalia and was taken in by the United States as refugees. Under America's refugee program, Omar was given every opportunity to succeed, and she parlayed that into her candidacy to become a prestigious member of the United States Congress. Omar's net worth is now $3 million, according to *Money, Inc.*, even though her annual salary as a congress member is just $125,000.

That these ladies have been given so much, yet proselytize for a socialist system that gives women so little is quite stunning.

So, how did Americans change their views on socialism so rapidly?

The late Andrew Breitbart said it best, "Politics flows downstream from culture."

Lefty liberals have already received favorable coverage in the media for decades. Yet AOC and "The Squad" were a different story. New on the scene, they were young, attractive, and fashionable, donning their "women's suffrage white blazers" during their first State of the Union.

Soon, every mainstream outlet tripped over themselves to glorify these young ladies. Glossy magazine covers once reserved for Hollywood starlets and the rich and famous were splashed with members of "The Squad." Cute sweatshirts emblazoned with "RGB" and "AOC" on them flooded the market. AOC could be found hopping into video game rooms and chatting with players, drawing a record number of users. Suddenly, socialism wasn't the scary thing that students read about in their high school history books.

It's not unlike the story of The Pied Piper. The people of a 13th Century German town hire a piper to help rid a town of rats, but instead the piper shows up wearing fascinating multicolored clothing, turns on the town, hypnotizes the children, and leads them astray. The analogy of the town of rats is of course Washington, D.C. and the modern-day pied pipers are the members of "The Squad."

The Unfortunate Opening

Pop culture causing socialism to be "cool" only explains *part* of the move toward socialism today.

Unfortunately, other events came into the play to help socialism improve its once dour reputation like the rancid soup at a Young Democratic Socialists soup-can drive.

I believe the COVID-19 pandemic was a major factor in opening the door to socialism.

The world witnessed America's capitalist system grind to a halt during the pandemic, and millions of Americans heard pedantically, every day, from mainstream media about the great disparities between the wealthy and the less fortunate.

Corporate offices were no longer open. No one sat at their desks anymore. No one witnessed the products of industry (with the exception of their Amazon delivery driver bringing boxes of goodies to their homes each day.)

Suddenly, telecommuters on laptops didn't need anyone. They didn't miss their bosses lingering in their doorways. They could sort of check out on Zoom calls and attend in pajamas (well, at least from the waist down.) And on Friday afternoons, they could slip out of the office without telling anyone.

Americans became acutely disconnected from the American capitalist system that has worked well for the last 100 years.

Additionally, capitalism quite glaringly appeared not to be able to solve some problems.

Americans' hearts broke at the images of cars pulling into food bank lines — sometimes in miles-long lines, even in places like Texas.

Headlines of past-due rents and shuttered businesses flashed on the news and soon — even though Democrat policies caused most of that in big liberal cities — millions of fear-paralyzed Americans began to question, "Why isn't the system we've known and loved for so long, not helping us?"

Enter AOC, Cori Bush and Rashida Tlaib who spoke loudly for their disadvantaged districts, on behalf of residents at risk of being evicted and the American systems they claim had failed them.

All of the ingredients of socialism were beginning began to bind together like the ingredients of loaf of bread in a Bernie Sanders bread line.

It was a recipe for disaster for American capitalism.

While major corporations grabbled with how to keep their employees safe and business owners scrambled to keep their doors open and their lights on, they didn't have time to share the great stories of capitalism from the last century.

Meantime, "The Squad" had already set the table for socialism for two years; then, when the pandemic hit they served it up to Americans hungry for something better.

Liberals once again took a page from Rahm Emanuel, the former adviser to President Barack Obama who once said, "Never let a crisis go to waste."

Using that mantra, "The Squad" capitalized on the panic of the pandemic and told voters that socialism would have helped them more than capitalism.

However, socialism isn't better.

In fact, it's deadly.

Sadly, "The Squad" is made up mostly of women, yet the socialism they push has hurt women the most throughout history.

Since its inception, Socialism has killed 100 people around the globe — the majority of whom were women and children.

Even in times when their lives were spared, women did not flourish in socialist societies, and they certainly did not advance like women of America. Any American woman who tries to tell you otherwise is either deluding herself, or lying to you.

Let's take a look at some specific examples of female life under socialism.

SOCIALISM'S NASTY TRACK RECORD AROUND THE GLOBE:

The Soviet Union

The Russian Empire was one of the most powerful governments that spanned multiple continents beginning in 1721. With more than 125 million citizens by the close of the 1800s, the Russian Empire had the third-largest population in the world only behind China and India, and it was a force to be reckoned with.

That is, until socialism came.

Socialist forces within Russia started a Civil War which was fought over the merits of capitalism, the rise of the worker, and the idea that a centralized, socialist government would serve society better. (Sound familiar?)

Russia's Civil War began in 1917 and ended 10 years later with socialism its only real victor. Her people would be the ultimate loser. The ten-year period of 1917 to 1927 saw Russia go from a powerful empire to a socialist state, which was re-named the Soviet Union. (Both

Vladimir Lenin and Joseph Stalin came to power during that time, and forms of socialism were also named after them.) For the next 60 years, under socialism the Soviet Union would see prices of goods skyrocket, nearly go bankrupt, starve its people, and cut off the rest of the world during the Cold War.

The advancement of women? Forget about it. People were too busy to think about women's equality; they were simply trying to survive.

According to the book, "Back in the USSR: What Life Was Like in the Soviet Union" by José Luis Ricón Fernández de la Puente and published by the Adam Smith Institute in 2017,[95] the Soviet Union was not exactly the best place for women.

Life expectancies fell in the Soviet Union during the 1960s and 1970s, when socialism was in full swing.

Under socialized medicine, Soviets experienced 30 times as much typhoid fever and 20 times as many cases as the measles as the United States.

Cancer detection rates under the socialist Soviet health system were only half as good as American detection rates. Many doctors in the socialized healthcare system could not even read a basic echocardiogram.

According to the author, other parts of Soviet life (outside of life and death crises) weren't exactly fun, either.

By 1976, only two-thirds of families in the Soviet Union had a refrigerator. By comparison, two-thirds of families in the United States had refrigerators by the early 1930s. Soviet families were forced to wait for years to get appliances and when they were finally granted one by the government, they were given a one-hour slot in which to pick up the appliance. If they could not accept delivery, then they would not receive the fridge. Not exactly the most fun form of bingo.

America had nearly 100 million cars on the road around the same time. The Soviet Union only had five million. While American women had just emerged from the hippie movement and were driving on "Ventura

Highway" as the song by America says, life for families — and women, in particular — wasn't exactly free and mobile under socialist rule.

Perhaps this is where AOC and friends got their big idea for the Green New Deal. However, they might be surprised to find out that even thought the socialist country could, indeed, keep cars off the road — they were not equipped to handle big issues such as pollution.

Despite the fact that it had 95 million fewer passenger cars on its roads, 15% of the population in the Soviet Union lived in areas with 10 times the average pollution levels.

When it came to buying power, the socialist system once again failed. Well over half of the population of the Soviet Union was poor — including approximately 25% of Soviets who couldn't afford a winter coat nor even a basic hat. Inflation was high, too. The garments cost an entire month's work wages, which is outrageous.

You see, AOC and "The Squad" want you to think it's a big fun game to live in a socialist country. However, living in squalor without transportation, appliances, nor even a winter coat while standing in a bread line with ration coupons for the most basic food— that's not exactly the definition of living, is it? We should want better for ourselves and our daughters.

Cuba

In 1959, Fidel Castro orchestrated Cuba to be a socialist state in order to closely align Cuba with one of its few allies, the Soviet Union.

The alignment worked for Cuba until the Soviet Union fell after Republican President Ronald Reagan urged, "Tear down this wall!"

The fall of the Soviet Union left Cuba to fend for itself in a global economy that by 1991 had moved on without the tiny socialist island.

Castro ccouldn't compete with other industrialized nations and with the United States' embargo on trade and tourism bearing down on Cuba, Castro stuck with the socialist construct in order to maintain control over his economy and his people so as not to have his own proverbial wall toppled.

For over 50 years, much of Cuba's human rights violations were out of the prying eye of the public and international human rights organizations. The result was a closed-off Cuba where human rights violations including torture, detention and imprisonment have been the order of the day, according to Human Rights Watch.[96]

Cuba's own legal system limits civil rights, freedom of speech, the freedom to assemble, and more. In the 1980s, Castro violently tamped down political protests and killed dissenters. In 2003, Castro had 75 political protestors executed without giving them any due process to a trial.

That's just another day at the office for socialism.

Even as Castro passed away, the communist tenets that he instilled in his leaders survived. Punishment today for protests still include internet disruptions, censorship, and schemes to cover up egregious civil rights violations. Punishment for American diplomats in the country have been far worse, including biological or ontological weapons.

Human rights abuses aren't the only challenges.

With socialism, a fight for resources always exists.

According to numerous news reports and human rights organizations, Cuba's socialist government responded very poorly to the COVID-19 crisis. Food supplies became an issue during the he pandemic. Its usual perennial shortages of medical supplies grew even worse. In 2021, it was widely reported that Cuba had run out of medicine to treat even the most basic and oldest of ills such as scabies, which was solved centuries ago in more industrialized, free nations. Under the stress of the COVID-19 pandemic, the country's system of socialized medicine entirely collapsed with the government failing to provide even the most basic supplies such as oxygen and other medicine to help alleviate the symptoms of COVID-19.

This does not sound like the socialist utopia described by AOC in any way, shape nor form.

As citizens began to get angry over Cuba's handling of the pandemic, protests erupted last July in the largest political dissent that Cuba has seen in the last 50 years. Right on cue, the socialist government swooped in — violently — to protect itself. According to Amnesty International, the government's response to the uprising was the harshest it's been in two decades, on "a scale we have not seen in 20 years." [97] The Cuban government shut off the internet, conducted widespread online censorship, and detained and jailed at least six citizens — including one woman.

Bottomline: A poor, socialist country that cannot care for its own like Cuba harms everyone — including the most vulnerable women and children. A country with a socialist economy which prohibits free markets and forces citizens to rely solely upon dictatorships for the most basic supplies that are traded freely elsewhere around the world also harms women and children. A socialist government that rules with a heavy fist, censoring its own citizens and limiting their contact with the outside world is a country that does not have the best interests of women at heart and fails to give a proper voice to young girls.

If AOC and "The Squad" were looking for a perfect poster country as a shining example of socialism, Cuba is not it.

Germany

Another example of failed socialism is Germany in the 20th century.

After Nazi Germany was defeated in World War II in 1945, the eastern part of Germany began to be barricaded off from the rest of Germany. The eastern part of Germany was aligned with the old, Soviet-style socialist economy, and the western part of Germany was more aligned with western, American-style capitalist systems. [98]

Between the years 1949 and 1961 at the time the Berlin Wall was built, there was a constant flow of Germans from the east to the west. Millions of Germans living under communist rule in an increasingly poor socialist economy, fled West to live a more free life.

As Hoover Institute Senior Fellow Russell A. Berman wrote, these millions of oppressed people in essence "voted with their feet."[99] Humans naturally want to be free, and Berman reported that East Germany's population decreased by at least 2 million people around the time while the population of West Germany increased by 12 million people. He said it was "an indisputable judgment on the failure of socialism" that so many people wanted to risk everything to escape socialism in order to live a life of freedom.

Think about it: If a government has to build a wall to keep its people in, instead of keeping others out, life is likely not great for those behind the wall. As conditions grew poorer and poorer under East Germany's socialist economy, other East Germans sought to leave but it was ultimately too late; they would have to run the gauntlet of armed guards surrounding the Berlin Wall and risk being shot on site.

Ultimately, the Berlin Wall fell in 1989 after urging from President Ronald Reagan to Soviet President Mikhail Gorbachev to "Tear down this wall." While this was great news for the millions of East Germans freed from socialist terror, the liberation came only after hundreds, if not thousands, of German citizens were killed in the process of trying to escape.[100] This is further proof that socialist systems are no walk in the park and aren't just bad for women, but devastating for men, women and children alike.

Why AOC or any member of "The Squad" would want to place Americans into such disastrous situations and allow history to repeat itself is beyond imagination.

China

No conversation about socialism is complete without mentioning its not-too-distant cousin, communism.

The primary difference between socialism and communism is that under socialism, citizens (allegedly) share equally in the ownership of economic resources. Under communism, the government owns and controls most of the property and economic resources.

However, both socialism and communism are terrible in that they advocate against private ownership of property, resources and the means of the distribution of goods. (The best way to describe this in American terms today is if the government owned all of the factories, stores, Amazon warehouses, Amazon trucks, and the like.) Both socialism and communism believe that the government ought to control all of those things from one central location: namely, on government property. (This would be the equivalent of Amazon trucks dispatching every morning from a U.S. government site.)

It might sound confusing, but quite often a "communist" government can have a "socialist" economic system — meaning, the government dictates and controls the means, but the people get to share a bit more in the outcomes of the economy.

This happens in countries such as China, Cuba and North Korea where "Socialist Market Economies" exist in that government controls the means of production and distribution of goods, but the country's goods are actually traded on the open market (steel, exported goods like electronic devices, etc.) with other countries.

These economic aspects of communism and socialist can sound less harmful. After all, much of the steel we build with in America today comes from China. Apple iPhones come from China. Harmless, right?

Wrong.

In terms of treatment of women, there is no more hostile friend to females than the Chinese Communist Party.

Throughout history, communists have let it be known precisely what they believe the value of females are — right down to their ability to exist at birth.

For decades, China made it known that sons were preferred over daughters. Sons, after all, could fight in wars to protect the homeland, sons were better earners who could take care of their elderly parents, and sons were the ones who could continue the family name.

In China, the preference for the birth of boys rather than girls became all the more severe when in the late 1970s (after the Cultural Revolution bolstered the Communist Party) China instituted its "One Child Policy." Through this policy, the Chinese government made it known that it strongly preferred each family have only one child and that preferably, it be a son.[101]

Chinese parents began to adhere to the wishes of their government, by reportedly engaging in sex-selective abortions as the rise of high-tech equipment such as ultrasound became available. In not-so-delicate terms, parents were in essence, snuffing out the lives of girls in order to please their communist government.

Under this national edict, the gender ratio at birth of boys in 1979 was 106 boys born for every 100 girls; in 1990, it was 111 boys born for every girl; in 2001, it was 117 boys born for every girl; and in 2005, it was 121 boys born for every 100 girl.

In a small town in America, that gender disparity might not be noticeable. However, due to China's enormous population of 1.4 billion people, these figures started to become enormous exponentially. For example, in 2005 there were an estimated 1.1 million more boys in China under the age of 20 than there were girls. This started to become problematic in terms of population control, dating, family structure, and more.

For now, China has relaxed its "One Child Policy" but for millions of girls, it's too late. Their lives were already snuffed out.

Scientists estimate that over the span of a few decades, there were literally a few million "missing" girls who were tragically aborted as parents as pressure grew to limit their children to just one child, preferably a son.

In a society today where the value of women and the encouragement of young girls is being sung from every feminist rooftop, it's odd that we hear so little criticism of China from the left. Perhaps liberals and the feminists of today want to be more like them, in everything from their central government to their squelching of free speech. However, limiting the female gender's ability to even be born is the ultimate statement on the lack of equality for women in China over the last 40 years, and this form of government should not be something we're aspiring to in America.

China is the textbook example of an authoritarian, communist, socialist regime that is not friendly — in fact, was deadly — to women and girls.

Socialism & "The Squad" — They Got It from Their Papa

"The Squad" members themselves have said that their love of socialism and their interest in pushing it in American politics came from their nearest and dearest supporter, self-proclaimed Socialist Bernie Sanders, who once stated in a TV interview that bread lines in socialist countries, where citizens actually have to line up for government food, are "a good thing." I'm not referring to the line you voluntarily stand in to get into Best Buy on Black Friday; this is for the most basic food that goes on your dinner table.

Any political leader who would shuffle people into line for basic supplies such as food is not a leader whose voice nor movement we ought to take seriously in contemporary American political dialogue.

On the feminist side alone, Sanders' brand of socialism would revoke from women the right to earn her own income from a hard day's work and spend her time as she wishes — you know, the foundational tenets of his generation's Second Wave of Feminism.

Yet here we are as the socialist conversation persists.

There are other troubling aspects of "The Squad's" mentor.

Bernie Sanders has bragged about visiting Cuba in 1985 and attending a parade to celebrate the Sandinista revolutionaries. At the time, Sanders was a mayor in Vermont but along with the rest of the world surely knew about the dastardly tactics of the Cuban regime. Sandinista soldiers were responsible for censoring law-abiding Cuban residents, forming "neighborhood watch" programs to snitch on neighbors, and not unlike the guards in socialist East Germany, reportedly shot Cubans who attempted to flee the socialist country.[102] Sanders boasted that he was the highest-ranking American official on the island at that time. The truth is, he shouldn't have been there at all.

Unfortunately, Sanders' adventures in socialism didn't end there.

Sanders appeared to bring the dark ideas of socialism home with him.

As Mayor of Burlington, Vermont, Sanders had the gall to suggest that Vermont needed to be more like Nicaragua, which was being run by the same Sandinistas who had shot citizens on site. Under their own reign of terror back home, the people of Nicaragua had their private property stolen, had their voices censored just like the Cubans, and their farmlands stolen and turned over to the government for national, centralized food production. You know, bread lines.

Sanders also applauded censorship of free press in the region at the hands of the Sandinistas, specifically the censorship of the Cuban newspaper *La Prensa*. The senator said that the censorship "makes good sense to me" because the newspaper had been critical of the Castro regime. If the newspaper was being censored, one can forget about the voices of the everyday man, woman or child. They had no chance.

Yet Sanders' love of socialism persisted.

"Vermont could set an example to the rest of the nation similar to the type of example Nicaragua is setting for the rest of Latin America," Bernie Sanders said at the time.

Five short years ago, it would be frightening to think that that sort of socialism could catch on in the United States of America, yet it indeed has through the popularity of Sanders and "The Squad."

Sanders' whole life has been a love letter to socialism, communism, Marxism and Leninism. He felt the love — literally — for a socialist nation, as a just-married socialist mayor honeymooning in the Soviet Union in 1988.[103] Though it was billed as a work trip, the fact that Sanders chose to spend the first days of wedded bliss in a socialist country speaks volumes about his life, in the same way that New York City Mayor Bill DeBlasio honeymooning in Cuba speaks about his.

While Sanders is now in the twilight of his life, "The Squad" unfortunately isn't going anywhere anytime soon.

According to the Cook Political Report, the four founding members of each preside over districts that have a hefty 20-point Democrat Party advantage. The likelihood that they'll be ousted by a Republican is not likely, and the chance that a fellow Democrat will step up to save their party and this country from socialism by challenging such popular members of their party is slim as well.

If "The Squad" is here to stay, then the debate over socialism will continue to be in the political dialogue.

It is shocking that a group of American female politicians would stand so fervently behind a socialist construct proven throughout history to be deadly and oppressive to women and children. However, it is up to all of us to wipe the surprise off of our faces and get to work to ensure that socialism does not further creep into American government under the sheep's clothing of six fresh-faced women on the block.

You see, "The Squad's" socialist proposals are really just the old policies of the Sanders-esque white, male, crusty, Socialist and Communist regimes who mistreated their citizens and never allowed the women of their societies to flourish.

Sorry, "Squad," but no matter how popular you become, America will not stand for the mistreatment of our mothers, sisters and daughters under these kinds of daunting regimes.

Conclusion: The next time someone tells you "Maybe Socialism isn't so bad," point them to the track record of Communist China, Socialist Cuba, the Socialist Soviet Union and East Germany. Women and children did not thrive in these economies, where basic survival was the goal of the day under the thumb of big dictatorial government. Life spans were shorter and more pain-filled. Medicines were hard to come by. Heck, refrigerators were hard to come by.

American capitalism, on the other hand, still remains the best system on the planet for the advancement of women, the empowerment of young girls, long life spans, and human rights for all mankind.

HOMEWORK
➤ Read Mark Levin's book, "American Marxism." The nationally-syndicated radio host and "the great one" examines how socialism is becoming more pervasive in our country today — from schools to corporations to the press. Let Levin awaken you and rally you to defend liberty.

➤ No homework is complete without again mentioning my colleague Cheryl K. Chumley; though, this time for her book "Socialists Don't Sleep: Christians Must Rise or America Will Fall." In it, Chumley points out the sneaky way that the left has pushed Socialism into American life today, and why Christians are the likely ones who can stop its further march.

REFERENCES:

[92] FOX News poll shows 60% of Democrats find Socialism favorable
https://www.yahoo.com/now/more-democratic-voters-favor-socialism-181600844.html

[93] Generation Z Have a 54% Unfavorable View of Capitalism
https://www.insiderintelligence.com/insights/generation-z-facts/

[94] Axios-Momentive poll: Capitalism favorability has plummeted in last two years
https://www.surveymonkey.com/curiosity/axios-capitalism-update/

[95] "Back in the USSR: What Life Was Like in the Soviet Union" – Adam Smith Institute – 2017
https://www.adamsmith.org/research/back-in-the-ussr

[96] Human Rights Watch. 1993. Cuba: "Perfecting" the System of Control: Human Rights Violations in Castro's 34th Year: January 1992-February 1993. New York, N.Y.: Americas Watch.

[97] Amnesty International on Cuba's July 2021 Protests
https://www.amnesty.org/en/latest/news/2021/08/cuba-amnesty-international-names-prisoners-of-conscience/

[98] Jaap Sleifer, Planning Ahead and Falling Behind: The East German Economy in Comparison with West Germany, 1936–2002 (Berlin: Akademie Verlag, 2006), 5

[99] Hoover Institute: Russell A. Berman Paper on Germany
https://www.hoover.org/research/leaving-socialism-behind-lesson-german-history

[100] Germans Who Died Fleeing Socialism in East Germany
https://www.dw.com/en/more-than-1100-berlin-wall-victims/a-1673538

[101] Zhu WX, Li L, Hesketh T. China's excess males, sex selective abortion and one child policy: analysis of data from 2005 national intercensus survey. BMJ 2009;338:b121 [PMC free article] [PubMed] [Google Scholar]

[102] Sandinistas, Cuba and the Soviet Union
https://www.brown.edu/Research/Understanding_the_Iran_Contra_Affair/n-sandinistas.php

[103] Bernie Sanders' "Honeymoon" in the Soviet Union in 1988
https://www.washingtonpost.com/politics/inside-bernie-sanderss-1988-10-day-honeymoon-in-the-soviet-union/2019/05/02/db543e18-6a9c-11e9-a66d-a82d3f3d96d5_story.html

MY BODY, MY CHOICE?

The feminist movement has always made the mantra "My Body, My Choice" the centerpiece of their agenda to protect a woman's body — from head to toe — from any government intrusion, lest some mean 'ole white Republican male tell them what to do with their bodies.

Over the past few decades, feminist leaders from Gloria Steinem to Cecile Richards have had a lot to say about the topic.[104]

Gloria Steinem said in a 2019 interview with Al-Jazeera, "Opposing women's right to control our own bodies is always the first step in every authoritarian regime."[105]

Well, well, well, Gloria… you don't say.

Cecile Richards has made a career of advocating for women's choice over their bodies first as the president of Planned Parenthood and now as the leader of her own political action fund simply called, "Supermajority."

Actresses from the self-proclaimed "nasty woman" Ashley Judd to Alyssa Milano have railed about the fact that a woman's body should be her own to do whatever she pleases with it.

"I'm so tired of having to continually prove that my body is my own," Milano said[106] outside of the 2018 Brett Kavanaugh Supreme Court nomination hearings.

Callie Khouri, creator of the movie "Thelma and Louise" likewise said that what women do with their bodies "belongs in the hands of women and their physicians."

TV mom and "Family Ties" actress Meredith Baxter said, "I'd like to know that my daughters would have the freedom if they find themselves in situations [that] no government is going to jump in and make decisions for them. It's outrageous. They have no place in that position. There is no question, it should be a woman's choice. It is not a religious thing, it's not a political thing, it's very simple—it's just a right, so don't f--k with it."[107]

Countless other feminists such as Hillary Clinton have chimed in over the years that a woman's health decisions are between she and her doctor — nobody else.

Feminist activist Camille Paglia went even further to say that anyone who tries to mess with a woman's body is a *fascist* — including Mother Nature.

"My argument has always been that nature has a master plan pushing every species toward procreation and that it is our right and even obligation as rational human beings to defy nature's fascism. Nature herself is a mass murderer, making casual, cruel experiments and condemning 10,000 to die so that one more fit will live and thrive." (Using Paglia's logic, then neither the government nor Mother Nature should tell us what to do with our bodes — even in the case of COVID-19.)

Last but not least, Speaker of the House Nancy Pelosi said at a press conference regarding Texas' new abortion law that a woman's right to choose "is about freedom. A woman's right to choose... is about a woman's freedom from the dangers of vigilantes..."[108]

However, feminists like Pelosi and others must not truly believe the words coming out of their own mouths; otherwise, they would have stood up for women everywhere during the COVID-19 pandemic as their brothers in the Democrat Party mercilessly told American women precisely what they had to put on — and into — their bodies.

A Woman's Right to Choose… What to Put into Her Body

The entire feminist belief system of "Women's Right to Choose" got flipped on its head during the COVID-19 pandemic.

During no other time in history have we seen government officials not just advising, recommending, and directing, but actually *ordering* what women they must do with their bodies.

In my view, Democrat Party leaders have forfeited their rights to *ever* claim again that government cannot have say over a woman's body.

First, Democrat Party leaders from Governor Andrew Cuomo to Bill DeBlasio and beyond mandated that Americans — 50% of whom are women — must slap a mask on their faces and over their mouths.

In New York City, that mask mandate was enforced for more than a year.

Nationally, Democrat Party leader and President Joe Biden (who refused to wear a mask at his own political events in the Spring of 2020, when it could have actually made a difference in stopping the initial spread of COVID-19) ultimately also instilled a national mask mandate during his "first 100 days in office." Didn't matter if you didn't want to don one, Uncle Joe said it was a must for any person on federal flights, trains and other government properties.

After masks didn't solve their COVID-19 crises, those same Democrat Party leaders then infringed on a "women's right to choose" by requiring citizens to put a vaccine into their bodies — even though it was not yet approved by the FDA. Once again, the leader of the Democrat Party in America said that any American federal worker, or any federal contractor, would have to take the jab.

In New York City, Mayor Bill DeBlasio required the same. Women could not participate in regular life in New York City, including dining at a restaurant nor going to a gym for physical activity, unless they put a chemical into their body.

Can you image if a Republican man had required women to do the same? We would never hear the end of it.

From liberal cities to Hollywood sets to TV networks like ESPN[109] the liberals in charge actually gave very few exemptions to women who simply wanted a "choice" due to concerns about their reproductive systems.

A deal between the Alliance of Motion Picture and Television Producers and several Hollywood unions allowed producers and directors to mandate vaccine injections as a condition of employment and even for visiting a movie set.[110]

In the sports world, ESPN reporter Allison Williams says she was "forced out" of her job at the network due to her "choice" not to take the vaccine. The real irony is she proclaims she is not anti-vaccine, she simply wanted to make that "choice" due to other reproductive decisions she intended to make in her life.

Not a single feminist came to her aid.

The silence of feminists during the COVID-19 crisis has been deafening. When American women looked down the barrel of overly-burdensome mandates on their bodies, Democrats and feminists proved once again that they only care about a woman's right to choose when it comes to liberal issues.

A Woman's Right to Choose… How to Defend Herself

As much as feminists and the Democrat Party have made "a woman's right to choose" one of their core priorities, they don't have the same belief when it comes to allowing a woman the right to choose how to defend herself.

For a while, Democrats and feminists succeeded in convincing women not to buy guns.

For decades, The Wall Street Journal reported that women only made up around 10-20% of gun owners.[111]

However, a Harvard researcher found that women now represent nearly half of all new gun owners.[112]

As Democrat politicians have "defunded the police," then greatly mismanaged crime in their blue cities and blue states, women have taken matters into their own hands. More than 70% of women[113] state that personal protection is the main reason they own a gun — not "duck hunting," as some well-meaning, right-leaning champions of the Second Amendment would have you believe.

However, women have historically *not* been rewarded by the left for their empowering choices.

In 2013, Democrats in the Colorado legislature took aim at restricting how much firepower women could have when they limited the magazine capacity that gun owners could have. In fact, some Democrats suggested they'd like to ban gun entirely in the Rocky Mountain state.

When questioned about the devastating effect that limiting the Second Amendment might have on women's safety, Democrat legislators suggested that women should just get "a rape whistle" or "urinate" on male attackers in order to protect themselves.[114] The suggestion came from a Colorado university bulletin that went out to students which suggested female students could pretend to "vomit" on a guy in order to stop a rape.

Yep, mark that down, Democrats think that "pee" is one of the best forms of self-defense for women. (I'm happy to report that my friends and I recalled and removed from office some of these very ridiculous elected officials just a few months later.)

One has to wonder why Democrats are so intent on not allowing women a "choice" on how to defend themselves and their families.

Perhaps the reason that Democrat Party leaders don't want women to find ways to protect themselves is that, as with so many other issues, Democrats want women to be forever reliant upon government.

A Woman's Right to Choose... Whom She Votes For

No one was more harassed after the 2016 election then Republican women for their choice to vote for Donald Trump.

From social media to the daily pedantic bullying on ABC's "The View," liberal mean girls just couldn't stop harassing conservative women over their "choice."

Countless skits on "Saturday Night Live" and the White House Correspondents Dinner portrayed Republican women as characters out of "The Handmaiden's Tale" as women who carried water for Republican men.

The Democrat Party and the feminist movement — both of which proclaim to pride themselves on giving women a "choice" — just couldn't stand the fact that Republican women actually exercised the right to theirs.

Unfortunately, this is nothing new for liberal feminists.

Feminist leader Gloria Steinem once said, "Women have two choices: Either she's a feminist or a masochist." Ironically, Steinem's binary choice suggest that if you're not a card-carrying member of today's Democrat Party-led feminist movement, then you have some sort of hatred for yourself. Her statement goes against everything she's ever tried to teach women and young girls about thinking for themselves.

She's not alone.

In the wake of the 2016 elections, former First Lady and Democratic presidential nominee Hillary Clinton suggested that Trump only won because women's husbands told them who to vote for.

As if women cannot think for themselves.

Hillary didn't just suggest that Republican women's husbands told them how to vote — she suggested that "white women's" husbands told them how to vote. Additionally, she suggested it wasn't just husbands, but really every man in women's lives who force them how to vote.

Speaking at a conference in Mumbai, India, Hillary said there is "an identification with the Republican Party, and a sort of ongoing pressure to vote the way that your husband, your boss, your son, whoever, believes you should..."

Sure, it couldn't possibly be that Hillary's favorability ratings were always under water (with both women and men) and that her unfavorable ratings never got out of the 45% territory (I've never seen any candidate, anywhere, get elected when their unfavorables never left the ballpark of 50%).[115]

Apparently, Hillary's loss had nothing to do with the fact that Americans viewed her as one of the most corrupt politicians of our lifetimes, proven when then-FBI Director James Comey suggested she might end up in jail.

No, Hillary still chose to rail about women's choices at the ballot box.

She did what so many other liberal feminists do — take a swipe at Southern women, in particular.

Hillary said that specifically women in "backward" parts of the country didn't vote for her, and that's another reason she lost.[116] She made it very clear she was talking about Southern, country, backwoods places far outside the glare of Washington, D.C., Los Angeles and New York City.

"What the map doesn't show you is that I won the places that represent two-thirds of America's gross domestic product. So I won the places that are optimistic, diverse, dynamic, moving forward," Hillary said in a speech. "And [Trump's] whole campaign — 'Make America Great Again' — was looking backward."

Hillbillies.

Hillary went on to suggest that Southern women aren't just from the "backward" places on the map, but that Southern women are also racist.

"You know, you didn't like black people getting rights; you don't like women, you know, getting jobs," the former First Lady said.

Racist. Misogynistic.

It is a mouthful coming from a woman whose Democrat Party for 100 years were *actually* responsible for keeping black people from "getting rights." It was also her party that was responsible for blocking women from "getting rights" to vote for another 50 years after Blacks did.

She also attacked American voters while she was on foreign soil, suggesting that American voters "don't want to, you know, see that Indian–American [person] succeeding more than you are…"

Outrageous.

Former First Lady Michelle Obama also piled on, suggesting that women who didn't vote for Democrats in 2016 are "still trying to figure out what it means to be women."[117]

That's right, at the United State of Women Summit in 2018 in an interview with actress Tracee Ellis Ross the former First Lady said, "We're still at that stage where we're trying to figure out what it means to be women and what we think of ourselves."

I can assure you, Mrs. Obama, conservative women know what it means to be women.

The fact that all of these self-proclaimed feminists can't believe that women didn't vote for their candidates of choice, means that they don't truly respect yours.

They're genuinely jarred by the notion that women dare to think differently when it comes to political choice. It shows how limited their beliefs are and how binary their choices actually are.

In a world where liberals usually herald "non-binary" choices, they seem to leave freedom of *political* choice off of their list. Why is that?

Well, the simple answer is that as with so many other causes, feminists only want women to have a choice when it comes to their pet issues.

Overblowing the Popularity of Roe v. Wade

Another thing feminists are lying to women about is the popularity of abortion in America.

Planned Parenthood and the rest of the abortion lobby would have you believe that abortion is as popular as apple pie.

While there are a stunning 800,000 abortions performed every year in the United States, the popularity has been on a steep decline.

A slew of polls taken over the last 18 months show that Americans no longer believe in the concept of on-demand abortion at every doctor's office on every corner.

Far from it.

An Associated Press-NORC Center for Public Affairs Poll[118] shows that a majority of Americans believe that abortion should only be legal in "some circumstances."

Moreover, a surprising 65% of Americans believe abortion should only be legal during the first trimester.

According to the AP-NORC poll, an even more surprising 80% of Americans now believe abortion should not be legal during the third trimester.

A Gallup Poll[119] taken around the same time period also shows that nearly half (48 percent) of Americans believe that abortions should only be legal during certain circumstances.

In fact Gallup asked a question with three choices: "Do you think abortions should be legal under any circumstances, legal under only certain circumstances, or illegal in all circumstances?" Respondents who replied that abortions should be "illegal in all circumstances" ranked closely to those who said "legal under any circumstances," which shows that the nation is actually quite split and that the pro-abortion lobby is anything *but* winning the war of public opinion.

Furthermore, when added together more than two-thirds of Americans (67 percent) responded to the Gallup Poll that abortion should be "illegal in all circumstances" and "legal under only certain circumstances."

Read that again: 67% of Americans believe that abortion should be "illegal in all circumstances."

That is a bad day at the office for Planned Parenthood.

When it comes to the morality of the issue, respondents were also split. In a recent Gallup Poll, just 47 percent of Americans believe in 2022 that abortion is "morally acceptable" while 46 percent believe it is "morally wrong."

Compare that to May of 2015, when 50 percent of Americans stated they would call proudly themselves "pro-choice" and to September of 1995 when 56 percent of Americans did so.

That is a double-digit plummet in public opinion.

Voter intensity on the abortion issue — meaning, abortion as a driving factor pushing Americans to the polls — has also been dwindling over the last decade.

While the pink-hat-wearing, hard-left feminists would have you believe that abortion is the #1 issue facing women today, just half (50 percent) of voters in the 2020 elections said that it was their top issue. Half of voters stated that abortion was just "one of many important factors" they would consider in choosing a candidate.

This sentiment is showing up in polling for the 2022 midterm elections as well.

While Planned Parenthood has spent millions of dollars canvassing neighborhoods and knocking on doors to speak with voters about the

U.S. Supreme Court's *Dobbs* decision to overturn Roe v. Wade, the American people have been grabbling with other, more important issues such as how to put food on the table and gas in their tanks.

In most 2022 midterm election polls, the issues Americans care most about are crime, the economy, inflation, education and creeping socialism. Abortion falls far down on the list as an important priority.

The trouble for Planned Parenthood doesn't stop there.

Abortion isn't just a top priority; it is now negatively thought of by the American people.

Gallup's polling in 2022 showed that 41 percent of Americans state they are now "dissatisfied" with "the nation's policies regarding abortion."

Twenty-two percent stated they were "dissatisfied, want stricter" laws when it comes to abortion, and 24 percent of Americans were simultaneously "satisfied" with the nation's current limitations on abortion including the national partial-birth abortion ban [120] which prohibits killing a baby as it's being born or as a woman is dilated.

As you can see from the flood of polling, America's increasingly negative viewpoint on abortion and the desire for stricter laws is a far cry from what Planned Parenthood and the abortion establishment would have you believe.

For nearly 50 years radical, far-left feminists sold a bill of goods to an entire generation of women from the 1960s into the 2000s that abortion was a necessary evil to uphold "women's rights," with little regard to the rights of the little baby forming inside of them.

Perhaps the most stunning development today is that 40 percent of Americans support a law in which abortions would be outlawed after a baby's heartbeat can be heard — placing nearly half of Americans in the camp of conservative republicans, southern states and Bible Belt states who have passed "heartbeat bills" [121] which protect babies beginning at 6 weeks in the womb.

This places hundreds of millions of Americans squarely on the conservative side of the issue. It would also, according to the ruling on *Dobbs v. Jackson Women's Health Organization*, show that America is actually aligned with the majority rule of the Supreme Court, not diametrically opposed to it as feminists have had Americans believe.

The next time radical feminists attempt to convince you that their quest for abortion is popular and should be the law of the land, you can share the most recent views of Americans which prove that nothing could be further from the truth.

Conclusion

Liberals often talk about the right to choose. After the pandemic, it's clear that statement only applies to their pet cause of abortion. From mandatory masks to government-mandated vaccines and boosters, liberals all the way from Hollywood to our nation's capital of Washington, D.C. have harassed Americans for more than two years now. When the next Women's March rolls into town and features Democrat politicians talking about the importance of "a woman's right to choose," you can be certain that they're only talking about choices on the issues *they* support. Just as they have proven on so many other issues, "choice" is apparently for thee, but not for the rest of us.

HOMEWORK
> ➢ Visit the website for the pro-life organization "Live Action." It presents the pro-life case with scientific facts and debunks Democrats' myths all in one place, and it also does so in a fresh, modern way. The young women leading the pro-life movement today including Lila Rose and pro-life strategist Alison Howard Centofante are impressive, in command of their message, and are precisely the messengers we need to reach the younger generation of women who might be considering abortion or simply want to have the tools to debate the issue in a more modern, populist way. The organization's website: LiveAction.org

REFERENCES:

[104] Pro-Choice Quotes throughout Time
https://www.goodreads.com/quotes/tag/pro-choice

[105] Gloria Steinem: "Opposing women's right to control our own bodies is always the first step in every authoritarian regime."
https://www.aljazeera.com/economy/2019/7/12/gloria-steinem-on-patriarchy-abortion-and-economic-independence

[106] Alyssa Milano: "Tired" of "Having to Prove" Her Body is Her Own
https://thehill.com/blogs/in-the-know/in-the-know/575110-alyssa-milano-says-its-the-most-dangerous-time-to-be-a-woman-in

[107] "Family Ties," "Thelma and Louise" Women Say Women's Choice Should Be between Women and Their Physicians
https://www.feminist.com/resources/quotes/quotes_choice.html

[108] Speaker Nancy Pelosi on Women's Right to Choose – PBS News
https://fb.watch/8WmsJXqqQO/

[109] ESPN's Allison Williams "Forced Out" of Job due to Vaccine Mandate
https://www.dailymail.co.uk/news/article-10138987/ESPN-broadcaster-tells-Tucker-Carlson-forced-refusal-follow-vaccine-mandate.html

[110] Vaccine Mandates in Hollywood
https://www.sacbee.com/news/coronavirus/article252899508.html
[111] Women Gun Owners Used to Be Just 10-20%

https://www.wsj.com/articles/women-are-nearly-half-of-new-gun-buyers-study-finds-11631792761

[112] Harvard Researcher: Nearly Half of New Gun Owners are Women
https://www.nraila.org/articles/20210920/harvard-researcher-about-half-of-new-gun-owners-are-women

[113] Pew Research Center: Women Buys Gun to Defend Themselves

https://www.pewresearch.org/fact-tank/2017/06/29/how-male-and-female-gun-owners-in-the-u-s-compare/

[114] Colorado Democrats: Women Should Just "Urinate" on Rapists to Protect Themselves
https://www.dailymail.co.uk/news/article-2281317/Colorado-college-sparks-controversy-advising-women-vomit-urinate-bid-stop-rapist-state-lawmakers-pass-banning-concealed-guns-campuses.html

[115] Newsweek: 53% of Women Didn't Vote for Hillary Clinton
https://www.newsweek.com/hillary-clinton-trump-voters-women-851013

[116] Hillary Clinton on Why Women Didn't Vote for Her
https://www.nationalreview.com/2018/03/hillary-clinton-white-women-pressured-husbands-vote-trump/

[117] Former First Lady Michelle Obama on Why Women Didn't Vote Democrat in 2016
https://www.youtube.com/watch?v=boB9modnMYQ&t=1256s

[118] Associated Press-NORC Poll on Abortion
https://apnews.com/article/only-on-ap-us-supreme-court-abortion-religion-health-2c569aa7934233af8e00bef4520a8fa8

[119] Gallup Poll on Abortion throughout the Years
https://news.gallup.com/poll/1576/abortion.aspx

[120] Partial Birth Abortion Ban of 2003
https://www.congress.gov/bill/108th-congress/senate-bill/3

[121] "Heartbeat Bills"
https://governor.sc.gov/news/2022-03/21-states-join-south-carolinas-fight-fetal-heartbeat-bill-file-amicus-brief

THE BIG LGBTQIA+ LIE

In 2008, I served as the spokeswoman for California's Prop. 8 — a ballot measure which gave voters the choice between traditional marriage and what was, at the time, the up-and-coming movement to institute gay marriage as a legal form of marriage.

Gay couples already had domestic partnerships, but they wanted more.

Prop. 8 was a Constitutional amendment that, if passed, would enshrine in California's Constitution that the definition of marriage shall be marriage between one man and one woman.

Sounds like a radical concept especially in a liberal state like California, doesn't it?

Well, it wasn't at the time.

It also wasn't the first time the battle had been waged in the Golden State with the traditional-values camp winning.

Ten years prior to the Prop. 8 campaign, 10 million voters in the liberal state of California voted "yes" on Prop. 22 in 1996 to define marriage as a union between one man and one woman. Conservatives believed at the time this was settled law.

Yet as the years slid by and more progressives won elected office, they brought with them the far-left progressive ideas of their base.

Two of those progressives were a guy named Gavin Newsom and a woman by the name of Kamala Harris.

At the time, Gavin Newsom was serving as the Mayor of San Francisco, and Kamala Harris was the District Attorney, and both of them began using the power of their pulpits to push for gay marriage. In their city, it made sense; after all, it was the city where gay rights were born.

In August 1951, the California Supreme Court ruled that gays had the right to assemble, which led to the opening of gay bars and eventually the formation of social and political groups in the city's gay community.

In 1961, a drag queen named Jose Sarria ran for San Francisco County supervisor, becoming the first openly-gay candidate to run for public office in the United States.

In 1964, Life Magazine named San Francisco "The Gay Capital of America."[122]

San Francisco's status as a gay destination was set.

Forty years later, in 2004 and just a month into his first term as San Francisco Mayor, Newsom began granting same-sex marriage licenses and he allowed the first same-sex weddings to take place at City Hall.[123] No doubt he saw this as an opening to stand out from other Democrats who also had their eye on the California governorship just two years away. However, Newsom was taking a risk because in doing so, the city would be breaking California law.

District Attorney Kamala Harris, always in competition with Newsom because they shared the same crowded political ecosystem in San Francisco politics, also put forth her edict: we will break the law and if anyone has a problem with it, they can sue me, the top law enforcement official in the city.

Together, the duo made national news. In some ways, they used each other to do so.

Gay couples lined up around the block of San Francisco City Hall for marriage licenses. Gays flew in from around the country to get hitched in the City by the Bay. By 2008, City Hall had become a carnival-like atmosphere with feather boas, men in drag, and gay and lesbian couples dancing in the streets in anticipation of gaining holy matrimony.

As the carnival-like atmosphere reigned, it was clear that San Francisco was making a mockery of California law as well as the 10 million Californians who had voted to enshrine traditional marriage in the law.

It wasn't that conservatives didn't support gay couples — they did. California was the first state in the nation to allow domestic partnerships in 1999, long before other states granted same-sex couples rights for hospital visitations, death benefits, and more.[124]

However, the push for equal religious determination was a Bay Area bridge too far for conservatives and for California voters, as progressive and open-minded as they were. Californians may be open-minded, but they didn't appreciate a group of citizens creating their own laws.

Conservative and family advocates ultimately sued, and a judge soon ruled that Mayor Newsom must halt the granting of marriage licenses to same-sex couples. However, Newsom — no doubt checking his hair in the reflection of his executive office window — admitted he saw TV trucks encircled around City Hall. He choose to continue breaking the law.

The legal battle went through the California court system like a ping pong game, back and forth, back and forth.

As the lawsuit reached higher courts, at least one liberal judge in San Francisco cast off all lines of objectivity and advocated from the bench in a shameless display of judicial activism that incensed conservatives. (His remarks would later be used in a Prop. 8 TV commercial.)

Frustrated and convinced that the courts were stacked against them, conservatives decided the only solution was to take it directly to the people of California and to let the people decide.

At that moment, Proposition 8 was born.

Today, it might seem that the fight is archaic but it was a true battleground between traditional values and the benefits that progressives wanted bestowed on a small percentage of the population.

The fight some days devolved between who wanted to be able to marry their cat (true story!) and Christian conservatives who wanted to keep the religious construct of marriage (in itself a religious term of holy matrimony) intact.

Despite being down more than 25 points, the Prop. 8 campaign ended up winning 52.24% to 47.76%.

Ultimately, the issue didn't end there. Leftists activists sued and their case went all the way to the United States Supreme Court, where same-sex activists won — not on the merits themselves, but because liberals were trying a new tactic. They would tinker with the system and have the representative who would normally defend state law for the State of California refused to show up to the U.S. Supreme Court to argue the case. That person was none other than Kamala Harris, who had been the District Attorney of San Francisco where the battle began and by that time had advanced to Attorney General of California. She, in essence, forfeited the case by not showing up to defend California law. (Clever, isn't it?)

Today, of course, opinions have evolved on same-sex marriage — part of that due to progressives pounding away at the issue, sometimes in the most bullying and hateful ways (I'll get to that shortly).

Now, support of same-sex marriage is at an all-time record high. According to a Gallup Poll, 70% of Americans now support gay marriage.[125] A majority of registered Republicans also support same-sex marriage today. Compare that to Gallup's first poll on the topic back in 1996 when only 27% of Americans supported the concept. There is no ignoring it, proponents of same-sex marriage ended up winning the messaging war.

However, there have been many latent effects that came from the landmark Prop. 8 fight that haven't been talked about much, if at all, since that fateful day on the steps of the U.S. Supreme Court. The biggest one is how the pro-gay lobby actually lied to the American people.

The Big LGBTQIA+ Lies

During the Prop. 8 campaign and on virtually every subsequent state-by-state battle over same-six marriage, progressives pleaded with voters that if they would simply give same-sex couples the right to marry, they wouldn't ask for anything else. (As the official spokeswoman for Prop. 8, I answered media questions ad nauseam over this *exact* claim.) *All they wanted was to get married and have the same marital rights as other couples, nothing more,* they said.

It was a lie.

It is a frequent trick of progressives to promise that they will only take an inch; however, after you give them an inch they end up taking a country mile. That's exactly what gay activists ended up doing to traditional American values on important issues such as adoption, sex education in schools, respect for private business, religious liberty and much more.

How exactly did progressives and the gay lobby lie to the American people? And how does it affect women and girls today? Let us count the ways:

Adoption

During the Prop. 8 campaign, one of the arguments we faced from proponents of gay marriage was that same-sex couples needed to be able to marry so that they could adopt children.

The gay lobby said they were certain that the passage of same-sex marriage *alone* would solve the adoption crisis and empty the orphanages across America. Gay advocates invoked images of Tiny Tim and little orphan Annie finally being freed from their fateful tenancies, to be let out into the streets to perform perfectly-timed dance routines with their gay dads. The kids would be loved, the dads would be happy — who could argue with that?

The adoption question was one of the tougher questions I had to field as the spokeswoman for Prop. 8; after all, how could I argue against something that would help so many orphaned children?

It's a question that I thought about for years afterward, then one day I looked it up

It turns out, gay couples never adopted as they promised.

Today, the adoption rate in the United States is the lowest it's ever been in history.[125]

In fact, in the years immediately following San Francisco's commissioning of same-sex marriage licenses in 2008 and the Supreme Court's overturning of Prop. 8 in 2013 which led to same-sex marriages across the land, the adoption rate actually *plummeted*.

The adoption rate in America fell a stunning 17% from the years 2007 to 2014, according to the National Council for Adoption.[127]

In 2007, the total number of adoptions was 133,737, and the figure for 2014 was 110,373. Even more surprising, gays didn't even account for most of the adoptions that *did* occur; in fact, nearly 50% of adoptions (41,023) were "within the family" — a term describing a situation in which the child was related to at least one of the adopting family members. This often occurs when grandparents adopt a child or extended family members adopt a child due to other family members not being able to care properly for a child.

The gay lobby also promised during the Prop. 8 campaign that not only would same-sex couples adopt, but they would adopt the children who have the most difficult time being adopted — handicapped children and older children who have been in the system for a long time. Gay couples were going to save them all. How magnanimous!

The truth: There was no positive movement in the effort to adopt older kids in post-gay marriage world. Today, only 16% of adoptions are of older kids. In fact, newborn adoptions — adoptions in which the adopted child is as young as one day old, up to two years of age — are still the #1 choice of adoption today, accounting for 84% of all adoptions in America.

However, even the rate of young babies being adopted in America fell sharply. Prior to the Supreme Court's decision on Prop. 8, about 9% of babies born in the U.S. were adopted; now, that figure is around just 1% of all babies born.[128] It is further proof that same-sex couples did not, in fact, rush to adopt children — not even babies who needed homes.

So, why exactly did same-sex marriage advocates not fulfill their promises to adopt? It's possible that once they achieved marital status, the prospects of adopting were just too burdensome.

However, I believe the answer is even more evident: vanity and, *ahem*, pride.

Instead of benevolently adopting desperate children as they promised they would, same-sex couples instead wanted something in their own image: their own babies.

In-Vitro Fertilization

Over the last decade since Prop. 8, same-sex couples have decided to forgo adoption in favor of experimenting with in-vitro fertilization instead.

According to Pew Research, 33% of Americans report that they or someone they know has used in-vitro fertilization.[129]

Compared to a decade ago, that number has skyrocketed in America particularly among — you guessed it — same-sex couples.

To be clear, this is not a critique of IVF nor of the children produced by it. I believe every child is a blessing and will leave their creation up to God and the courts. I'm here merely to point out the intellectual argument in the historical context of Prop. 8 that the adults in the room were intellectually dishonest about the means to an end (i.e., activists promising they'd adopt America's orphaned children in order to pass same-sex marriage, then immediately abandoning that plan after they got it.)

Today, not only are same-sex couples utilizing in-vitro fertilization but same-sex couples and their doctors are experimenting with it in ways that are pushing the boundaries of ethical science. The internet is filled with no shortage of IVF websites with entire sections dedicated to "LGBTQIA" reproduction.

"Reciprocal IVF allows lesbian couples to share in the parenting process by using one partner's eggs to create embryos & implant them in the other partner," one site in New Jersey boasted.

"Same-Sex Couple Carries Same Baby in IVF Treatment First," blared *USA Today*.[130]

"An L.G.B.T.Q. Pregnancy, From DIY to IVF: Our Absurdly, Occasionally Maddening, yet Ultimately Successful Path to Parenthood," the headline read in *The New York Times*.

In at least one of these cases, two lesbians desired to have their own "biological" child rather than adopt. *USA Today* reported that the couple used "radical technology" to give themselves a child.

Instead of eggs being placed into "incubators in a lab" where IVF embryos would usually go, instead mother #1 would have her eggs harvested, then embryos created (using an unknown father's sperm) would be implanted into the other mother using a "plastic vaginal device."[131]

After the embryos incubated for a while inside mother #1, the embyros were then implanted back into the body of mother #2 who w carried the baby to term. Mother #2 compared it to a track meet: "Almost like passing the baton, like it's a relay race."

Yeah, it's a regular track meet.

Stories began to emerge of one "miracle baby" after another.

But were these procedures miracles? A miracle, after all, is a faith-based phenomenon thought to be derived from God.

To be clear, I'm not suggesting that all children aren't a gift from God; they are. However, the methods that their *parents* have gone about to bring them into the world have definitely pushed the boundaries of science and safe to say all boundaries of Christianity.

In a story in *The New York Times*, a couple self-identifying as "LGBTQ" in 2020 described their IVF process. It began at home with "failed D.I.Y. attempts at home using a drugstore syringe" filled with sperm, after a male friend of theirs from college emailed and offered up his "genetic material."[132]

You can't make this up, folks. Rather than adopt children in orphanages as they promised, same-sex couples instead began playing God in their bathrooms.

The New York Times article also detailed the harrowing trek of another couple, Lisa and her "husband" Alex — a transgender who was biologically born a woman — and had trouble at the local sperm bank. A friend of theirs showed up to the sperm bank and sought to make a "direct donation" of sperm to the couple in order to make a child, but the sperm bank refused to turn over the sample, citing no relationship to the couple. Lisa and her transgender "husband" threw a fit and demanded that they be given their friend's sperm.

This is the world in which we are living just 9 ½ years after the Supreme Court spiked Prop. 8.

I hate to say we told you so but, we told you so.

Forcing Medical Providers to Perform Same-Sex Reproductive Services

For all of this "science" to take place, states first had to ensure that same-sex couples were granted "equity" in reproductive rights.[133]

Naturally.

Remember, same-sex marriage advocates said all they wanted to do was get married.

Quickly after the Supreme Court struck down Prop. 8 and opened the door to same-sex marriage across the land, California passed a bill in 2013 to ensure that same-sex couples could not be discriminated against in the formation of embryos or anywhere else in the process of reproduction.[134]

Maryland followed suit and passed a bill in 2015.

New York, surprisingly, pulled up the rear by passing legislation just last year[135] after much lobbying from the likes of Bravo TV star and single gay dad Andy Cohen who testified that he had to go out of state to create his son, Benjamin, with a surrogate.

As it is often the case, America set the trend for the world.

Just one month after the Supreme Court paved the way for same-sex marriage in June 2013, the United Kingdom passed The Marriage (Same Sex Couples) Act 2013. Same-sex marriage became law in the UK on March 13, 2014 and just 16 days later, the first same-sex wedding took place across the pond.[136]

Naturally (or in this case, perhaps not-so-naturally), the spike in same-sex-couples utilizing IVF in the UK also followed closely behind.

Just six years after gay marriage became the law of the land in the UK, Reuters reported in 2019 that IVF for same-sex couples hit an all-time record high.[137]

Data from the Human Fertilization and Embryology Authority (HFEA) showed that during the time period, same-sex IVF rose by 12% compared to just 2% among heterosexual couples. This correlates with the increase in same-sex marriages around the same time period.

Furthermore, the HFEA reported that the biggest growth in IVF use was attributed to same-sex couples, single women and surrogate carriers, who found themselves carrying a baby for male-same-sex couples.

Once again, instead of adopting children who already needed homes as same-sex marriage advocates promised they would, the quest for same-sex IVF had gone global.

Given the numbers, it appears that the same-sex marriage lobby peddled a big lie that if America would simply allow same-sex couples to marry, society would be a better place and every child would have a warm, happy home with a chicken in every pot.

Instead, liberal activists really ended up vastly altering the definition of "motherhood" to such a degree that it takes the title away from women. A "mother" can now include two women together, transgenders, men, and others who wish not to identify with any particular gender or whose "gender fluidity" (favorite new phrase of the left) may change with the tides.

In shifting the definition of motherhood, progressive advocates have likewise pushed the boundaries of medical ethics to please people who selfishly wished to see more images of themselves in the world.

As for those homeless orphans? You guessed it, they were left behind in the wake of this great experiment.

"Drag Queen Story Hour" and Gay Sex Education for Three-Year-Olds

Another big lie that the gay lobby told America was that if we simply allowed same-sex couples to marry, they would not push their own sexual agenda onto American children.

As Maury Povich might say on his show, "That, too, was a lie."

During the Prop. 8 campaign in California, one of the campaign managers called me and briefed me on intelligence they had received from an educator stating that progressives behind the scenes in the education establishment had drawn up a proposal to introduce gay sex education to children as young as kindergartners. The proposed curriculum for kindergartners that the person witnessed included the topic of anal sex.

Surely this could not be true, I said. Why would any kindergartner need to know about sex of *any* kind, let alone anal sex? It made no sense to me.

Armed with the intel, I shared it with media by way of a formal press release and boy, did I get clobbered by same-sex marriage activists and reporters who called to see if we had lost our minds.

I assured them we hadn't.

It didn't stop them from calling us and specifically, me, crazy.

We were validated a few years later when progressives began to push the envelope of their big gay agenda.

It started to creep in at the most innocent of places — neighborhood libraries where young children would go for story time before retiring sweetly to their afternoon naps.

What happened next, however, was a nightmare.

Drag Queen Story Hour began to crop up at neighborhood libraries across America.[138]

The idea, created in 2015 in San Francisco at the behest of an activist named Michelle Tea, was meant to "inspire a love of reading, while teaching deeper lessons on diversity."

The big problem?

Drag Queen Story Hour's target stated audience is three-year-olds.

You don't have to take my word for it.

Materials for the drag queen events are listed as "geared for children aged 3–11" — that's right, children starting at age three — and "hosted by drag queens who read children's books and engage in other learning activities in public libraries."

Even more astonishing is how the content has evolved during story time. Today, Drag Queen Story Hour's own materials state that the program strives to 'instill the imagination and play of gender fluidity of childhood and gives kids glamorous, positive, and unabashedly queer role models."

Gender fluidity at three years old?

At the same time they were growing Drag Queen Story Hour, gay advocates were also pushing same-sex sexual education in elementary schools, just as we had predicted during the Prop. 8 campaign. They were pushing it on — you guessed it — kindergartners!

On one hand, I felt relieved that we hadn't inadvertently spun some tall tale about the motives of the same-sex marriage lobby back in 2008. Our predictive powers were in firmly intact.

On the other hand, I once again felt sick this was truly happening.

In New Jersey, Governor Phil Murphy signed a bill into law requiring education of "diversity of gender and sexual orientation" to be taught from grades K-12.

Also in New Jersey, the State Board of Education mandated that "students should be able to identify oral, vaginal and anal sex by eighth grade."

In its "California Healthy Youth Act"[139] California enacted new sex education requirements that kindergartners must be taught about gender diversity and same-sex relationships while high school seniors are taught about "bondage," "oral sex," "blood play" and more. Teaching violent sexual play to youth who barely even understand their own bodies sounds like anything *but* healthy.

All of this age-inappropriate content made its way through America's school systems and publicly-funded libraries.

In 2019, a group of dedicated parents finally won a victory when the California State Board of Education dropped four books from its "recommended reading" lineup for K-12 students. Those books, according to the California Family Council, included: "telling kindergartners they could be two genders at once or no gender at all; "showing third graders large and close up illustrated pictures of the sex act; "introducing fourth graders to sexual fantasies, masturbation, and slang words for sexual organs; "and presenting high schoolers with a detailed how-to sex manual that included instructions on anal sex for all sexual orientations, BDSM (bondage, domination, sadomasochism), body fluid (urinating on each other)... and fisting."[140]

Yes, fisting.

I don't know about you, but I can't think of a worse way to introduce sexuality to our young girls today than by suggesting to them that they can be a variety of genders by kindergarten — and suggesting violent sexual play in high school before girls even fully understand their own bodies.

Yet it has been happening in liberal states.

The creeping LGBTQIA+ sexualization of our kids is something that gay advocates promised they wouldn't do — yet it's one of the *first* places they went. That alone should inform every parent that the radicals in the movement can't be trusted.

Assault on Private Businesses

Another lie that same-sex marriage proponents told was that business would boom if they could just get married.

Specifically, gay activists cited that the wedding industry — a $54.3 billion industry around the time — would experience a new windfall from same-sex weddings. Countless news articles ran during the Prop. 8 campaign featuring winery owners from Napa Valley to Honolulu,

Hawaii who would benefit from a boom economy of gay weddings, as well as cake bakeries and photography studios.

I have to hand it to the gay lobby — they figured out a way to craft a fiscal conservative message within a far-left social battle.

It was genius.

They predicted that the hospitality industry would go from bust back to boom following the bursting of the housing bubble in California, the collapse of the subprime lending market in August 2008, and the fall of big firms such as Lehman Brothers in mid-September which happened just a month out from the November election where Prop. 8 would be decided.

The foreclosure crisis was ravaging California at the time, as 1 in 4 foreclosures nationally came from the Golden State. This would solve a multitude of financial problems, they promised. It would help keep the economy afloat.

As with everything else the activists promised, a few years down the line they were once again proven to be liars.

What actually ended up happening was businesses who opted not to engage in same-sex weddings began to get sued (at the suggestion of left-wing activist groups) for declining to host same-sex weddings and receptions or for merely declining to cater them.

In 2013, a cake baker in Colorado was sued for declining to bake a cake for a same-sex wedding. [141] The bakers were Christian and felt uncomfortable catering the affair. They achieved a partial victory at the United States Supreme Court after having to fight for their religious rights. The same cake bakery was sued again in 2021 over "alleged LGBTQ bias" for declining to bake a birthday cake for a transgender individual. It's hard to believe it's a coincidence that one bakery could be targeted twice for the same type of lawsuit.

An Oregon bakery called Sweet Cakes by Melissa was fined $135,000 for declining to bake a cake for a same-sex wedding. [142] The U.S.

Supreme Court also ruled in favor of the bakery, though part of the case was also sent back to an Oregon court.

In many of these cases, Alliance for Defending Freedom came to their aid. If it hadn't been for ADF, these business owners would have had to have spent tens of thousands of dollars, maybe more, just to keep their businesses open.

Companies and creative artists from New Mexico to New York went through horrific legal challenges. In Kentucky, Trump's Department of Justice in 2020 came to the aid of a Louisville photographer who declined a same-sex wedding.[143]

These are textbook examples of further lies that were perpetrated by gay activists who promised they wouldn't usurp other people's beliefs nor abilities to do business.

Nothing could have been further from the truth.

Attack on Religious Liberty

One of the other big lies that advocates of same-sex marriage told America was that if they were granted the right to "marriage" — itself a religious term to describe the sacred covenant between one man and one woman — they promised not to sue churches and other religious institutions if those institutions ultimately declined to officiate their weddings. (After all, they had those fabulous wineries where they would get married, right?)

That, too, turned out to be a lie.

Just two months after the Supreme Court struck down Prop. 8, the Associated Press reported that churches were rushing to change their bylaws due to a flood of legal threats over their religious rights to decline to officiate same-sex weddings.

In Coeur d'Alene, Idaho ministers were told in 2014 that they must perform same-sex wedding ceremonies. The punishment if they continued to decline on the basis of religious grounds? For every day they declined to perform a same-sex wedding, ministers faced up to 180 days of jail time and up to a $1,000 fine.[144]

Although the Roman Catholic Church and Pope Francis reaffirmed its policy in 2021 that the church cannot bless same-sex marriages, the church and other religious institutions continue to look over their shoulders, knowing that the target is eternally on their backs. While many churches now officiate same-sex weddings, the Catholic Church does not officially sanction them. They probably haven't been forced into it legally because the Vatican has more money than, well,… God.

Assault on Free Speech

Gay activists also went after Americans' right to free speech. This is despite the fact that they have advanced their own movement on the back of First Amendment rights to creative expression, free speech, and freedom of assembly since the 1960s.

However, when it comes to the free thought and speech of those who might not be in lock-step with their views, the gay lobby sought to crack down on speech.

In 2016, the New York City Human Rights Commission enacted a mandate to issue $250,000 fines to individuals who "misgender" an LGBTQIA+ person.

According to *The New York Post*, the edict required anyone "providing jobs or housing" to use "individuals' preferred gender pronouns."[145] Those pronouns weren't limited to simple he/she monikers; they included pronouns such as "they" (to describe gender-fluid individuals who don't wish to be limited to he/she choices on any given day) and even the pronouns of "ze" (third person singular) and "hir" (third person plural).

NYCHRC claimed that individuals who accidentally misgendered tenants or people in their employ would not be fined.

However, the die was cast. The quarter-million-dollar fine was enough to put a chill on speech and make New Yorkers think twice about saying, "Yes, ma'am."

I went through my own winter of discontent after the Prop. 8 campaign, with gay activists following me to new jobs and ruthlessly "doxxing" me to new employers, calling me a "bigot" (even though I am not one), and attempting to get new campaigns not to hire me. They specifically did this in June 2013 upon my hiring at the Colorado recall campaigns over the Second Amendment. It had zero effect on my new campaign boss, who had already done a deep dive of background research on me. Around that time, I also had evidence which led me to believe the so-called "gay mafia" as they affectionately refer to themselves, successfully got me shadow-banned on Twitter. It was only in 2022 after Elon Musk threatened to buy Twitter that my account began to be seen widely by my followers again, but of course that followed 8 long years of being throttled. There is no way to estimate how much business I lost during those years due to the quelling of *my* free speech.

As with so many progressives, it is a textbook case of free speech for thee, but not for me.

Taxpayer-Funded Sex-Change Operations

The gay lobby's lies didn't stop at the cake baker's door; in fact, they went all the way into American taxpayers' wallets.

Remember, gay advocates initially argued they simply wanted to get married. They pledged that their life choices and sexual preferences wouldn't impact anyone else.

However, not long after same-sex marriage became the law of the land, requests began to flow in for Uncle Sam to pay for the lifestyles and sexual preferences of those in his care.

In 2017, just four years after the Prop. 8 ruling, a convicted murderer in a California prison became the first inmate in American history to have a gender reassignment surgery.[146] True to Democrat Party form, taxpayers footed the bill for it.

In 2016, a U.S. Army private by the name of Bradley Manning was granted approval for gender reassignment surgery even as "she" was incarcerated for espionage after leaking 750,000 documents to Wikileaks. Because Manning was allowed to keep health care benefits while serving a multi-decade prison sentence, the U.S. taxpayers footed the bill for Bradley Manning to become Chelsea Manning.[147]

Yep, liberal activists promised that their quest for LGBTQIA+ equality wouldn't affect others' lives, beliefs or financial livelihoods. However, forcing the rest of America to pay for personal sexual preferences and elaborate surgeries with taxpayer dollars is anything *but* equitable.

Conclusion

There's no other way to say it: The far-left, pro-gay activists lied. They said all they wanted was marriage for themselves and for their own households, but once they got it they quickly moved to infuse gay sex education for little kids, intolerance for religious liberty, and hateful intimidation into the American bloodstream. The lesson here is: never believe what a progressive promises. Progressives by their very nature tell you that they want a little bit of progress but when you give them an inch, they'll end up taking a mile. In most cases, they'll take your children with them.

It might surprise many Americans that progressives' ability to shift public opinion on same-sex marriage rarely, if ever, came from ballot-box victories — it came from legal activism[148] (i.e., suing), it came from Hollywood and the media, and it came from activists ramming it down the throats of Americans who felt intimidated that if they said no, they would be called a bigot, a hater — just as we were called on the Prop. 8 campaign, just as the cake bakers were, and just as the photographers were. We were the first official targets of the "Cancel Culture."

Despite all of the daunting stories here, there is a bright side. There is a lesson we can learn from how swiftly LGBTQIA+ activists moved to get state laws changed, push sexual curriculum into schools, get businesses to capitulate to their demands, and to get government (i.e., you the taxpayer) to fund their entire radical agenda. If the left can move that quickly, imagine what could be set right if faithful Americans stood up and did the same.

HOMEWORK

> On marriage and all things religious liberty, follow Ryan T. Anderson. Ryan is the former William E. Simon Senior Research Fellow in American Principles & Public Policy at the Heritage Foundation. While that is a mouthful, Ryan's specialty was straightforward: studying traditional marriage and the impact of its disruption on America. While he is no longer at the think tank (he has since moved on to become the founding editor at Public Discourse), Heritage has benevolently kept all of his writings on their website, which you can read here: https://www.heritage.org/staff/ryan-anderson *(Be sure to scroll below his photo for the entire library on everything from marriage to transgenderism.)*

REFERENCES:

122 San Francisco's PRIDE Timeline
https://projects.sfchronicle.com/2018/sf-pride-timeline/

123 CNN: 2004: Mayor Gavin Newsom Defends Same-Sex Marriage
https://www.cnn.com/2004/LAW/02/22/same.sex/

124 Domestic Partnerships in California - 1999
https://leginfo.legislature.ca.gov/faces/billTextClient.xhtml?bill_id=199920000AB26

125 Gallup Poll: Americans' views on same-sex marriage: 1996 versus 2021
https://news.gallup.com/poll/350486/record-high-support-same-sex-marriage.aspx

126 Adoption Rates in the U.S.
https://creatingafamily.org/adoption-category/adoption-blog/adoption-cost-length-time/

[127] Adoption Numbers in the U.S.
https://adoptioncouncil.org/themencode-pdf-viewer-sc/?tnc_pvfw=ZmlsZT1odHRwczovL2Fkb3B0aW9uY291bmNpbC5vcmcvY29udGVudC91cGxvYWRzLzIwMjEvMTAvQnktdGhlLU51bWJlcnMtMjAxNy5wZGYmc2V0dGluZz3M9MTExMDEwMTAxMDAxMDAxMDAwMCZsYW5nPWVuLVVT#page=&zoom=page-height&pagemode=thumbs

[128] Infant Adoption Rate Dropping
https://adoption.org/adoption-rate-dropping

[129] Pew Research: In-Vitro Fertilization in America
https://www.pewresearch.org/fact-tank/2018/07/17/a-third-of-u-s-adults-say-they-have-used-fertility-treatments-or-know-someone-who-has/

[130] USA Today: Same-Sex Couple Carries Same Baby in IVF Treatment First
https://www.usatoday.com/story/news/nation-now/2018/10/29/same-sex-couple-carries-same-baby-ivf-fertility-treatment-first/1804554002/

[131] Same-Sex Couples' Babies Being Implanted into "Plastic Vaginal Devices"
https://www.ncbi.nlm.nih.gov/pmc/articles/PMC6357699/

[132] The New York Times: LGBTQ Pregnancy: From DIY to IVF
https://www.nytimes.com/2020/04/15/parenting/fertility/lgbtq-pregnancy-ivf.html

[133] States Moved to Ensure "Equality" in Health Insurance for Same-Sex Couple Reproductive Rights
https://www.baltimoresun.com/politics/bal-in-vitro-mandate-bill-for-samesex-couples-passes-both-chambers-20150324-story.html

[134] States Moved to Ensure "Equality" in Health Insurance for Same-Sex Couple Reproductive Rights
https://www.baltimoresun.com/politics/bal-in-vitro-mandate-bill-for-samesex-couples-passes-both-chambers-20150324-story.html

[135] New York Moves to Expand Access, Ensure Insurance Coverage for Same-Sex Couple Fertility Treatments
https://www.dfs.ny.gov/reports_and_publications/press_releases/pr202102111

[136] "Bulldozed:" Same-Sex Marriage Rights Pass in the United Kingdom
https://www.bbc.com/news/uk-politics-23338279

[137] Same-Sex IVF Spikes in the UK
https://www.reuters.com/article/us-britain-fertility-lgbt/same-sex-couples-and-singles-use-of-fertility-treatment-hits-uk-record-idUSKCN1SF1QH

[138] Drag Queen Story Hour
https://www.dailysignal.com/2020/01/27/how-drag-queen-story-hour-expanded-across-america/

[139] "California Healthy Youth Act" Requires Gender Diversity Teachings
https://www1.cbn.com/cbnnews/us/2019/may/downright-sickening-ca-preps-graphic-sex-ed-with-bondage-blood-play-and-k-3-gender-queer

[140] California Sex Education Books Taught Kindergartners They Could Be Two Different Genders, Taught High Schoolers about Violent Sexual Acts
https://www.californiafamily.org/2019/state-officials-remove-several-books-from-sex-ed-guidelines-after-parent-protest/

[141] Colorado Cake Baker Sued
https://apnews.com/article/us-supreme-court-jack-phillips-lawsuits-colorado-denver-a589873d7c2be64d07e1dc0433b13f64

[142] Oregon Bakery Sued
https://www.opb.org/news/article/sweet-cakes-by-melissa-oregon-appeals-court/

[143] Trump DOJ Backed Kentucky Photographer

https://www.nbcnews.com/feature/nbc-out/doj-backs-kentucky-photographer-who-won-t-do-gay-weddings-n1144516

[144] Christian Ministers Told to Perform Gay "Weddings" or Face Jail Time
https://www.catholicnewsagency.com/news/30760/christian-ministers-told-to-perform-gay-weddings-or-face-jail-time

[145] NYC to Fine Individuals $250,000 if They Don't Use Preferred Gender Pronouns
https://nypost.com/2016/05/19/city-issues-new-guidelines-on-transgender-pronouns/

[146] California Convicted Murderer Becomes First Inmate in U.S. to Have Gender Reassignment Surgery
https://www.latimes.com/local/lanow/la-me-ln-inmate-sex-reassignment-20170106-story.html

[147] Chelsea Manning to Undergo Gender Reassignment Surgery
https://www.militarytimes.com/news/your-military/2016/09/14/chelsea-manning-to-undergo-sex-reassignment-surgery/

[148] Massachusetts Same-Sex Marriage Came about by Court Decision, Not the Ballot Box
https://www.mass.gov/info-details/massachusetts-law-about-same-sex-marriage#related-

BIDEN'S BORDER BUNGLE: THE TRUE COST OF ILLEGAL IMMIGRATION TO AMERICA, WOMEN, AND GIRLS

Americans have not been able to turn on the news during the last year without seeing the surging border crisis, as our Southern U.S. border has teemed with migrants and organized crime bosses determined to test the limits of the best national security system on the planet.

The magnitude of the crisis is stunning.

According to the Pew Research Center, illegal border crossings are at a 21-year high.[149]

During President Joe Biden's first year in office, an estimated 4 million illegal immigrants came through our southern U.S. border. It is quadruple the amount who came here during the year prior, during the administration of President Donald Trump.

The number of illegal immigrants who streamed across our border during just the first year of Biden's administration is equivalent to half the population of New York City, the largest city in America.

The numbers alone are staggering — however, what has been done with those 4 million illegal immigrants is just as shocking.

According to reports, tens of thousands (possibly hundreds of thousands) of illegal immigrants have been whisked away in the dark of night never to be seen by Customs and Border Patrol agents again, sometimes on flights chartered by the Administration's agencies into states unknown.

While we don't know exactly where these illegal immigrants have gone, nor when we will encounter them again, we do know one thing: Americans will be astounded by the multitude of issues that will surely be brought on by this class of illegal immigrants infiltrating the American population.

Illegal immigration complications are vast, they come with a high price tag to the American people, they impact our public safety, our most fundamental right to vote, and they are *all* downright offensive to women.

The Humanitarian Crisis

First and foremost, the border crisis is a humanitarian crisis — especially for women and young girls.

As millions of migrants have marched (and continue marching) toward America, women and young girls are the ones who pay the highest price.

U.S. Customs and Border Protection estimates that a stunning 40 million people are enslaved in some type of human trafficking.[150]

CBP describes human trafficking as an act that occurs "when a person is induced by force, fraud or coercion to:
- Work under the total or near-total control of another person or organization (slavery or involuntary servitude)
- [Be] Forced to pay off a loan by working, but instead of paying money, for an agreed-upon or unclear period of time (debt bondage) or even without an agreement as to the timeframe (peonage)
- Perform a sex act for money or anything of value (if under 18, force, fraud or coercion is not required)"

When you see the technical definitions laid out so clearly, it is sickening. It is also easy to see how organized crime groups, gangs, coyote smugglers, and even sexual predators are taking full advantage of the chaos brought on by lax immigration policies and a porous border under the cloak of night.

Among the 40 million people who are trapped in human trafficking, nearly 25 million people have found themselves in forced labor — either in domestic situations (such as housekeeping) or farm labor where they remain trapped, handing over part of their earnings to the very people who trafficked them.

However, the greatest toll of our broken border comes to women and girls in the form of sex trafficking — being kidnapped or even merely transported across the border, only to end up a sex slave to those who helped the women gain safe passage to America. Women represent 99% of people trafficked to the sex industry.

But that's not all.

More than 15 million of the people trafficked end up in forced marriages. These are often underaged girls. Devastatingly, 1 in 4 humans who are trafficked are underaged children.

As shocking as all of these figures are, they are from 2016 — the last year that statistics were available. It is a near certainty that these numbers have skyrocketed after President Joe Biden's big border surge of 2021.

Unfortunately after nearly two years of free reign under the Biden administration, human trafficking is now far too profitable for the gang bosses and coyote smugglers to give it up.

The Texas Public Policy Foundation reports that human trafficking surrounding the migration crisis "has become a multi-billion dollar business, trapping thousands into modern-day slavery."[151]

It will take years, possibly even decades to untangle the mess that has been made.

It is odd that the Democrat Party of today would allow such slavery to happen on their watch, particularly to the very women and children they so often claim they protect. Democrats constantly preach about the need to protect women and on virtually every policy issue they put forth, liberals claim it's "for the kids."

It's also odd that Democrats have allowed "people of color" to become so damaged in the border fight.

When you consider that most of the victims of human trafficking streaming across the border today are people of color, Biden's border crisis demonstrates that Democrats have utter disregard for women of color and children of color.

It's even more bizarre that while the Democrat Party over the last year has feigned concern over slavery that happened on their watches 400 years ago, Democrats' current-day policies will place another generation of millions into a lifetime of slavery. The fact that the enslaved will be predominately women and girls speaks of an even greater depravity.

By the Numbers

Over the last 20 years, politicians in charge have been trying to obfuscate the figures of exactly how many illegal immigrants reside in America.

Thankfully, conservative stars from Ann Coulter and former President Donald Trump to think tanks such as the Center for Immigration Studies [152] have tackled the issue head-on despite its political incorrectness.

Experts estimate that the illegal immigration population inside America is somewhere between 11 million and 21 million people. Of course, radical pro-illegal-immigration activists balk at those figures, mostly because they don't want unsuspecting Americans to know just how big the problem has become.

Besides, radical activists suggest, it's racist to even *discuss* it.

For a clear and unbiased picture, then, let's jump into the "way back machine" and take a look at the last clear figures that a Democrat-run Department of Homeland Security provided the public in 1996, long before this became a political hot potato.

To illustrate *just how long ago* it was acceptable to discuss illegal immigration without being screamed at, let's set the stage: Cindy Crawford had just walked to the Pepsi machine in those tiny cutoff jean shorts; the late Presidential candidate Bob Dole was preparing to surprise audiences with those famous Viagra commercials at the Super Bowl that year, and the Democrat Party's favorite Democrat at the time, Bill Clinton, was President.

That same year, DHS reported that as many as "5.4 million" illegal immigrants resided inside the United States.[153] At that time DHS also reported that the illegal immigration population was growing exponentially, at a rapid clip of at least 275,000 new illegal immigrants per year. By the Clinton administration's own math, over the last 25 years, 6.875 million new illegal immigrants came to America.

That equals 12.275 million illegal immigrants living in America, which falls within the exact range that Coulter, Trump and the conservative think tanks estimated.

Add in the border crisis of 2021 which added an additional 4 million to that tally, and it equals roughly 16 million illegal immigrants living in America today.

This figure ought to be the *starting point* for any conversation about illegal immigration today.

An Assault on Voting Rights

For all of its humanitarian concerns, Biden's open border is at risk of creating other looming crises.

With 16 million foreign nationals now residing inside America, one could see how that could easily become a threat to the integrity of America's elections.

Ironically, radical left Democrat Party leaders such as Stacey Abrams have been busy attacking and undermining the integrity of the vote (by pushing for vote-by-mail programs which have a higher fraud rate), as Americans' rights to vote are now potentially at risk due to the influx of millions of illegal immigrants.

Some conservative pundits have asserted that the left is *purposely* inviting illegal immigrants into the country in order to change the makeup of the electorate in time for the next Presidential election.

I used to think that was a conspiracy theory.

However, Democrats are demonstrating, week by week, month by month, and now year over year, that their plan is to grant at least some non-citizens the right to vote, and they are moving at a pace far faster than anyone initially thought.

Liberal leaders in the most radical cities ended 2021 by dipping their toe into that very scheme.

In the final month of 2021, the New York City Council voted to allow 800,000 foreign nationals (non-citizens) to vote in city elections.[154] That's nearly 1 million new voters who are not legally otherwise allowed to cast a ballot in the United States of America because (even though they are here legally) they are not citizens.

However, New York agreed to welcome them with open arms to cast votes for mayor, city council members, and city issues.

It is not insignificant.

Allowing foreign nationals to vote in highly-consequential elections in America's largest city could have significant consequences.

The mayor of New York City presides over the most populous city in the nation and presides over the largest municipal budget in the United States at more than $99 million annually.[155] Non-citizens would be voting on how to spend that budget. New York City also hosts some of the world's best hospitals and the world's global financial headquarters on Wall Street.

Giving non-citizens the right to vote in New York City is an idea so bad that even radical former Mayor Bill DeBlasio opposed it.

Allowing foreign citizens to vote in New York City's elections grants a great deal of power to residents who have not yet pledged allegiance to this country of ours. Heck, most non-citizens aren't even fully accustomed to important traditions of ours such as law and order, policing, capitalism, and many more issues on which they will be allowed to vote.

At nearly 1 million new voters, non-citizen voters would make up roughly 10% of the electorate of New York City. That's a lot of power at the ballot box. It's certainly enough to change the outcomes of elections.

So, where exactly did New York get this bright idea?

As is often the case with liberal cities trying to outdo one another, it appears that the Big Apple is emulating a proposal passed in San Francisco in 2016 which allowed non-citizen parents to vote in school board elections. [156] The premise is that since the population of schoolchildren who come from non-citizen parents is so high — one-third of children in San Francisco public schools are of non-citizen descent — then the parents ought to have a say in who governs their kids.

Sounds fair enough, right?

Let's take a look at how the slippery slope began.

If California hadn't been so lenient on harboring illegal immigrants in the first place, the numbers of schoolchildren coming from non-citizen parents wouldn't be so high in the first place.

San Francisco was the first city in America to consider itself a "sanctuary city" which attracted hundreds of thousands of non-citizens and then harbored them from the federal government.

The state of California was not much different.

In 2012, none other than California Attorney General Kamala Harris bucked even her own party's leadership when she refused an order from the Obama/Biden administration to bear down on illegal immigrant activity in the state. Harris outright rejected the administration's Safe Communities Act directives, which set forth that law enforcement must report illegal immigrants if they came across them during a routine traffic stop or other law enforcement activities.[157]

Harris did the same when it came to an Immigrations and Customs Enforcement detainer request in 2014 which would have required California's local law enforcement agencies to detain illegal immigrants. Ever defiant and apparently as thirsty for more illegal immigrants as her hometown of San Francisco, Harris didn't just deny the ICE detainer request, she went so far as to pen a memo to law enforcement agencies in all 58 of California's counties stating that *they* would be subject to legal liability if they dared to comply with the federal ICE order. Ask any law enforcement officer today who served in California during that time period, as they remember the detainer well.

Around the same time, San Francisco officially declared itself a sanctuary city[158] (though they had unofficially been operating as such for decades). Los Angeles followed with its own declaration of sanctuary status soon thereafter.[159]

It was official: Californians were then placed on the hook for their new residents' activities from the cradle to the grave including pre-k education, public schooling, healthcare, housing, the feeding of families, and a litany of social services.

After all, under the Democrats' philosophies if you invite people into your cities, then you have to make it livable for them.

If you've ever read the book *If You Give a Mouse a Cookie* you know how this goes. Once you let the mouse into your house, it stays for a while and then it wants more. (The premise goes, *If you let a mouse into your house, then he'll want a cookie. If you give a mouse a cookie, he'll then want a glass of milk. After he's had the milk, he'll need a place to lie down…* and so forth.)

As such, California liberal officials began pushing for "drivers licenses for illegal immigrants." Naturally, after creating sanctuaries for non-citizens and inviting them to stay, those non-citizens would need drivers licenses to get "to and from work."

So, in 2013, California drivers licenses for illegals were granted after Governor Jerry Brown signed Assembly Bill 60 into law. It stated that in order to gain a drivers license, you no longer had to be a U.S. citizen, you merely had to present proof of residence (such as a lease or utility bill) and proof of insurance.

But wait, there's more.

From there, California's liberal leaders began to push for an automatic "motor voter" program which would automatically register to vote everyone who has a driver's license. The California driver's license database would be given to the Secretary of State, and those not already registered to vote would — surprise! — be registered automatically by the state.

How very convenient! Except, of course, if you're a legal American citizen and a registered voter in California about to get your lawful vote cancelled out, in effect.

Thankfully, this last step of California liberals' grand plan to grant the right to vote to millions of illegal immigrants was discovered and halted by a crack Constitutional lawyer by the name of Harmeet Dhillon. (Full disclosure: Harmeet was my client during this time.)

Upon learning that this maneuver was about to take place, Dhillon intervened and issued a cease-and-desist letter to the Secretary of State, demanding a halt to any automatic transfer of voting rights to illegal immigrants.

Had it not been for Dhillon and her team, millions of illegal immigrants would likely have been *automatically* granted the right to vote vis-à-vis the DMV — no citizenship test required, no 10-year waiting period for citizenship as so many legal immigrants have accomplished, nope, just skipping to the front of the line thanks to the keyboard strokes of some liberal bureaucrats in California.

Outrageous.

An Assault on the Women's Right to Vote

It's worth mentioning that for every illegal immigrant and non-citizen who dares to vote, it erases the vote of a law-abiding American citizen.

Now imagine disenfranchising millions of American women who were the *very* last group of American citizens to gain the right to vote. Women have had the right to vote the *shortest* amount of time as legal voters, yet our leaders in big cities and sanctuary cities are poised to allow non-citizens to erase our sacred vote.

That's unfair.

Women have only just commemorated our 100th year of having the right to vote. We were granted the right to vote a stunning 140 years *after* white American males were able to vote and 40 years after the last Black American males were granted the right to vote.

Allowing non-citizens to jump the line is a slap in the face to the suffragettes who fought so hard to win American female citizens the right to vote.

Long before Gloria Steinem and Cecile Richards ever ascended a stage, American women in the 1920s fought with blood, sweat and tears to win us the right. Women including Susan B. Anthony, Elizabeth Cady Stanton, Lucy Stone, Alice Paul , Ida B. Wells, and others sacrificed greatly in the fight. To usurp those rights by even giving non-citizens the right to vote is to denigrate our foremothers' valiant efforts on behalf of all American women.

However, the reality now is that our sacred vote could disappear in a heartbeat because millions from Guatemala, Honduras, Venezuela, or another Socialist country broke into our country via our broken southern border. That is no different than a burglar breaking into the south window in your house, squatting there, and claiming that they have rights to your home, your children, your budget, and everything you've worked for.

To allow foreign citizens — via the liberal politicians who aid and abet them — to illegally gain the right to vote, would be to dishonor the First Wave feminists in America who fought so hard to win our right to vote, and it would be deeply offensive to today's female voters who so cherish their role as America's "swing voters" who not only have the right to have their voices finally heard, but so often see their voices as defining ones in contests across the country.

The Drain on Red States & Congressional Districts

To be sure, the influx of illegal immigrants since Biden took office is shocking.

However, even more shocking is how clandestinely the Biden administration made these migrants disappear in the dark of night.

Long before Republican governors began busing migrants to sanctuary cities, a few observant members of the media and presumably vigilant airport workers made it known to the world that Biden officials were flying migrants into the interior of the country — specifically, to red states. Most of those flights happened under the cover of darkness and without the permission of either the congressional delegation of those states nor their governors.

At least one Florida Congress member, along with Governor Ron DeSantis, are asking the White House for answers after airport records show that the Biden administration flew illegal immigrants to Jacksonville, Florida at least 70 times.[160]

In Tennessee — another red state — Senator Marsha Blackburn is asking questions after flights reportedly landed in the state she represents, under the same conditions, in the dark of night outside of the public's view.[161] A local FOX television affiliate also reported that migrant children and teens were riding buses into Tennessee in late

2021[162] and that the effort was "just getting ramped up." Blackburn accused the Biden administration of "trafficking" these migrant children into the state.

Then there's the Lone Star state — another red state. It can't go without mention that the red state most assaulted by the border surge during the first year of Biden's presidency is none other than Texas. Perhaps not so coincidentally, Texas just so happens to be a state that the Democrat Party is salivating to flip[163] in future elections.

In each of these red states, the likelihood that the flow of illegal immigrants could demographically alter particular electoral districts forever, is actually reasonably high.

In some small towns and districts in red states across America, critical elections are sometimes won by small margins — in some districts, as little as 2,500 voters vote in municipal elections, and in some red U.S. House districts, as few as 400 votes made all the difference.

Imagine if there were 10,000 new potential voters flooding into those areas. It would make an impact.

With no voter ID requirements in elections, it is plausible.

The funny game that the Biden appears to be playing with our electoral politics is not funny at all. It could change the makeup of not only local school board races, but also city council, Congressional, U.S. Senate, and even statewide elections such as governor. It's not unreasonable to suggest that it could change the makeup of the United States forever.

Perhaps that's the plan.

If you were writing a novel about a sinister plot to alter the makeup of the American electorate over the course of 18 months to 3 years, this would be it.

The Price Tag

In addition to the Constitutional rights that radical Democrats appear to be trampling with their border crisis, liberals are also placing a hefty bill at the feet of the American taxpayers.

The overall cost of illegal immigration to America is estimated to be approximately $116 billion [164] according to the Federation for Immigration Reform. To be clear, FAIR's figures are from 2017. (They are certainly much higher now.)

During his administration, President Trump estimated the actual cost to be higher, coming in at around $200 million according to his administration's estimates. [165]

Even NBC News admitted, "A precise cost is hard to ascertain."

The figures after Biden's first year of border bungles are even higher than they were four years ago.

One thing is certain: it costs taxpayers an inordinate amount of money to keep up the lifestyles of those who come here illegally, or those whom come legally initially then overstay their welcome, which makes up about 41% of non-citizens.

The costs are insidious and they stretch into virtually every aspect of our lives. In order to support millions more people, it stretches the limits of our most basic systems.

Illegal immigrants' use of America's schools, roads, and other infrastructure has a direct cost correlation.

Democrats have long claimed that illegal immigrants are simply here to work, "doing the jobs Americans won't do" and that they're paying back into society more than they're taking. However, analyses by think tanks suggest that's not quite the case. Illegal immigrants are, in reality, taking more than they're putting back into our systems.

As FAIR describes it, "Illegal aliens are net consumers of taxpayer-funded services and the limited taxes paid by some segments of the illegal alien population are, in no way, significant enough to offset the growing financial burdens [they] impose on U.S. taxpayers."

As a starting point, we can look back to 1994 when one of the first reports estimated that the cost of illegal immigration was between $2 billion and $19 billion, according to the Government Office of Accountability in its report to Congress members.[166] That is chump change compared to today's exorbitant costs.

Over 30 years, a lot of extras have been tacked onto those costs.

For example, sanctuary cities have ushered in even enormous costs. According to former Congressman Tom Tancredo, who has studied illegal immigration and its costs extensively, the annual financial burden of sanctuary cities adds up to more than $14 billion nationally; $1 billion in California and Texas alone; and more than $100 million annually in over 10 U.S. states combined.[167]

Texas Attorney General Ken Paxton reports that illegal immigration costs Texas taxpayers a stunning $850 million annually.[168] Other think tanks have that figure at an even higher level, including FAIR which once reported that illegal immigration actually costs Texans upwards of $11 billion.

All of these figures are pre-2021 border surge, by the way.

Our government has not yet reported nationally just how much the 2021 border crisis has added to the annual cost of illegal immigration, but you can be sure it is a hefty price.

The other price, of course, is the "opportunity cost" to Americans; in particular, American women and their children.

The hundreds of billions of dollars — that's hundreds of billions, with a "b" — spent on illegal immigrants could be going to American women and their children to provide for a brighter future, better school systems, improved healthcare access, and entrepreneurial opportunities in disadvantaged neighborhoods is enormous. Sadly, it goes against everything that Second Wave Feminism taught us that we should be: *demanding our rightful share.*

Drain on Hospital & Healthcare Systems

During ordinary times, the high cost of illegal immigration is tough on our American systems.

This is acutely true of our hospital and healthcare systems.

Even before the COVID-19 pandemic, America was paying the healthcare costs of *millions* of illegal immigrants.

Uncle Sam wasn't the only one footing the bill.

States are bearing the burden of healthcare costs for migrants as well — especially the two biggest border states.

According to a report by Texas Attorney General Ken Paxton, Texans pay between "$579 million and $717 million each year for public hospital districts to provide uncompensated care for illegal aliens."

Texans pay another $62 million to $90 million every year "to include illegal aliens in the state Emergency Medicaid program."

The state also pay an additional $30 million to $38 million per year on "perinatal coverage for illegal aliens through the Children's Health Insurance Program."

They've always said things are bigger in Texas, but the media never mentions just how big this price tag has gotten.

California fares exponentially worse.

A stunning 1.3 million California children — approximately 15% of California's children — are on the Children's Health Insurance Plan as of 2017.[169] This comes at a cost of $2.6 billion annually, traditionally split between the federal and state governments.

The cost of "free" healthcare for adult illegal immigrants is even more shocking. The cost of Medi-Cal coverage to the state of California is $22.5 billion annually, as of 2020-21.[170]

I can't even imagine what the cost is now with the onset of COVID-19. We likely won't know for a few years the full costs of the pandemic care that American hospitals provided to other nations' citizens, at the risk to our own citizens who died.

These costs aren't only measured in dollar amounts; there are also opportunity costs to American citizens in terms of proper care.

With all of the COVID-era talk of "finite bed capacity" and ICU capacity, it is reasonable to ask how many Americans were turned away as non-citizens were treated in our hospitals and emergency rooms predominantly in America's largest cities, where the death rates also happened to be higher.

In fact, elected officials from then-Governor Andrew Cuomo of New York to California Governor Gavin Newsom based their most important public health decisions on bed capacity and ICU capacity! Those numbers matter when it comes to our healthcare and hospital systems. Those figures were the very thing liberal officials were utilizing to determine lockdowns, business closures, mask mandates, vaccine mandates and warning levels during the pandemic. Those bed availability figures mattered.

That's not to say we can't be benevolent to others. America is. For perspective, America has been a benevolent nation to many throughout our history, sending medical supplies large and small to underprivileged nations in their times of need. In keeping with our founding Christian principles, it is the Godly thing to do.

However somewhere along the way our desire to help others trumped keeping ourselves safe.

Media and BLM activists talked a lot about the "disparity" of health care treatment during the pandemic, yet not one word was uttered about how many Black Americans could have been better treated in hospitals and emergency rooms if our healthcare systems hadn't been serving illegal immigrants from foreign countries. Not one word. In a world of finite resources, that conversation matters.

There has been no conversation about the liberal policies which allowed non-citizens to stroll right through the emergency room doors and rob American women of the system they paid into. To freely give away the resources, ventilators, medical supplies, N95 masks and world-class expertise of American doctors and nursing staff at a time when it was in the highest demand is just not "fair" nor "equitable" to us.

However, the Democrat Party of today doesn't appear to care about fairness to American women in healthcare.

Every single one of their presidential primary candidates raised their hands at the first debate in support of providing more money for free healthcare to illegal immigrants. Every. Single. One.

That show of hands represents tens of billions of more money that will be paid for by Americans to take care of those who are in our country unlawfully.

Imagine for a moment if the United States of America invested tens of billions of dollars into its female entrepreneurs and girls in disadvantaged areas like East L.A., the Bronx and Chicago instead. Imagine if those tens of billions of dollars went toward women's healthcare systems in order to help disadvantaged aunties and grandmas with COVID, to cure breast cancer, increase survival rates, and improve the overall health of American women. Instead, Democrats are inviting more people to come here at a time when we can afford it least.

Impact on Education

The cost of educating illegal immigrant children in America is also costly.

An analysis in *The Atlanta Journal Constitution* by Lance Izumi shows that it takes tens of billions of dollars to educate illegal immigrants' children right here in the U.S.[171]

Why is the cost so high?

It has to do with demographics.

Izumi reports that nearly half, or 47 percent, of illegal-immigrant households are parents who have children. This is more than double the makeup of U.S.-born households, where only 21 percent of households consist of parents with children.

As more illegal immigrants arrive to America, they are bringing exponentially more children.

Izumi reports that nearly 20 years ago, there were 4.3 million children of illegal immigrants in the United States. By 2008, that number had climbed to 5.5 million[172] which was more than the entire population of the state of Colorado. With figures like that, there can be no denying that the large number of children of illegal immigrants does indeed impact our public schools and education costs.

The average cost-per-pupil of educating a child in public school today is more than $12,000 per pupil. The estimated costs, then, of educating children of illegal immigrants in America today are more than $66 billion.

The tens of billions of dollars paid to educate children of foreign nationals are tens of billions of dollars that are not going to America's most challenging schools, in the roughest neighborhoods, in the most underserved areas.

As Americans constantly look for ways to improve education for their own children and the children of underserved neighborhoods, there is no question that footing the bill for children of illegal immigrants is unfortunately a zero-sum game. For every billion dollars spent on illegal immigrants' education, that's a billion dollars not spent in America's worst-performing schools in The Bronx, Harlem, East Los Angeles, Mississippi and elsewhere.

For that, America deserves an "F" — a failing grade.

Impact of on Women's Safety

Illegal immigration also has a negative impact on crime rates and the safety of women.

As unpopular as it might be to say, then-candidate Donald Trump was right when he launched his presidential campaign in June 2015 by suggesting that Mexico was "not sending us their best."

I wrote about it for *TheBlaze* at the time that Trump was right and that the crime statistics backed him up.[173]

Democrats have long pushed the theory that illegal immigrants are coming to America strictly for the jobs. However, the House Committee on Homeland Security debunked that theory in a 2006 majority report: "Not all illegal aliens are crossing into the United States to find work... Law enforcement officials indicate that there are individuals coming across the border who are forced to leave their home countries because of criminal activities. These dangerous criminals are fleeing the law in other countries and seeking refuge in the United States."[174]

Read that again. These criminals are not able to stay in their own home countries due to the crimes they've committed, so they instead come to America to slip in through the proverbial unlocked doors at our southern border.

Once they're here, they don't magically stop committing crimes.

According to the Center for Immigration Studies, 95% of all outstanding warrants for murder in Los Angeles are for illegal immigrants. In addition, "Up to two-thirds of all fugitive felony warrants (17,000) are for illegal aliens." Those figures were reported back in 2004 and while it's not considered politically correct to discuss them nowadays, the figures are likely even higher today.

CIS crime expert Heather Macdonald also reports that 60% of L.A.'s infamous 18th Street Gang and the murderous, racketeering, drug gang around MacArthur Park are illegal immigrants.

An FBI Statistical Report on Undocumented Immigrants dating back to 2006 showed that in addition to the 95% figure for warrants for homicide in L.A.,[175] a stunning 83% of warrants for murder in Phoenix were for illegal aliens. 86% of warrants for murder in Albuquerque were for illegal aliens. A shocking 75% of those on the most wanted lists across Los Angeles, Phoenix and Albuquerque were illegal aliens.[176]

In addition to the human cost of day-to-day crime, the cost of illegal immigration are also steep on America's prisons, jails, and criminal justice systems and ultimately that is additional bad news for American women.

A report from the U.S. Senate in the 104th Congress shows that 25% of all prisoners incarcerated in the United States federal prisons are illegal immigrant criminals[177] and the Federation for American Immigration Reform reports that state and local facilities hold an approximately 16% population of illegal immigrant criminals. To be clear, these are not individuals thrown into prison simply for the crime of being here illegally, but rather committing other heinous crimes after they are here.

According to the FAIR, the annual cost to house these criminal illegal immigrants nationally is $1.6 billion and growing each year.[178]

In Colorado, for example, a 2016 report by the state Department of Corrections revealed that state prison system was holding "2,039 criminal aliens at a cost of $37,958 per inmate. That is a total cost of $77,396,362. The federal reimbursement grant was $2,077, 720. That is a grant of 2.7 cents for every dollar of actual cost. Those 2,039 criminal alien inmates were 14% of all state prison inmates: One in every seven felons in the state prison system is a criminal alien." That was back in 2016, when the last statistics were available. The figures are likely even higher now.

After Biden's border bungle of 2021, these figures will undoubtedly continue to grow.

With today's defunding of police and crime spikes across the nation, even if illegal immigrant criminals are caught, there is no guarantee they will stay in jail. So-called bail reform programs, long-term costs of incarcerating illegal immigrant criminals on our soil and pressure from activist groups make it less likely that leaders facing cost constraints and constant pressure to be re-elected will be willing to keep criminals locked up.

The Effect on the American Worker

As millions of illegal immigrants flood our southern border, they place at risk the jobs of working-class Americans who find themselves in desperate financial straits in a post-pandemic economy.

That's not a racist trope; there are statistical facts to back it up.

Illegal immigrant workers drive down wages for American jobs [179] particularly service industry jobs like the restaurant industry, where over half of the restaurant staff positions are held by female workers. This means less take-home pay for the moms and single ladies who often work as wait staff, hostesses, and more.

At a time when 2 million women are already missing from the workforce post-pandemic, the fact that Democrats would welcome in millions of additional illegal immigrants tells you an awful lot about what they think of the female American workforce.

It's also ironic that illegal immigrant labor drives down wages as that's directly in conflict with Democrat Party perennial campaign promises to raise the minimum wage to $15 an hour, and now $20 in some places. Real-life immigration policies run contrary to their own campaign pledges.

Border Walls Work

Sadly, much of the high costs to our American systems — from schools to hospitals — could be solved with simple borders walls or fences.

Border barriers work, and Democrats once believed that, too. You know how I know? They once voted for them.

Long before their radical, far-left caucus including "The Squad" was sworn into office in 2018, Democrats actually voted for border security.

Then-Senate Minority Leader Chuck Schumer voted for the 2006 Secure Fence Act which required the construction of border barriers along 700 miles of the southern U.S. border.[180]

Then-Senators Hillary Clinton and Joe Biden also voted for the Secure Fence Act. So did a young community-organizer-turned-Senator named Barack Obama, who gave an impassioned speech on the floor of the U.S. Senator on its behalf.

Ultimately 64 Democrats in the House voted for the Secure Fence Act, and 26 in the Senate voted for it.

The result of that act? In places like Yuma, Arizona illegal border crossings plummeted 70%.[181]

It is proof that even Democrats know that border fences and barriers work.

In a post-pandemic economy, with limited resources for our own people, the time has come to support stronger immigration policies again. During the Trump administration, illegal immigration hit a 20-year low. It's time we get back there. Our healthcare systems, our hospitals, our school systems, our public safety, and our national security all depend upon it.

Conclusion

America is a special place. It is one where liberty and freedom have been granted upon us in large part due to our founding fathers' commitments to God and where hundreds of millions of Americans are working hard every day to continue those blessings. Today, the evidence is clear that our nation is under attack, from outside and from within, not only by the asylum seekers who wish to take advantage of the American system but by those in American leadership who wish to alter the makeup of our country.

Benjamin Franklin once stated that America is a Republic… "if we can keep it. We are on the precipice of not being able to keep it.

However, it's not all bad news. We can keep our Republic, but only if we only if we step up and stop our elected leaders from giving away our country to citizens of socialist countries who don't understand our founding, our values, nor have yet worked to earn her all of her blessings.

HOMEWORK

- ➤ Check out the National Border Patrol Council. You'll appreciate the expertise of its president Brandon Judd, who has served as a Border Patrol agent for 22 years. He has testified before Congress about border security. The organization's website is a wealth of information for anyone who wants to stay up to date with everything going on at the border: BPUnion.org
- ➤ Make your voice heard. Call your Congress member and U.S. Senators today, or write them an email or letter to tell them that they must hold the Biden administration accountable for the influx of illegal immigrants. These offices track their Constituent mail and keep tabs on what the people in their states and their districts are most concerned about. Your letter can make a difference and affect the policies that receive your elected officials' attention.
  - o To find your Congress member:
    https://www.house.gov/representatives/find-your-representative
  - o To find your U.S. Senator:
    https://www.senate.gov/senators/senators-contact.htm

REFERENCES:

[149] Pew Research: Migrant Encounters at the Border at 21-Year High
https://www.pewresearch.org/fact-tank/2021/08/13/migrant-encounters-at-u-s-mexico-border-are-at-a-21-year-high/

[150] Customs and Border Protection: Human Trafficking
https://www.cbp.gov/border-security/human-trafficking

[151] Texas Public Policy Foundation:
https://www.texaspolicy.com/multimedia/article/border-crisis-human-trafficking

[152] 2021: Center for Immigration Studies
https://cis.org/Immigration-Topic/Illegal-Immigration

[153] DHS: 1996: Estimated Number of Illegal Immigrants in America
https://www.dhs.gov/xlibrary/assets/statistics/illegal.pdf

[154] Proposal to Allow 800,000 Illegal Immigrants Vote in New York City
https://www.foxnews.com/politics/new-york-city-council-approves-measure-to-allow-nearly-800000-non-citizens-to-vote-in-local-elections

[155] Annual Budget of New York City
https://www1.nyc.gov/site/omb/index.page

[156] San Francisco Allows Illegal Immigrants to Vote
https://www.sfexaminer.com/news/san-francisco-supervisors-approve-non-citizen-voting-in-school-board-elections/

[157] Then-Attorney General Kamala Harris Bucked Illegal Immigration Orders from Obama Administration
https://www.newsmax.com/jenniferkerns/border-crisis-illegal-aliens-illegal-immigrants-undocumented/2021/04/08/id/1016875/

[158] San Francisco Becomes a Sanctuary City
https://sfmayor.org/sanctuary-city

[159] L.A. Becomes a Sanctuary City
https://www.latimes.com/local/lanow/la-me-ln-city-of-sanctuary-cedillo-20190208-story.html

[160] Florida Congressmen Ask Questions about Dark-of-Night Flights
https://webster.house.gov/press-releases?id=9FD50F8D-2A92-4EE7-82F2-43E13F16A67

[161] Sen. Marsha Blackburn Suggests Biden Administration "Trafficking" Migrants into Tennessee
https://www.blackburn.senate.gov/2021/5/blackburn-hagerty-fleischmann-speak-out-against-biden-administration-trafficking-migrant-children-to-tennessee

[162] Migrant Children, Teens Flying, Riding Buses into Tennessee: FOX 17
https://fox17.com/news/local/they-are-just-getting-ramped-up-migrant-children-flying-riding-buses-into-chattanooga-nashville-knoxville-tennessee-immigration-southern-border-marsha-blackburn-bill-lee-hagerty

[163] Democrats Aim to Flip Texas
https://www.vanityfair.com/news/2019/12/beto-orourke-second-act-flipping-texas

[164] FAIR: 2017: Illegal Immigration Costs $116 Billion per Year
https://www.thecentersquare.com/national/report-illegal-immigration-costs-taxpayers-116-billion-annually-californians-texans-floridians-pay-the-most/article_f942e522-c5b0-11e9-93e6-0ff213e44ae5.html

[165] President Trump: 2019: Illegal Immigration Costs $200 Billion or More per Year
https://www.nbcnews.com/politics/donald-trump/fact-check-how-much-does-illegal-immigration-cost-america-not-n950981

[166] GAO Report on the Cost of Illegal Immigrants in 1994
https://www.gao.gov/assets/hehs-95-133.pdf

[167] Breitbart: 300 Sanctuary Cities Costing State, Local Taxpayers $7,000,000,000 Annually
https://www.breitbart.com/politics/2017/01/28/tancredo-300-sanctuary-cities-costing-state-local-taxpayers-7000000000-annually/

[168] Texas Attorney General Ken Paxton: Costs of Illegal Immigration
https://www.texasattorneygeneral.gov/news/releases/ag-paxton-illegal-immigration-costs-texas-taxpayers-over-850-million-each-year

[169] The Cost of Free Healthcare in California – The Most Populous Border State in America
https://www.ppic.org/blog/million-california-children-rely-chip/

[170] Medi-Cal Costs to California
https://lao.ca.gov/Publications/Report/4373

[171] Atlanta Journal Constitution: OPINION: Educating Illegal Immigrants is Costly
https://www.ajc.com/news/opinion/educating-illegal-immigrants-costly/Iafsqvt6ydowmSvgX9C4TM/

[172] The Washington Post: Illegal Immigrant Children in America's Schools
https://www.washingtonpost.com/news/answer-sheet/wp/2014/11/21/how-many-k-12-students-are-illegal-immigrants/

[173] TheBlaze: KERNS: Donald Trump is Right on Immigration
https://www.theblaze.com/contributions/is-donald-trump-right-on-immigration

[174] 2006 House Committee on Homeland Security
https://books.google.com/books?id=H37hCgAAQBAJ&pg=PT318&lpg=PT318&dq=%22Law+enforcement+officials+indicate+that+there+are+individuals+coming+across+the+border+who+are+forced+to+leave+their+home+countries+because+of+criminal+activities.%22&source=bl&ots=OwKlzC9lJf&sig=0lRouE7w1JfXtHRWYOrbmztQ_sA&hl=en&sa=X&ved=0ahUKEwi-6ajQ86zXAhUM02MKHe28AfYQ6AEIJjAA#v=onepage&q=%22Law%20enforcement%20officials%20indicate%20that%20there%20are%20individuals%20coming%20across%20the%20border%20who%20are%20forced%20to%20leave%20their%20home%20countries%20because%20of%20criminal%20activities.%22&f=false

[175] Center for Immigration Studies: Warrants for Arrest in Homicide Los Angeles are 95% for Illegal Immigrants
https://cis.org/Report/Crime-and-Illegal-Alien

[176] FBI Uniform Crime Report Statistics, by Year
https://www.fbi.gov/services/cjis/ucr/publications

[177] U.S. Senate Committee Report from the 104th Congress: 25% of Incarcerated in America are Illegal Immigrants
https://www.congress.gov/104/crpt/srpt48/CRPT-104srpt48.pdf

[178] Federation of American Immigration Reform: Cost of Incarcerating Illegal Immigrant Criminals
https://www.fairus.org/issue/societal-impact/criminal-aliens

[179] POLITICO Magazine: Yes, Immigration Drives Down Wages
https://www.politico.com/magazine/story/2016/09/trump-clinton-immigration-economy-unemployment-jobs-214216/

[180] Democrats Voted for Border Fence
https://wjla.com/news/nation-world/2006-secure-fence-act-vs-trumps-border-wall

[181] USA Today: OPINION: Border Walls Work. Yuma Sector Proves It
https://www.usatoday.com/story/opinion/2017/08/22/homeland-security-secretary-border-walls-work-yuma-sector-proves-it-elaine-duke-column/586853001/

TRANSGENDER ATHLETES or TITLE IX: YOU CAN'T SERVE BOTH

Second Wave Feminists fought for their sisters' rights to "play ball!"

Winning young ladies the right to play sports was one of the more impressive cornerstones of the American feminist movement of the 1960s and 1970s — a proud trophy of accomplishment.

In the 1960s, as more young women entered the world of collegiate sports they found themselves disadvantaged to their male counterparts. Everything from their very ability to participate in team sports to their access to university training centers were restricted to men. Even after they gained access to sports, fancy workout rooms and high-tech ultrasound machines intended to help athletes were usually afforded to male athletes, but not women.

Feminists of the era thought that was highly unfair, and they set out to amend the education statutes in America.

Prior civil rights legislation addressed discrimination, but nothing had yet risen to the level of banning discrimination specifically against women in this arena. The Civil Rights Act of 1964 addressed discrimination based on "race, color, religion, sex, or national origin" but only in public accommodation and employment matters. Similarly, Title VI was enacted around the same time in regard to Federally funded entities, but it left out women.

Feminists got to work lobbying Congress to add sex — or as we are supposed to say today, "gender" — as a protected class of citizens.

The National Organization for Women (NOW) leaned on President Lyndon B. Jonson to issue an executive order prohibiting sex discrimination in Federal contracts. That was a close step.

Soon after, "Title IX of the Education Amendments"[182] was born. In 1972, it was signed into law by a Republican president — Richard M. Nixon. (So much for suggesting Republicans don't support women!)

Title IX stated, "No person in the United States shall, on the basis of sex, be excluded from participation in, be denied the benefits of, or be subjected to discrimination under any education program or activity receiving Federal financial assistance."

While Title IX is best known for helping girls in sports, its protections span to areas off the field as well. In fact, early reports about Title IX didn't even mention sports. It provided a great umbrella of protection for young women throughout multiple institutions — universities, female professorships, sports complexes and the like.

In essence, Title IX ensures that no institution receiving Federal funds could discriminate against women in any way, shape or form.

Decades later President Barack Obama would light the match to burn down Title IX protections when he issued a letter to members of Congress informing them of his guidance that "transgenders" should be seen as equal to women in Title IX consideration.[183]

President Trump would ultimately undo Obama's advice by having Attorney General Jeff Sessions rescind the Obama order.[184] Yet, the die was already cast. Transgender activists had gotten a leg up on the competition — literally — and as most things with progressives go, they weren't going to give up a perceived advancement.

Today, transgender athletes are jockeying to take their positions next to young women in sports all across the country. Thanks to Obama and his supporters in the feminist movement of our era, protections have gone far afield of the original intent of Title IX. It's just one more way that Democrats have abandoned our girls. Instead of protecting our girls, liberals push the outrageous idea that somehow a boy can "become" a young girl, then summarily compete against other young girls in sports.

Scholarship Money Down the Drain

By allowing transgender athletes to compete against America's girls, liberals and their feminist enablers are also ripping hard-earned scholarship money out of the hands of young female athletes who have worked hard for years to go to college. In many cases, a scholarship is the only way that some girls can afford college or the college of their choice.

Athletic scholarships are extremely competitive. According to college athlete recruitment sites, less than 2% of athletes are offered scholarships each year — which would explain why male athletes might want to compete against female athletes... for the better odds!

Even athletes who win scholarships are likely to receive just $10,000 per year on average. Less than 0.02% of student athletes receive scholarships above $25,000. So, one can see just how precious these slots are and how scarce the resources are. It stands to reason that we ought to protect biological girls from being eclipsed by transgender athletes.

Olympic Games

Beyond college scholarships, there is another destination for young female athletes: the Olympics.

Unlike college sports, the propensity to make big money in endorsement deals exists at the next level (though that is changing due to new National College Association of Athletes (NCAA) rules on college athletes' pay.) However, endorsement deals for Olympic athletes are the best bet as those can range in the millions to multi millions.

Gold medalist Michael Phelps' net worth was an estimated $80 million in 2021, largely from endorsement deals from companies including

"Louis Vuitton, Visa, Colgate, Omega and Under Armour." [185] According to the South Morning China Post, bathing suit company Speedo also paid Phelps a $1 million bonus for his gold medal finish at the Beijing Olympics.

Endorsement deals for female athletes are lucrative as well.

Yahoo! News reports that tennis star Naomi Osaka's "marketing might" rings up at $55 million.

Serena Williams' is not far behind at $35 million.

Olympic gymnast Simone Biles clocks in at $6 million.

Soccer star Megan Rapinoe is not far behind with $4.1 million with an additional half million in endorsement deals, salaries and bonuses. [186]

Yet, if young women don't first win titles in collegiate sports, many of them likely can't proceed to the next Olympic level.

If young girls in middle school and high school are snuffed out early in their athletic careers, it could mean the loss of potentially millions of dollars over a lifetime, not to mention the dreams that would tragically be crushed in the process.

Intersectionality

The feminist movement of today has most certainly abandoned our girls in an effort to please their radical, left-wing bosses who push a relatively new construct called "intersectionality" [187] — a belief that a person's social, gender, sexual and political identities all intersect to create different modes of discrimination or privilege.

Under the construct of intersectionality, liberals believe that who you identify as, the race you are, the gender you are (or the gender you choose to be). leads to the amount discrimination which will be heaped upon you.

The only solution, of course, is for social justice warriors to swoop in to prevent or remedy this discrimination. It is a never-ending cycle of liberal madness.

The creator of the theory of intersectionality, by the way, just so happens to be the creator of Critical Race Theory, Kimberle' Williams Crenshaw.

In the world of intersectionality, today's social justice warriors believe that transgenders who identify differently than their biological gender are at risk of *greater* discrimination than biologically-born girls and therefore need more accommodation than the girls who were originally protected under Title IX.

Wrap your head around that for a moment.

No matter how you slice it, intersectionality in this arena is the ultimate betrayal of our biologically-born girls.

Transgender Bathrooms in Schools

With transgender rights gaining momentum in pop culture, liberals did the one thing they do best — they sped it along it by jamming it into the systems that they control, along with funding that they control: America's schools.

Soon, American parents began seeing rules passed in favor of transgenderism at local schools. For example, allowing transgender/biologically-born boys into girls' locker rooms among other things.

The policies were so ill-conceived and not thought through, that they've actually had disastrous consequences for girls.

In Loudon County, Virginia — a posh suburb of Washington, D.C. — a "skirt-wearing" high school boy entered into a "gender fluid" bathroom[188] and raped a female student.[189] That young lady's life will never be the same.

Much of this has been on the news so I won't go into further details. But it's worth noting that Democrats added insult to literally injury in this case. Rather than assist the young girl and her outraged parents, at least one school official sat quietly on the matter, transferring the biological male student to another school where he committed sexual assault *again*.

The second sexual assault lays firmly at the feet of the school official, but also Democrat Governor Ralph Northam, who signed into law Virginia House Bill 257 which enabled schools to *not* disclose the sexual assault of girls in schools.[190]

All down the line, the officials failing girls in schools belong to one party: the Democrat Party.

If these shameless policies don't fly directly in the face of the Title IX protections that Democrats were supposed to be providing our schoolgirls, I don't know what does. This is a literal "War on Women," and it's happening in the most delicate of all places: our schools and the private places where our girls go to the restroom.

With all of these assaults (both proverbially and literally) happening to young girls today, it is no wonder what I call "Mad Dads" are showing up at school boards in droves.

Not-So-Planned Parenthood: Transgenders Set to Give Birth... Using Surgical Pouches

As if transgender athletes competing against our daughters wasn't enough, liberals are now attempting to change the definition of *everything* feminine — right down to the definition of a mother, and a uterus.

On the heels of liberal educators teaching boys as young as kindergarten that they can be girls, now they're trying to tell the world that men can actually get pregnant and carry a baby to term.

I'm not referring to women who now identify as men. I'm talking about biological men — men born "sans uteri" — if that's now what passes for a definition of what a man is.

Transgender activists are now looking into whether men can have the opportunity to do so by having uteri (that's plural for uterus) implanted onto their bodies.[191]

The idea is that transgender women (men who became women) now want to show their partners and the world that they can get pregnant and be great "mothers."

This idea involves basically building a womb or conducting a womb transplant.

As with most things, liberal activists are using radical science experiments to further their goals.

The scientist who conceptualized the procedure, Mats Brännström, says that he initially came up with the concept to help biological women who were naturally infertile or previously had to undergo hysterectomies. He also thought it would be especially helpful for women in Sweden, where surrogacy is not allowed. He tested the procedure in lab rats, then larger animals, then in five women who all gave birth to bouncing baby boys and girls. Excuse me, I mean humans who viciously had their "genders assigned at birth," according to Democrats.

The procedure was helpful for women who were no longer able to have children, through no fault of their own.

However, it wasn't long after word of the successful "womb" procedure spread that Scientific American reports doctors from Boston Medical Center to the Cleveland Clinic saw an uptick in transgenders requesting this external "womb."

In fact, one physician reports that a transgender woman (a man transitioning to a woman) even inquired if she could do both the gender reassignment operation and receive a "womb" implant on the same day.

The doctor said, "No."

The procedure itself is extremely complicated. The patient has to find a donor who will donate a uterus (either a live person who doesn't need their uterus anymore, or a uterus from a cadaver (i.e., a dead person).

Next, the transplant of the organ would have to take place very quickly. If the procedure is successful, then menstruation would begin shortly after in the host body (yes, even if it were a man or a former man).

A year later, IVF could actually be attempted and if successful, the man would be on his way to giving birth and carrying the baby in this transplanted "womb."

This is *Animal Farm* type of stuff, folks.[192]

Like so many of the policies that progressives push, the suggestion that men can give birth is highly offensive to natural-born women.

Whether you believe it or not, it is a scientific fact that mothers were granted the organs (from either God or Mother Nature, whomever you pray to) in order to fulfill the sacred privilege of motherhood. Suggesting that a man named Steve can be a man one day, cut off his genitalia the next, then implant a "womb" onto his body two days later and instantly become a "mother" requires some incredible mental gymnastics.

It is all an offense to the God-given, traditional, feminine sanctity of "motherhood."

Conclusion

Today, the U.S. Department of Education's Office for Civil Rights (OCR) states that it "enforces, among other statutes, Title IX of the Education Amendments of 1972. Title IX protects people from discrimination based on sex in education programs or activities that receive federal financial assistance."[193]

Oh, really?

If that were truly the case, Biden's Department of Education and his Democrat friends around the country would be helping families of young women today. Yet, they're doing everything except that. If Democrats and feminists truly care about young women in sports, universities, and other federally-funded programs, they would use their power to prevent the many disadvantages brought about by the acceleration of transgender athletes where girls exist in our nation's schools, locker rooms and beyond.

Feminists today could certainly pressure Biden to do so. They helped him get elected, and they have political capital to spend. The fact that they haven't further proves that today's Democrat Party and liberal feminists don't truly care about the girls they claim they once did, back in their Title IX glory days.

The gall of progressives today — and the lack of feminists willing to stand up and say anything about it — shows that feminism of our time might not actually value the promise and potential of young women as much as they once did. Perhaps to feminists, women have simply been the means to an end to gaining political power, media attention, a litany of taxpayer-funded goodies (read: free abortion, free healthcare, free daycare) and swanky parties in the White House with friends who were once women but are now men.

Now that they're there at the top, maybe the feminist power brokers don't actually need women anymore.

HOMEWORK
- ➢ Familiarize yourself with the full text of Title IX, as signed into law in June of 1972 here: https://www.justice.gov/crt/title-ix-education-amendments-1972 However, see for yourself on the Biden administration's Department of Justice website that the protection of "girls" has been replaced instead with the protection of "transgenders." This is a far cry from the original intent of the federal law, and this discrepancy should have been addressed by feminists today: https://www.justice.gov/crt/fcs/titleix-sexdiscrimination
- ➢ I'd like to challenge parents and enterprising Civil Rights attorneys to look into suing the Department of Education for not

doing their duty in upholding Title IX for your daughters. It's a stretch, but so were many things that Democrats have pushed uphill to the Supreme Court over the last half century like same-sex marriage, Roe v. Wade, and more. It's worth a shot for their future. If you're looking for representation, one of my favorite Civil Rights attorneys is Harmeet Dhillon, founder of the Center for American Liberty.

REFERENCES:

[182] Title IX
https://www.britannica.com/event/Title-IX

[183] President Obama's Civil Rights Division Letter on Transgenders and Title IX
https://www2.ed.gov/about/offices/list/ocr/letters/colleague-201605-title-ix-transgender.pdf

[184] Trump Administration Reverses Obama-era Guidance on Transgenders and Title IX
https://www.documentcloud.org/documents/4067437-Sessions-memo-reversing-gender-identity-civil.html

[185] Olympic Medalist Michael Phelps' Net Worth
https://www.scmp.com/magazines/style/celebrity/article/3144538/michael-phelps-net-worth-how-olympic-swimmer-made-his

[186] Yahoo! News – Highest-Paid Female Athletes
https://www.yahoo.com/now/highest-paid-female-athletes-2021-040150450.html

[187] Definition of Intersectionality: PragerU
https://www.youtube.com/watch?v=rc7VUoytoU4

[188] "Skirt-Wearing" Male Student in "Gender Fluid" School Bathroom Rapes Girl
https://www.dailymail.co.uk/news/article-10114809/Loudoun-County-board-member-seeks-inquiry-claim-girl-raped-bathroom-skirt-wearing-male.html

[189] Loudon County Student Rape in Gender Neutral Bathroom
https://wjla.com/features/i-team/teen-suspect-found-guilty-in-loudoun-county-public-school-stone-bridge-high-bathroom-assault

[190] Northam-Signed House Bill 257 Allows Schools to Hide Sexual Assaults in Schools
https://lis.virginia.gov/cgi-bin/legp604.exe?201+sum+HB257

[191] Scientific American: How a Transgender Woman Could Get Pregnant
https://www.scientificamerican.com/article/how-a-transgender-woman-could-get-pregnant/

[192] Animal Farm – George Orwell
https://www.britannica.com/topic/Animal-Farm

[193] Department of Education's Office for Civil Rights on Title IX
https://www2.ed.gov/about/offices/list/ocr/docs/tix_dis.html

BIG TECH BULLIES & THEIR FEMINIST HANDMAIDENS

Feminism in all of its iterations throughout history sought to give women a voice.

Therefore, one would expect feminists today to be extremely concerned about their liberal brothers in Big Tech increasingly squelching the free speech of Americans.

After all, no one has squelched nearly 100 million voices faster and more effectively than Silicon Valley in the lead-up to the 2020 elections.

As the November 2020 Presidential election drew nearer and nearer, conservatives on social media began to complain of their posts being limited or blocked, and conservative stars with hundreds of thousands of followers — if not millions — were just plum thrown off of social media platforms, placed in "Twitter jail," and so forth.

In October 2020, news broke that the laptop of Hunter Biden, then-candidate Joe Biden's son, had been found along with some very compromising information contained on it.

No one believed it *less* than the so-called champions of the free flow of information at Meta (formerly called Facebook), Instagram and Twitter. In fact, they didn't want anyone to even *discuss* it.

The New York Post Tweeted posted a report that Hunter's laptop contained bizarre emails discussing money splits for consulting gigs in foreign countries, with China and Ukraine suspected to be among them. Hunter's laptop also reportedly contained graphic images of him reportedly doing illegal drugs. Twitter not only blocked the Post story, but it made the rare move of blocking *The New York Post* entirely from its platform. It also prevented most other users from being able to even share the story.

I won't elaborate further as the story has been covered ad nauseam on TV news, but in retrospect it's hard to believe this wasn't some sort of purposeful, biased, electioneering at the hands of the tech gods.

It was a move that left 80 million Americans frustrated.

Almost a year after the *Post* ran the Hunter Biden story, more liberal news outlets reported that the story was, in fact, true. Yet there was no apology from social media companies for hiding a truthful story from the American electorate.

Election Integrity

Soon after the 2020 presidential elections wrapped, Americans began to get very frustrated again with the counting of votes — in particular, information they saw on the news such as reported spikes in numbers of ballots after-hours in places like Philadelphia and poll workers unpacking ballots from suitcases stored under tables in Georgia. Americans — well, at least half of them — at least wanted more information about the events to make up their own minds about election integrity.

Meta, however, had different plans and that included tamping down the opinions of users who posted about recounts, election audits and anyone who was on the wrong side of what Meta deemed "election integrity."

I guess election integrity only goes one direction? Who knew!

As weeks went by and Americans grew more tense, President Trump chimed in on the matter on social media as he did with most populist matters. Word began to spread online about a "Stop the Steal" protest at the U.S. Capitol on January 6, the same day that Congress was scheduled to certify the electoral vote. Trump determined that he would show up in person to speak at the rally down the street from the Capitol.

After Trump spoke and in a separate incident, angry mobs stormed the Capitol — mobs that we now know, according to FBI details of their arrests, had planned the riot "several months" before Trump agreed to speak on that fateful day.

After the riots and the swarming of the U.S. Capitol on January 6, liberals demanded that Trump be suspended from social media entirely. Hosts in liberal media wrung their hands on national TV and suggested that if he was allowed to stay in the social discourse, more scary violence would ensue.

The next day, without a shred of evidence as to whether he knew about or participated in the planning of the riot, Meta suspended him. They called his speech a "risk to public safety" and suggested that his social media posts had "incited a violent insurrection."[194]

In June of 2021, Meta announced that Trump would be suspended from the platform for nearly two years until January 2023. Any account run by the Trump organization was banned as well. They added one caveat, that Trump will only be let back onto their platforms after that time if "the risk to public safety has receded."[195]

What is most interesting about the Meta ban is that the Silicon Valley "judge and jury" tried Trump before any investigation began, many months before any January 6 congressional committee was seated, and before a single piece of testimony was heard on Capitol Hill as to his innocence or guilt.

In fact, members of the January 6 committee weren't even announced until July 26, 2021[196] — seven months after Trump's ban on Meta which occurred on January 7.

No matter what you believe happened, that series of events should tell you exactly who has more agility and power in this country today: Big Tech, or Congress.

I think we all know the answer.

Big Tech shenanigans haven't gone unnoticed among the American people. A recent Pew Research Center poll showed that 52% of Americans believe that social media is biased [197] and 90% of Republicans or Republican-leaning Independent voters believe that Big Tech censors conservatives.

A majority of Republicans and Republican-leaning Independents, at 69%, believe that tech companies favor the views of liberals over conservatives and that those views make a difference in Big Tech's permitted flow of information.[198]

According to a Harvard University/Harris Poll, 65% of Americans are concerned about bias on Big Tech platforms. A Harvard CAPS/Harris Poll shared exclusively with *The Hill* revealed that a majority of Americans — 54% — actually want lawmakers to "spell out" what standards they would use to make social media companies accountable[199] for whom they censor and which content they censor. How that accountability would occur is also still up in the air, unfortunately.

As they often do, the American public knows exactly what it going on. Pew Research reported that 64% of Americans believe that Big Tech actually is having a negative effect on the political discourse today.

Unless an epiphany occurs which allows more free flow of information, this will be Big Tech's legacy.

Big Tech Whistleblower

Every once in a blue moon, heroes step forward to blow the whistle on something they've witnessed in society that they feel the broader public needs to be aware of.

Meta product manager-turned-whistleblower Frances Haugen was that person, and she testified on Capitol Hill last fall.[200]

What she shared was nothing short of shocking.

I understand that some in the conservative movement thought she was a plant; but based upon the information I am about to share below, I want to make it clear that I believe her. I truly feel that what she witnessed in Big Tech was so alarming regarding gaslighting within political discourse that she felt she had to come forward. *(I also believe she felt such compassion about how young girls were being treated that she felt compelled to risk her own livelihood and career to come forward. More on that in a moment.)*

Haugen testified that managers at Meta, in particular, are making decisions regularly that lead to increased civil unrest online and in the real world. She also testified that Meta regularly "intentionally hides" vital information from its users, from the American government, and from its own investors that is harmful. That information includes, but is not limited to, the assertion that the intelligence service within Meta cannot protect the American public from outside forces that are preying upon our citizens, in numerous ways that go far beyond what any American outside the halls of Meta initially knew.

Meta Gaslit Americans. Did Zuckerberg Light the Match?

If you listen to the Big Tech bosses, they'll tell you that it's their job to police the fighting among users, as if they're white knights coming to save the day.

However, befitting of the classic deflection that the left does so well, according to the Meta whistleblower Americans didn't just decided to start gaslighting each other.

According to the whistleblower, it turns out Meta may have been lighting the match for us.

Haugen came forward last Fall to share that Meta participated in political agitation *purposefully* during the 2020 elections,[201] knowingly steering users toward more "explosive" political arguments on their platform because that's what made them profits via higher click rates, ad traffic, and advertising rates.

This means that all the while Meta founder Mark Zuckerberg and others were chastising Trump and testifying about the dangers of radical speech on social media, they *themselves* were behind the curtain practically guaranteeing that the speech was becoming more and more radical every time users logged on.

According to Haugen, Meta users argued about the 2020 elections, specifically grew increasingly frustrated over the slow results of audits after the 2020 elections, and just before the January 6, 2021 certification of the 2020 elections, the speech on the platform according to Haugen was at its most dangerous level.

Hmm, an astute observer would be tempted to think that Meta — not President Trump — incited the "insurrection."

Global Unrest

If Meta could get away with fomenting agitation in America — the greatest and most watchful country in the world — then they could surely do it elsewhere.

Sure enough, whistleblower Haugen claimed in her testimony that Meta was responsible for fanning the flames of ethnic violence and ethnic cleansing in countries such as Myanmar and Ethiopia, where people were literally being killed over what was said on Meta.

Now *that* is power.

The evidence — among 10,000 pages of documents that Haugen smuggled out from her product manager "pod" at Meta — shows the Big Tech giant at the behest of Mark Zuckerberg literally has the power to start wars around the globe.

If Zuck is able to gaslight foreign countries, what makes any American think he wouldn't do it right here in this country to favor his own political beliefs?

After all, Mark Zuckerberg spent $419 million in the 2020 elections[202] to affect the outcome in favor Democrats — not Republicans. The money he raised went to raise awareness of his pet issues in swing districts where the races were close, and his funding undoubtedly affected outcomes.

Whistleblower Haugen said that immediately after Election Day (once Zuckerberg's pet candidates were either elected or re-elected), Meta immediately removed what they called "the guardrails" from election content censors. She testified that over the 90-day-period *immediately following* the tense election, Americans experienced gaslighting like never before.

While whistleblower Haugen's testimony wasn't focused on who exactly caused the riots on January 6, it raises serious questions about what the January 6 Select Committee has been missing as they've examined the circumstances surrounding the insurrection at the U.S. Capitol.

Trump has ultimately paid a stiff price on social media platforms for it.

However, it now seems plausible that the angst over the election and the subsequent teeth-gnashing was fomented by Meta itself.

Beyond Politics: Meta's and Instagram's Bullying of Young Girls

If tens of millions of Americans didn't like what Meta did to President Trump and conservatives around the country and foreign countries around the globe, they certainly won't like what the Big Tech company is doing to innocent, trusting, young girls.

Meta staffers reportedly now admit that the Big Tech giant knowingly targets everyone around the globe from adults "armchair arguing" over politics, to teens and young girls. Sadly, while we adults can certainly figure out how to govern ourselves more accordingly, teens and young girls are an entirely different story.

As Meta whistleblower Frances Haugen testified last fall, the mental manipulation of teens and young girls at the hands of Meta and Instagram programmers is beyond what the public has previously known.

At a Senate hearing on the matter, Sen. Marsha Blackburn of Tennessee pointed out Meta's own data on the matter, which glaringly shows that the boys in Big Tech are not looking out for America's youth.

Meta's own research shows that 66% of teenage girls and 40% of teenage boys experienced negative "social comparisons" while on the Instagram platform.

Among teenage girls, 52% reported that their negative feelings over social comparisons were caused by "images related to beauty."

The event of social comparison is reportedly worse on Instagram because it is "perceived as real life" more than Meta and because it has more influencers on its platform making it look like real life (think: beauty photos, swimsuit poses and airbrushed celebrity perfection).

Instagram reportedly did nothing to change this.

Even more disturbing, Meta — which also runs Instagram — did its own research that found social comparison actually "mimics the grief cycle" among young adults including bringing up feelings of depression, jealousy, body dysmorphia and a "downward spiral" of mental health.

Yet according to Haugen, they did nothing about this, either.

Neither did feminists who proclaim to care so much about young women's "body images" and mental health.

Meta research also showed that the Big Tech giant knew that its platform was creating "Meta addiction" — a hard and fast habit which teens found impossible to break on their own, a habit as hard to break as nicotine — and that it was most prevalent in teens, peaking at age 14 when they are most impressionable.

Yet Meta did nothing about it.

Neither did feminists, who have complained about other addictive substances for teens of that age group including cigarettes, vapes, pornography and (yes, Tipper Gore) rap music.

Why not?

Because Meta and the feminists work together to elect Democrats. Feminists couldn't make waves with one of the newest, largest power brokers in Washington, D.C.

Meta made many of their gains in revenue off of getting young people hooked — just like liberals accused Big Tobacco of doing back in the 1990s. Yet, there's been no real reckoning along the lines of what Democrats did to the tobacco companies.

Most members of Congress have been too busy hiding under their desks as the lobbyists of Meta and other Big Tech giants roam the halls pressuring them to betray American moms and dads. There are a few heroes, however, such as Sen. Ted Cruz, Sen. Josh Harley (R-MO), GOP Leader Kevin McCarthy, and others mostly on the Republican side have pushed back.

Sen. Marsha Blackburn (R-Tenn.), the Ranking Member of the Consumer Protection Subcommittee and Sen. Richard Blumenthal (D-CT), Chairman of the Consumer Protection Subcommittee, along with Sen. Ed Markey (D-Mass.) have been digging into this issue to investigate just how Big Tech is preying upon young children — young girls, especially.

Their work has been nothing short of heroic.

Most Democrats however, who stand to profit greatly from Zuckerberg's nearly half-a-billion-dollars in election-year spending, haven't done much to stop it.

Putting Young Girls' Lives at Risk

Placing teens in harm's way reportedly didn't stop there with Meta and Instagram.

Haugen claimed that Meta is acutely aware that its algorithm can lead otherwise healthy teenage girls into dark accounts that promote eating disorders such as anorexia and bulimia.

The algorithm — called Engagement Based Ranking[203] — can do it in record time as well.

According to Haugen, teenage girls searching for "healthy eating" or recipes would soon be led down a dark path to accounts offering tips for fast weight loss, bulimia and anorexia.

Engineers at Meta were allegedly so aware of this that it had done its own testing to see just how quickly a user who searched for healthy eating could be led to sites and other accounts that obsessively focused on weight, appearance, and dangerous eating disorders.

That is truly sick.

Meta's own resident feminist at that time, Chief Operations Officer Sheryl Sandberg, regularly holds court at boardroom tables and convention halls with talks about female empowerment — even coining the phrase, "Lean In." But it doesn't appear that she leaned in to defend girls while others in the company were reportedly aiding and abetting her white, male, billionaire boss in his company's alleged online abuse of young girls and teens.

As with so many other issues today, feminists all over the country have been absolute hypocrites as they've stood with their brothers in Big Tech.

While feminists rail about "toxic masculinity" and "white male power" as the #1 threat in America today, feminists have said nothing about the white males such as Zuckerberg and Jack Doyle who run Silicon Valley today.

Why not? Because feminists are enjoying all of the fruits of these guys' labor when it comes to their progressive push for more liberal policies. That's why they are carrying these guys' water.

Speaking of water, lastly — but perhaps most shamefully, with the health of young girls at stake — Meta founder Mark Zuckerberg dodged the U.S. Senate's Consumer Protection Subcommittee's questions about teens and girls according to its Chairman, Sen. Blumenthal (D-Conn.), a rare Democrat hero on the issue. Meta advised lawmakers that Zuck was going "sailing" instead of making himself available for questions. Although Zuckerberg wasn't there to speak for himself against the allegations from Haugen, his absence ought to speak volumes to American parents about what Meta really thinks of their young daughters.

The Metaverse Doesn't Look Any More Promising

Lest you think that Meta has learned anything from the criticism and the whistleblowing in its prior iteration at Facebook, reports are already emerging that at least one of the Big Tech giant's "Metaverse" is already showing signs of abuse to women.

A report released by the non-profit organization and online watchdog SumOfUs alleges that women are already "being sexually assaulted and harassed" in the new virtual reality community hosted by Meta.

A 21-year-old woman alleges that she was "raped within one hour of being in the metaverse" according to the group's report titled, "Metaverse: another cesspool of toxic content." The report looked into issues such as being "gang raped," being the target of "hate speech" and lack of content moderation at Meta as it boasted that users could live amazing alternate realities inside its online communities.[204]

Doesn't sound too amazing to me.

Another woman, 43, reported a similar experience.

"Within 60 seconds of joining — I was verbally and sexually harassed — 3-4 male avatars, with male voices… virtually gang raped my avatar and took photos — as I tried to get away they yelled 'don't pretend you didn't love it,'" wrote Nina Jane Patel, a mother from the United Kingdom.[205]

She said that even though it was virtual reality, it was shocking, a "horrible experience" and a "nightmare."

More harassment for our young girls to look forward to from the boys who probably couldn't even get a date in Silicon Valley.

In response to the alleged online sexual assault, Meta offered a new feature called Personal Boundary which prohibits other avatars from being able to touch you; though, it's unknown if that also limits users (predominantly women) from being able to participate in normal activity inside the metaverse, such as shaking hands for business and hugging a friend.

It's a sad statement on our society that Meta even has to offer such a feature.

It's even more ironic when you consider that Silicon Valley liberals were among the first to demand "safe spaces" from mere words and conservative viewpoints in the real world, while allowing such awful violations to occur in its online spaces.

Meta Sells Out Americans & Their Kids on Privacy

On the issue of privacy, Meta is not much better.

It turns out, Zuckerberg and his clan have been selling us all down the river. Probably the Yangtze River, at that.

Meta has reportedly been selling our personal data and it turns out when they weren't selling it, they were allowing it to get hacked.

The Senate subcommittee on the matter reports that 1.5 Billion users' Meta data was being sold on a hackers' auction site online, putting at risk not only adult users' data but our kids' data as well, which could haunt them well into adulthood. These bits of information that were swept up in hacks include the email addresses with which you or your kids signed up for Meta, home phone numbers, cellphone numbers, relatives' information, occupation information, workplace names, hobbies, and a whole cadre of personal information.

If Meta truly cared about Americans' privacy and personal information, it would do a better job of protecting it. Yet they are reportedly leaving Americans vulnerable to hackers who could be from nefarious countries including those who wish Americans harm.

Imagine if AT&T or Southwestern Bell or Pacific Bell telecommunications companies back in the day had allowed the likes of China, North Korea, or Russia to hack its customers' personal phone numbers and home addresses. Americans would have been outraged! There would be televised hearings breaking into Days of Our Lives every day. The telecom and public utilities companies' bosses would be standing before a full session of Congress, raising their right hands.

To some extent, Congress did attempt to do that in 2020. Yet, with COVID-19 restrictions in place, the American public only got to see awkward, Zoom-like video calls with the likes of Meta founder Mark Zuckerberg, Twitter founder Jack Dorsey, and a few others. Nothing really came of the hearings. No Section 230 privileges were affected.

In their quest to "put profits before people" according to whistleblower Haugen, Meta has abandoned the trust which Americans placed in it and they should no longer be afforded that blind trust.

A Different Time on Sand Hill Road

Silicon Valley wasn't always this way. When the valley came into its own from the late 1970s through the early 2000s, the founding fathers of tech — Tom Perkins, Brook Byers and John Doerr — were the ultimate diplomats.

Perkins was the co-founder of Kleiner Perkins Canfield and Byers, the legendary venture capital firm on Sand Hill Road, now the Mecca for Big Tech funding.

While they incubated industries such as microchips, the start of the internet, and funded such companies as Genentech, Amazon, Google and more, these gentlemen also engaged in politics.

However, unlike their successors today (the Zuckerbergs, etc.) the O.G. venture capitalists believed in dialogue and healthy debate of ideas. They supported Republicans — though moderate ones, such as Governor Arnold Schwarzenegger and one of my former bosses, Steve Poizner, who invented the GPS chip for cellphones and later ran for the California State Legislature. (Poizner's technology today allows you to do everything from check into locations on Meta and Instagram and to be located when you call 9-1-1 in an emergency.)

My brief time in Silicon Valley working for both of these moderate public officials was both enlightening and just plain fun. I remember renting a cottage in the village of Los Altos (the next-door neighbor to Palo Alto) and I spent my days at press conferences and my evenings at cocktail receptions rubbing elbows with icons of industry.

Marc Andreessen, the founder of Mosaic and Netscape and well, the modern-day internet (sorry, Al Gore) came to one of my big press conferences to support the candidate, whom he had known for years. I had no idea if Marc was a Republican or a Democrat, and you know what? It didn't matter. He was there to support a person who had bold ideas.

So did a guy by the name of Reed Hastings, founder of a small company at the time called Netflix. I recall Reed telling me that he was going to put Blockbuster Video out of business one day. When I asked him how, he explained this system of checking out movies on CDs and sending them back in, then being able to check out more CDs. I remember thinking, "This is interesting, but it'll *never work.*" Which is why I'm in journalism and Hastings is personally having his staff read this to him.

One of my favorite stories I also chuckle about today is being at a cocktail party in Palo Alto one evening and being served mini quiche by waiters who cruised around with aromatic trays. One of my more liberal colleagues Nielson Buchanan had organized the soirée, and he asked if I had met the host, whom he simply referred to as Nancy. "She makes the greatest quiche," he said.

It turns out that Nancy was literally the founder of Nancy's Quiches, the mini version of the 1980s treat in a party-sized, cocktail-napkin-sized portion to go and sold in virtually every store's freezer section today.[206] As I looked around, I realized that almost everyone at the party (except me) was a giant in their industry. I also realized that Republicans and Democrats were mingling and exchanging ideas about how to create better government.

I can't envision today's Silicon Valley gurus endorsing any Republican, even a moderate Republican — and that's not because Republicans suddenly became more radical as the media would have you believe.

In fact, as I've laid out in the pages in this book, quite the opposite is true. Democrats are the ones who've gone rogue against everything that American capitalists should stand for (free markets, capitalism, etc.)

The political u-turn in the valley, I believe, can be traced back to a 2014 opinion piece that Perkins penned in *The Wall Street Journal* comparing the Occupy Wall Street movement in America to Nazis in Germany.[207]

Even though "the Occupy movement" in America (much like Antifa today) was using similar fascist tactics to intimidate, harass and shout people down in the streets, and they clearly stated their intentions to go after the "one percent" just as the Germans had in their time, Silicon Valley went nuts on Perkins for making such a suggestion.[208]

His own firm that he had built and that had helped build Silicon Valley, abruptly disowned him. He ended up having to apologize to the creeps at Occupy Wall Street for his remarks, which would be the equivalent of Jeff Bezos having to apologize to Antifa today.

Perkins died two years later of what I believe was a broken heart.

After that, the die had been cast. With one of the beloved godfathers of Silicon Valley diplomacy gone, no moderate would dare speak out in Silicon Valley again. We now see it has enabled an entire generation of young tech founders to run amok as the very fascists that Perkins warned us about.

My hope is that Silicon Valley someday returns to what it once was — a place where no idea is dumb and political ideologies are welcomed and that our American rights of free speech are fully protected.

Conclusion

For now, we must deal with the realities of what Silicon Valley is today. The sooner you realize that today's sniveling, snarky, spoiled, soy boys of Silicon Valley are targeting your young girls, the sooner you will get fully engaged with your kids' Meta and Instagram accounts or if you're the parent of a young child, to prevent them from getting hooked on the crack of Big Tech in the first place.

Big Tech feigns to the public that it cares about oh-so-much about online bullying — as witnessed by their dumping of Trump from their platforms. The real irony is that Big Tech turned out to be the biggest bully of all.

Sadly, today's feminists haven't said a word about Meta's treatment of young girls. They can't challenge the Big Tech giants, because its founder is spending hundreds of millions of dollars to win them races that they care about winning. Feminists today have literally allowed a billionaire Silicon Valley boss to *buy* their complicit silence.

Unfortunately, Meta whistleblower Haugen suggests that changes to Section 230 laws — which have previously been thought would reign in Big Tech — won't be enough to regulate Meta to ensure it is safer for children. She suggests that Meta's closed-design engineering is prohibiting Congress and regulators from seeing what is actually going on at the tech giant.

In terms of Congressional oversight of marketing campaigns and products that are addictive to kids, Mark Zuckerberg runs circles around the few Big Tobacco ads that were shown to kids in the 1980s. In fact, Mark Zuckerberg puts the Marlboro Man to shame.

HOMEWORK

- ➤ I've referenced it throughout this chapter, but it's worth mentioning again: Meta whistleblower Frances Haugen's testimony to Congress is something every parent should watch in order to gain a full understanding of what is in their child's inbox. Watch the full testimony to Congress here via C-SPAN: https://www.youtube.com/watch?v=GOnpVQnv5Cw
- ➤ Once you know the dangers presented to your children by Meta, Instagram, etc. limit or monitor their time on social media. Family psychologists suggest setting up a computer terminal or a fun iPad pit in the family room so that youth — especially young girls — can be monitored while they're on social media.
- ➤ *Parents* magazine recommends "7 Best Parental Control Apps to Monitor and Limit Screen Time" including apps that let you track which websites your kids are going to and to automatically limit time during critical hours like bedtime and homework hours.
- ➤ Last but not least, now that you know how Big Tech may be abusing your children, treat them just as you would any other intruder in your home — kick their butts to the curb when they abuse their power.

REFERENCES:

[194] Meta Oversight Board on January 7 Suspension
https://www.npr.org/2021/05/05/987679590/Meta-justified-in-banning-donald-trump-social-medias-oversight-board-rules

[195] Meta Suspends Trump, Gives Maximum 2-Year Suspension
https://www.npr.org/2021/06/04/1003284948/trump-suspended-from-Meta-for-2-years

[196] January 6 Committee Members Announced
https://www.usatoday.com/story/news/politics/2021/07/26/january-6-select-committee-who-its-9-members/5375766001/

[197] Pew Research Center: Most Americans Think Social Media Sites Censor Political Viewpoints
https://www.pewresearch.org/internet/2020/08/19/most-americans-think-social-media-sites-censor-political-viewpoints/

[198] Pew Research Center Poll: 64% of Americans Think Big Tech Has a Negative Affect on Public Discourse
https://www.pewresearch.org/fact-tank/2020/10/15/64-of-americans-say-social-media-have-a-mostly-negative-effect-on-the-way-things-are-going-in-the-u-s-today/

[199] Harvard CAPS/Harris Poll: 54% of Americans Want Lawmakers to Hold Social Media Companies Accountable for Censoring Content
https://thehill.com/policy/technology/534840-poll-most-americans-want-legislation-governing-social-media-policiesB

[200] Meta Whistleblower Testifies to U.S. Senate Subcommittee LIVE – C-SPAN, 10/5/2021

[201] Whistleblower Opening Statement to U.S. Senate Consumer Protection Subcommittee
https://www.commerce.senate.gov/services/files/FC8A558E-824E-4914-BEDB-3A7B1190BD49

[202] Mark Zuckerberg Spent $419 Million on 2020 Elections
https://nypost.com/2021/10/13/mark-zuckerberg-spent-419m-on-nonprofits-ahead-of-2020-election-and-got-out-the-dem-vote/

[203] Meta Whistleblower Frances Haugen Testimony
https://www.commerce.senate.gov/2021/10/protecting%20kids%20online:%20testimony%20from%20a%20Meta%20whistleblower

[204] Disturbing Reports of Sexual Assaults in the Metaverse: "It's a Free Show"
https://nypost.com/2022/05/27/women-are-being-sexually-assaulted-in-the-metaverse/

[205] Meta Adds "Personal Boundary" to Metaverse after "Virtual Gang Rape"
https://nypost.com/2022/02/04/meta-adds-personal-boundary-to-metaverse-after-virtual-gang-rape/

[206] The Queen of Quiche – Nancy Mueller

https://www.sfgate.com/business/article/The-Queen-of-Quiche-Nancy-Mueller-s-frozen-3034236.php

[207] Thomas Perkins Dies at 84
https://www.thewrap.com/thomas-perkins-venture-capitalist-who-backed-amazon-and-google-dies-at-84/

[208] Thomas Perkins Apologizes for Comments about Occupy Wall Street
https://www.youtube.com/watch?v=Vux0S6tHEag

IT'S THE SUPPLY CHAIN, STUPID

Political strategist James Carville uttered one of the most famous lines in politics when he advised President Bill Clinton's 1992 presidential campaign team to stay focused on one of the biggest issues in the race.

He simply said, "It's the economy, stupid."[209]

Today, 30 years down the line from Carville's famous phrase there is so much stupidity happening in Washington it's hard to pick just one thing to advise President Joe Biden to maintain as his focus.

Yes, it's the economy, stupid — but it's so much more troubling than that.

Skyrocketing inflation, a supply chain crisis, a sharp rise in food and gas prices, a shortage of willing workers — these have all become trademarks of the Biden economy.

While the White House has attempted to shift the blame for the flailing economy by suggesting that Biden somehow inherited a terrible economy from President Donald Trump, it's just not true.

The Trump Economy

First, it's important to point out that under President Donald Trump, America experienced a booming economy.[210]

Participation in the workforce was enthusiastic and at an all-time high and accordingly, unemployment was also at a record low.

I wrote about this in *The Daily Caller* back on Labor Day, appropriately, in 2019 when Trump had just 2 ½ years in office under his belt, and the Trump economy was humming along nicely.

American jobs were coming back under Trump's "America First" plan.

By the midway point in his administration, Trump had already created a stunning 6.3 million jobs.

The gains that he created were enjoyed by every sector of the American workforce, regardless of gender or race.[211] Women's participation in the workforce reached 76.3% — the highest it had been since right after 9/11.

Overall labor participation was 63.2%.

Minorities also shared in the success like never before: Hispanics reached their lowest unemployment in history, and the unemployment rate for Black Americans also fell to the lowest point in 50 years, since the first time it was ever recorded. Unemployment overall was also the lowest it had been in 50 years.

Americans were also earning more. Pay had grown by 3.2% which means people weren't simply in the workforce like never before, but they were also earning more and feeling a more powerful punch in their paychecks. Much more so than during the Obama administration.

Midway into the Trump administration, American confidence was high as well. 51.2% of Americans said they felt good about jobs being "plentiful."

By the time that his second Labor Day as president rolled around, Trump had achieved the unthinkable: 107 consecutive months of job gains. He hadn't missed a month of momentum.

While the mainstream media never gave him credit, that didn't matter — America's economic engine was firing on all cylinders.

While the onset of the COVID-19 pandemic in Trump's last year certainly disrupted much of the his job gains as American workers were asked to "pause" for two weeks (then two years in some liberal states!), Trump was able to steer it back.

By September of 2020, jobs were beginning to surge back, with a stunning 661,000 jobs added.

Trump also worked with Congress, the Federal Reserve, the Department of the Treasury and others to provide a whopping $3.4 trillion in relief to American workers — the largest in our nation's history.

America was poised for the great American comeback.

Then, the 2020 elections happened.

With the election over and the pandemic starting to subside by January of 2021, Trump handed Biden an economy as gilded as the entrance to Trump Tower.

It's hard to believe, but Biden squandered it in a matter of just one year.

As a result, inflation skyrocketed and Americans are now suffering — including millions of women and girls.

Obamanomics 2.0

Unlike his predecessor Trump, Joe Biden was a lifelong politician for 50 years who had never signed the front of a paycheck.

Additionally, the last time Biden was in the White House he was the vice president for President Barack Obama who presided over one of the worst economic downturns in American history.

Simply put, Biden wasn't exactly versed in how to run great economies.

For all of his pop culture success, President Barack Obama was not a great economist. Under Obama, Gross Domestic Product (GDP) — the amount America was producing — fell to its lowest point in 50 years.

Unemployment — which was relatively low when his predecessor President George W. Bush handed him the baton — skyrocketed under Obama to a stunning 10% by October 2009. (By comparison, as the U.S. was still dealing with COVID-19, the worst pandemic in 100 years, unemployment in 2020 under Trump was just 6%.)

Obama's economic woes weren't helped by the housing market collapse of 2008. The Democrat Party contributed greatly to its downfall. Liberal leaders such as Speaker Nancy Pelosi, the Congressional Black Caucus, Rev. Al Sharpton, Rev. Jesse Jackson, and yes, even Republicans in the Bush administration suggested that everyone should own a home (fact: not everyone is ready for that kind of commitment).

Proof that big government can't solve all of life's problems or societal injustices, the bottom eventually fell out of the government-fueled housing bubble and lenders were left holding the bag. It had reverberating effects through other industries and state economies as well.

At one point during the Obama administration, 1 out of every 5 homes in California went through foreclosure.

In response, Obama went overboard. He introduced the $1 trillion American Recovery & Reinvestment Act, spent billions to create slush funds and boondoggles for companies like the failed Solyndra solar plant, and banked on "shovel-ready projects" though the only thing Americans were left shoveling was, well, a pile of crappy promises ten feet high.

Many Americans won't remember this and it never came up, not even once, during the presidential debates in 2020 — but one of the pushiest salesmen of the massive government-spending plan was none other than Obama's veep at the time, Joe Biden.

As an ambassador for the White House's spending programs, Biden hit the road during the summer of 2010 pledging that it would be "The Summer of Recovery."

However, the sun set quickly on that summer, without much recovery.

Then-Vice President Biden vowed that the economy would bounce back and that economic growth would boom to 4% between 2011 to 2013; however, as reported by economists Stephen Moore and Art Laffer for The Heritage Foundation, Obama's economic growth barely even topped 2% more than two years after the massive American Recovery & Reinvestment Act.[212]

Worst of all, with all of its government spending the Obama administration appeared not to have even helped the poorest among us but rather, gave a leg up to some wealthy supporters.

In his book, "Obamanomics: How Barack Obama Is Bankrupting You and Enriching His Wall Street Friends, Corporate Lobbyists, and Union Bosses," author Tim Carney writes about how Obama enriched his Wall Street supporters while giving mostly lip service to his rank and file base, all the while pushing expensive propositions like nationalizing the automobile industry ("cash for clunkers," anyone?) and creating expensive global climate change regulations.

As Biden rattled on, the Obama administration's economic growth was sinking.

During the first quarter of 2015, Obama produced just 0.2% growth for the economy — the worst economic growth in 50 years.

Sadly, Biden appears to be making the exact same overtures of big government spending while suggesting that the middle class and the poor will benefit. He surely knows these are empty promises given his experience with the same failed economic policies in the Obama White House that he touted for 8 years.

Then again, maybe he doesn't remember it.

Jimmy Carter 2.0

The list of Democratic leaders who have presided over economic calamities is fairly long.

With the exception of President Bill Clinton, most Democratic presidents have not had much luck creating the kind of strong economies that Republicans have historically created.

Republican presidents seem to do quite well with the economy, even in times of adversity.

America experienced economic prosperity during the Ronald Reagan administration (despite the Cold War and an assassination attempt on the president), the George W. Bush administration (despite the 9/11 terror attacks) and the Trump administration (despite the COVID-19 pandemic).

A dismal Democratic leader who didn't fare well in times of crisis is Jimmy Carter.

Though Carter has become an affable character since leaving office, largely due to his work in the charitable world — including winning the Nobel Peace Prize in 2002 — his time as president is generally viewed by analysts on both sides as a dismal failure.

The Carter administration truly became the example of "what not to do" in the White House. He liked to talk softly and carry a not-so-big stick. He bumbled foreign relations by allowing Americans to remain hostage in Iran. He attempted to push Americans onto a strict national energy conservation plan rather than compete globally on energy. However, the Carter's economic policies were the most calamitous of the Democrat's administration.

While the oil crisis of 1979[213] wasn't initially Carter's fault — that was caused by a labor strike of Iran's nationalized petroleum workforce — how Carter responded to it was a disaster.

As international forces cut the global oil supply, Carter's reaction exacerbated the problem. In true liberal fashion, Carter attempted to use the crisis to push Americans off of fossil fuels and onto "alternative energy sources."

Sound familiar?

Rather than call upon American energy companies to step in to help solve the oil and gas shortage, he instead introduced a new nationalized energy program. It went over like a lead balloon, with Americans preferring to sit for hours in lines at their local gas stations rather than end their love affair with the pump.

That's right, rather than roll up his sleeves and get to work finding an American energy solution to the Iran oil crisis, Carter instead suggested Americans turn down their thermostats and "put a sweater on" if they were cold.

Now *that's* cold.

For the record, women and Black Americans didn't do too hot in Jimmy Carter's America either.

They seriously lagged in employment opportunities.

While unemployment for white males was a respectable 4.5% during the better years of the Carter administration, Black Americans suffered a stunning 11.8% unemployment rate.[214]

With women, he didn't do much better. Despite Carter touting his appointment of women to key roles in the White House, women across America were also less-employed than men during Carter's administration, at 6% unemployment.

The feminist movement, which had just worked so hard in the prior decade to gain advancements for women in the workplace, weren't thrilled with the Democrat's policies.

By the fall of 1979, with designs on the 1980 presidential election contest, the feminist movement — led by the National Organization for Women — began to turn their focus toward economic issues, rather than the traditional feminist issues of the past such as abortion.

They began to turn on Carter.

The New York Times in 1979 reported that feminist leaders were concerned[215] that Carter had not delivered on key issues that voters — especially women voters — cared about, such the economy and jobs.

Sounds a lot like Biden's presidency today.

"We're the first to get fired and the last to get hired," NOW's president Eleanor C. Smeal said of the economy, citing record inflation, unemployment, riding energy prices, a shortage of supply and other daunting economic issues facing women.

Feminists had said the ugly part out loud. Jimmy Carter was going to have to improve, or answer to women at the ballot box.

As minorities and women weren't faring well during the Carter administration, children weren't either.

By 1977, 3.8 million families with children lived below the poverty line. To show just how hard Democrat inflation was hitting families, one-third of the parents had at least one part-time job and often more than one, but they still couldn't make ends meet because inflation was quickly outpacing wages.

Again, sound familiar?

By March and April of 1980, inflation had hit a whopping 14.6% — a record high which would ultimately hurt Carter's chances being re-elected.

While Carter's presidency became a joke along with his advice to Americans on their winter wardrobes *(cable knit vs. wool, anyone?)*, he did have some sage advice. He famously advised that we should all "Live as though Christ is coming this afternoon."

As Biden's America now begins to mirror Carter's America — complete with a financial crisis, energy crisis and inflation crisis — it certainly feels like Jesus might come sooner than one thinks.

BidenFlation

Compared to Carter, Biden has not fared much better.

Just 18 months into Biden's administration, the annual inflation rate already spiked to 7.1%. Granted, that's only half of what inflation was at the worst point in Carter's administration, but Biden was just getting warmed up.

By Summer of 2022, Biden's rising inflation represented the highest 12-month increase since June of 1982 — coincidentally, during the smoldering aftermath of the Carter administration.

It's odd that inflation rose so quickly, as Biden promised Americans that his "American Rescue Plan" — a $1.9 trillion stimulus bill passed by a Democrat majority in March of 2021 — was the answer to our economic woes. It gave $1,400 stimulus checks to Americans, expanded unemployment insurance coverage, and more. However, it turns out that all of that not-so-free money he printed likely exacerbated the problem.[216]

If only he had listened to advice from economists.

Macroeconomist Mitch Roschelle said one could spot the inflation coming from a mile away.

"Beginning in early 2020, shutdowns across the U.S. economy and around the world were a shock to the supply-side of the economy," said Mitch Roschelle, founding partner of Macro Trend Advisors. "The policy moves that followed, from the Fed (monetary) and Congress (fiscal) all served to stimulate the demand side of the economy. With too much demand and too little supply, the seeds for inflation were planted. In March of 2021, the Biden administration poured fertilizer on the seeds of inflation by further stimulating demand when it wasn't needed. Fast forward to today, inflation stands at the higher level in two generations, and there have been no policy advances to tackle the problem."[217]

The suggestion that there's even a problem hasn't been easy for the Biden administration to agree upon.

Biden initially denied there was an inflation problem, and his Treasury Secretary Janet Yellin underestimated it, suggesting it would be very "short-lived" and that it would "dissipate" by the Fall of 2021.

They were both wrong.

With inflation appearing to go nowhere but up, Biden and the Democrat Party began to attempt to pass off high inflation as Russian Federation President Vladimir Putin's fault, suggesting that the invasion of Ukraine was to blame for the rising price of gas and goods.

That was a convenient lie.

One big reason Putin wasn't to blame: First, inflation was already on the rise during Biden's first year in office, well before Putin fired the first shot in Ukraine. Second, oil prices aren't even included in what economists and the U.S. government consider "core" inflation numbers. Decades ago, food and gas prices were removed from the inflation equation as the Federal Reserve and some economists determined that the two were too volatile to be considered in the equation. So, that alleged Putin price hike? Not even in the equation.

The Democrat Party's perennial "blame Russia" game is a day late and an inflationary dollar short.

The only thing Biden has told the truth about regarding the economy is how voters may react to his performance in the 2022 midterm elections. Speaking to a group of donors in Chicago, Biden warned of the messaging challenges for Democrats as they are left defending his record. To put it bluntly he said, inflation is "going to scare the hell out of everybody."[218]

Yes, Uncle Joe, it is.

Women's Wages Wipeout

Among the Americans hurt by Biden's skyrocketing inflation, women bear the brunt of the pain.

Ironically, with all of the talk from the left about "gender wage gaps" and "income equality" the Democrat Party oddly doesn't pick leaders who deliver on the issue.

Just like Jimmy Carter, Joe Biden has done the opposite.

You don't have to take a conservative's word for it. Even left-leaning CNBC reported as early as November of 2021 that inflation was wiping out American workers' wage gains.

CNBC pointed out that even though wages had gone up 0.4%, inflation had outpaced it at 0.9%. Therefore, Americans actually saw their purchasing power go down -0.5%.

This meant that Americans "on paper" were making more, but that it took more money to live. (Remember, that doesn't even include food and fuel, which rose even higher during Biden's first two years.)

In 2022, CNBC doubled down on its analysis by pointing out that the inflation-to-wage gap had gotten even worse.

"Despite higher wages, inflation gave the average worker a 2.4% pay cut last year," the liberal network sang out.

By that point in Biden's administration, inflation had already grown 7% over the previous December. Although hourly wages had grown more than 4% as well, they still couldn't keep up with Biden's inflation figures. The inflation gap had grown even wider, equating to that nearly 2.5% pay cut.[219]

Sadly, women took the brunt of the inflationary hit.

Not every industry was hit as hard during the pandemic as female-dominated industries (restaurant industry, hospitality industry, etc.) Conversely, after the pandemic, male-dominated industries were the first ones to bounce back and in fact, go into overdrive during the supply chain crisis. The demand for truck drivers, construction workers and warehouse stockers was high, and the industries hiring were paying more to attract workers. According to CNBC, "rank-and-file workers in transportation and warehousing saw their annual pay rise 8.4%, to $25.04 an hour in December [2021]." The pay growth for male-dominated industries was still at least higher than the 7% inflation rate; therefore under Biden, men were getting hit less hard than women in the workforce. This created an even larger wage gap between men and women, at time when women's wages were not quite able to outpace high inflation.[220]

Normally, you'd hear feminists on the left screaming about this inequality; however, the feminist establishment has learned to look the other way when it comes to their liberal friends in order to get the other things they want at the ballot box (free abortion, free social services, etc.) In a red pill vs. blue pill world, the pink-hat ladies clearly swallowed the blue pill.

FoodFlation

Facing down high inflation in every other corner of their lives, Americans have also faced with higher prices at the grocery store thanks to President Biden.

It impacts products that American families use every day.

In March of 2022, a dozens of eggs cost $1.40; however, just one month later they had jumped to $2.90.

In the U.S., the price of sugar in 2021 was 26.66 percent higher than in 2020.

In 2021, the price of whole milk per gallon was nearly 40 cents higher than it was in 2020.

American families weren't the only ones who noticed.

Restaurants noticed as well.

The rising cost of food was cited by the National Restaurant Association as a major challenge. This dilemma can also be tied back to failed Democrat leadership. In just the first year of Biden's presidency, restaurants began to feel the pinch.

Despite what some liberals might like for you to believe, the spike in food prices cannot be blamed on President Trump. Food prices were stable during Trump's tenure — even during the pandemic.

In the Spring of 2020 when Americans and people around the globe were panic-buying food, Trump convened the CEOs of national grocery chains and major fast-food restaurants to ensure that Americans would not be price-gouged. At the time, Trump reported during a press conference that Americans were shopping every day in record numbers that rivaled Christmas and Black Friday shopping. Yet Trump kept the supply lines moving, and he kept the costs of goods down.

However, in January of 2021 — the same month in which Biden was inaugurated — wholesale food prices began to climb across the U.S. Even worse, they have risen at least 1% every month(!!) since Biden was inaugurated. The U.S. Bureau of Labor Statistics reports this is a trend they have not witnessed since 1973.

The liberal publication *New York Magazine* reported that restaurant research firm Technomic estimates that typical annual "menu inflation" any given year is around 2.5 percent. However, in 2021 according to the U.S. Bureau of Labor Statistics, prices at restaurants rose 4.3 percent. It represents the biggest 12-month increase on record.

Across many other areas, "foodflation" has skyrocketed under Biden.

In mid-2021, the USDA reported that food prices across the board were 2.4 percent higher than the year prior.

With America leading the way, the United Nations reported that food costs globally also rose nearly 40 percent over last year as well.

Furthermore, the cost of getting food from the farm to table also increased under Biden.

The price of gasoline spiked in June 2021 to a 45% increase over 2020. Forbes also reported a seven-month spike in gas prices during the first seven months of the Biden presidency. This means increased transportation prices for the food which is already experiencing increasing costs. By Spring of 2022, gas prices had hit $9 in Southern California. That makes for one expensive truck trip to the grocery store.

Energy Prices

In Trump's America, gas prices were low and energy was abundant. So much so, that America was a net-exporter of energy. We not only had enough supplies for ourselves, but we no longer had to rely upon the bad guys around the world to give us oil. We had so much surplus energy that we could sell our extra supply on the open market.

When Trump was sure that America's energy supply was secured, he then took his show on the road in an attempt to help other countries also wean themselves off of energy from dictatorial countries.

In the Summer of 2017, Trump traveled to Poland where he spoke about the importance of energy independence for the NATO nation and how critical it was for Poland to get off of the Russian oil teet, especially during the brutally cold North Atlantic winter months. Trump understood the geopolitical economics of being dependent upon foreign oil. He knew that if a country like Poland needed Russian oil in the dead of winter, they'd be less likely to buck their Putin's demands. Trump was not only helping our allies become more independent from their former Soviet Union bosses, he was also helping stabilize the region.

The Democrat Party today doesn't appear to be interested in energy security, nor global security.

One of Biden's first acts as president was to cancel the Keystone XL pipeline, which would have allowed for more free flow of oil between Canada and the U.S. In shutting down the pipeline, Biden cost the U.S. in more than just monetary measure — he sent a signal to the world that America would not be a net-exporter of energy as long as he was in office. He had gone fully green, bending to the demands of the left flank of his party.

In California, another high-profile Democrat has done the same. Despite owning stock in major oil companies such as BP, including owning interests in BP's "Deepwater Horizon" oil drilling rig which literally blew up, Governor Gavin Newsom has completely capitulated to the far left in his party who insist on eliminating fossil fuels and not building any new power plants. Funny, liberals don't seem to cry every time a tree loses its life to become a corrugated Amazon box.

As a result of his own cow-towing to the radical enviros, Governor Newsom announced ahead of the summer that California would be unable to provide power to at least 1 million residents. This means rolling blackouts, brownouts, and rationing of the electric grid.

Talk about slipping into third-world-country status.

The power shortage, ironically, comes at a time when women are feeling their "power" in the golden state. Women now outnumber men in California, representing 50.3% of the population. They are feeling their political power, too: the single female voter has just overtaken her fellow man as the largest single voting bloc in California.

From Biden to Newsom, women ought to expect better living conditions from their leaders.

Power means precisely what it says it is: *power*. It's the power to do, the power to travel, the power to live your life freely, and to care for your children in the way you best see fit — with the lights on and the air conditioner or heater on if you so choose. *(There's that word "choice" again.)*

That's right. Fuel equals freedom. At the most basic level, oil and gas allow women to be independent. A free flow of energy means that women can go to work if they so choose, go to job interviews, participate in networking, seek advancement and that they can get there on their own schedule.

Having plentiful energy also equates to safety for some. Look at the headlines. You can't turn on the TV these days without seeing that young women are being shoved in front of trains, losing their lives, and being raped, beaten, and sexually assaulted on the subway on their way to and from work. High gas prices negatively affect a woman's freedom. The more expensive the gas is, the less further away from an

The majority of Americans say they have experienced a supply chain issue, and 82% of Americans believe it will "ruin their life plans." 89% percent of Americans believe "supply chain disruptions will continue to negatively impact their futures."[222]

Sadly, 97% of Americans believe further supply chain delays will plague the country in the near future, and 66% believe supply chains will never catch up.

That's more than "rich people's problems."

That's a lack of confidence in the American economy and our ability to move goods.

Working-class Americans, minorities and women are always impacted more disproportionately by these disruptions, which is ironic because these are the groups that Democrats claim to care so much about.

These groups have far less disposable income and far less of the most valuable commodity — *time* — to go hunting for the most basic products because they've just worked two jobs, picked up their children and come home with dirt under their fingernails and in need of a shower.

Beyond women and working-class Americans, the most fragile among are being disrupted by Biden's supply chain woes: *babies.*

Babies are at risk of not having enough food in 2022 due to a shortage of baby formula and supply chain issues. That's right, just 18 months into the Biden administration, mothers have had to scramble to find enough baby formula to feed their children, as stores nationwide reported a stunning 40% drop in supply. The shortage comes after Biden's Food and Drug Administration shut down a major baby formula manufacturing plant without warning the public that a shortage would be the likely outcome.

While Psaki and Klain joked about the victims of Biden's supply chain crisis, Biden's Transportation Secretary Pete Buttigieg took paid family leave at the height of the crisis to join his husband when their twins were born.[223] *The New York Post* reported that Buttigieg — the person whose portfolio as transportation secretary includes oversight of things like the supply chain — went "AWOL on paternity leave amid the US's crippling supply-chain crisis."

Buttigieg also missed the mark when he predicted that the supply chain issues of 2021 would be "short-lived," predicting they'd continue after Christmas of 2021 but not much further than that.

A year out from his parental leave, the issues were still dire.

While Buttigieg's babies undoubtedly had plenty to eat, babies elsewhere in America did not. Yet, the administration's answer to the crisis was to laugh, crack jokes, and sneer down their noses at moms and the working class.

It tells you what Democrats truly think of the people who elect them.

Amid Crises, Lectures on a "Woke" Economy

While Rome is burning, one would think that the Biden administration would be scrambling to find top-notch economic advisers to turn the ship around.

They're not.

Instead, Biden has nominated and appointed the most radical liberals to run America's financial institutions.

As they prepared to be seated, they proved that their main focus is to have a more "woke" economy.

For starters, Biden nominated Soviet-born Saule Omarova to be the United States' comptroller of currency.[224]

There were some problems with the nomination.

Omarova had written on previous occasions that she wanted to "end banking as we know it" in the United States. It turned out that her academic writings were littered with what she even ended up having to admit were "radical" ideas.[225]

In 2020, just months before she was tapped by Biden to head up America's currency, Omarova proposed that the United States maintain a "people's ledger" which would give the federal government the ability to see every Americans' checkbook ledger and banking activity, and it would even grant the federal government the responsibility for "clearing checks" rather than letting private banks such as Citibank, Wells Fargo, and Chase Bank handle that.

She also criticized America's "gender pay gap" while complimenting the former Soviet Union for never having such a thing (nevermind that the country has a history of overall problems with wages and jobs themselves!) Like many Socialists in the Democrat Party today, she also critiqued America's Wall Street, suggesting that America's markets don't always 'know best.'

It doesn't appear that Omarova believes in capitalism which would be odd for someone working in, say, capitalism.

She also publicly expressed an interest in seeing America's energy companies go "bankrupt." As if the means justified the ends, Biden's choice to oversee banking transactions in America dared to said, "We want them to go bankrupt if we want to tackle climate change, right?"[226]

No, ma'am. Wrong.

Biden's radical picks to run America's economy didn't stop there.

The new Energy Secretary, Jennifer Granholm, made waves when she nearly laughed herself off the stage during a Bloomberg television interview. When asked what her plan was to reduce gas prices, Granholm rolled with laughter.

"That is hilarious," she said. "Would that I have the magic wand."

What America needs is not magic; it needs someone who will do the job they were nominated to do, managing energy policy and not simply towing the party line when it comes to bankrupting energy companies.

Sadly, Biden's nominees are themselves a laughing matter.

Even Secretary of the Treasury, Janet Yellin, is not immune to the "woke" culture.

Although she previously served as the Federal Reserve Chair and produced positive results for former President Bill Clinton, today's "woke" version of Yellin is something else to behold.

Yellin broke her own rule of tipping her hand on politics by scorching a University of Chicago faculty member for critiquing the Black Lives Matter riots. She even waded into the debate over defunding the police.[227] She took the opportunity of Martin Luther King, Jr. Day (which was signed into law by a Republican) to state, "From Reconstruction, to Jim Crow, to the present day, our economy has never worked fairly for black Americans — or, really, for any American of color." (One wonders if she is aware that Democrats are on-record as the ones who steadily voted down civil rights during that 150-year time period?)

Yellin also suggested there is a detrimental "racial wage gap" in America and in essence suggested to the world — as the head of the world's most powerful Treasury Department — that the American economic system is a patently unfair place.[228] All of this, of course, was spoken as our nation struggled greatly to get out from under the pandemic and back onto our feet. Nothing like kicking America while she's down.

It's difficult to tell if this is a new Janet Yellin, or if she was told that the condition of her landing the post was that she had to moonlight as a social justice warrior.

Tragically, unless the Biden administration gets serious about economics and brings more "adults" back to the table, America is not likely to climb out of its economic crisis anytime soon. Meantime, millions of people will continue to suffer.

The only thing that is likely to help America dig out of this economic chaos is a complete regime change in 2024.

HOMEWORK

- One of my favorite resources is Stephens Moore's book, "Return to Prosperity: How America Can Regain Its Economic Superpower Status." Moore, who currently serves as a Distinguished Fellow in Economics in the Executive Vice President's Office at The Heritage Foundation, lays out the fundamentals of a strong economy — and (spoiler alert!) they don't include big-government spending where Uncle Sam is the primary driver of the economy. Moore has a style of laying out complex economic terms in street-level language for everyone to understand. He wrote the book with his friend and fellow economist Art Laffer back in the midst of the dismal Obama-era economy, but with Biden's big spending the book is as relevant today as it was in 2010.

- My favorite institute in Washington, D.C. and perhaps my favorite person in D.C. is Americans for Tax Reform and its founder, Grover Norquist. He founded the group in 1985 at President Ronald Reagan's request. Grover talks about complex tax policy in a way that's understandable, and he illustrates every day how increasing taxes and regulatory burdens actually affect the rest of the economy. Visit their site regularly at: ATR.org.

REFERENCES:

[209] "It's the economy, stupid"
https://politicaldictionary.com/words/its-the-economy-stupid/

[210] Trump Economy – White House Archives
https://trumpwhitehouse.archives.gov/issues/economy-jobs/

[211] Trump's Economy Was a Win for Women and Minorities
https://dailycaller.com/2019/09/08/kerns-trump-women-minorities/

[212] Obama's Bad Stimulus Example – 2009 American Recovery & Reinvestment Act
https://www.heritage.org/budget-and-spending/commentary/obamas-bad-stimulus-example

213 1979 Oil Crisis
https://www.brookings.edu/wp-content/uploads/1979/06/1979b_bpea_verleger_okun_lawrence_sims_hall_nordhaus.pdf

214 Unemployment Rates during the Jimmy Carter Administration
https://www.nytimes.com/1978/03/11/archives/unemployment-rate-fell-to-61-for-february-lowest-in-3-years-jobless.html

215 Feminists Turned to Economic Issues in 1980 Election
https://www.nytimes.com/1979/10/23/archives/feminists-turn-to-economic-issues-for-80-meat-and-potatoes-issues.html

216 Biden's American Rescue Plan Worsened Inflation. The Question is How Much
https://www.vox.com/23036340/biden-american-rescue-plan-inflation

217 Macroeconomic Issues with Biden's "American Rescue Plan" – Interview with Mitch Roschelle, May 13, 2022

218 Biden: Inflation is Going to "Scare the Living Hell Out of Everybody:
https://nypost.com/2022/05/12/president-joe-biden-warns-dems-over-inflation/

219 CNBC: "Despite higher wages, inflation gave the average worker a 2.4% pay cut last year"
https://www.cnbc.com/2022/01/12/higher-pay-eclipses-inflation-bite-for-some-.html

220 CNBC: "Inflation Has Taken Away All the Wage Gains for Workers and Then Some"
https://www.cnbc.com/2021/11/10/inflation-has-taken-away-all-the-wage-gains-for-workers-and-then-some.html

221 Jen Psaki: "The Tragedy of the Delayed Treadmill"
https://www.dailymail.co.uk/video/news/video-2528823/Video-Tragedy-delayed-treadmill-Psaki-jokes-supply-chain-crisis.html

[222] Oracle Survey: 82% of Americans Say Supply Chain Issues "Will Ruin Their Life Plans"
https://www.oracle.com/news/announcement/survey-of-americans-scared-of-supply-chain-issues-2021-09-29/

[223] Transportation Secretary Pete Buttigieg Takes Parental Leave amid Supply Chain Crisis
https://nypost.com/2021/10/17/buttigieg-defends-being-on-paternity-leave-amid-supply-chain-crisis/

[224] Biden's Pick for Bank Regulator Set for Rocky Hearings over 'Radical' Ideas
https://www.cnbc.com/2021/11/17/biden-occ-nominee-omarova-set-for-rocky-senate-hearing-as-gop-protests-her-.html

[225] Biden's Controversial, Soviet-Born Pick for Banking
https://www.rferl.org/a/saule-omarova-biden-soviet-union-comptroller/31524305.html

[226] Biden's Choice for Comptroller of Currency Said She Wants Oil and Gas Companies to Go Bankrupt
https://www.dailymail.co.uk/news/article-10188847/Bidens-comptroller-currency-nominee-said-wanted-oil-gas-companies-bankrupt.html

[227] Janet Yellin Weighs in on Black Lives Matter, Defunding of Police
https://www.cnbc.com/2020/06/11/yellen-joins-chorus-against-economist-who-criticized-black-lives-matter.html

[228] WSJ: Janet Yellin Joins Democrats in Peddling Sour Grapes
https://www.wsj.com/articles/janet-yellen-joins-democrats-in-peddling-sour-grapes-treasury-blacks-economy-systemic-racism-progressive-woke-biden-georgia-speech-11642948826

DEMS' FOREIGN RELATIONS ARE AN ABUSIVE RELATIONSHIP FOR WOMEN AND GIRLS AROUND THE WORLD

No one has given more elaborate speeches overseas yet delivered such stunning failures on the international stage than Democrats. From Afghanistan to North Korea to Libya to Egypt to Iran, there isn't a single foreign policy deal in the last 40 years orchestrated by Democrats that didn't end in disaster.

Sadly, the people that have been left behind in the wake of these failures are victims of a Democrat Party whose foreign relations are like an abusive relationship where the good guys give in and the bad guys always end up winning. Women are often left behind in the dust.

Afghanistan

Prior to August of 2021, "leave no man behind" was the gold standard of the United States military, as well as U.S. diplomatic operations at the U.S. State Department which boasts 70,000 employees both stateside and at 270 posts around the world at any given time.[229]

Sadly, America's vow to never leave a fellow man (nor woman) behind came to an abrupt end one hot, fateful, summer month in the middle of the South Asian desert.

On July 8, 2021 President Joe Biden astonished Americans — and the world — when he announced[230] that troops would withdraw from

Afghanistan no later than August 31, 2021 — a decision which left Americans and our allies there scrambling for the exits.

To be fair, Biden was simply abiding by a treaty — informally called *The Doha Agreement* — which was signed in February of 2020 that stated that American troops would leave the country by the 20th anniversary of 9/11.

However, in politics as with most things in life, it was the *manner* in which the Biden did it.

Rather than announcing troop departures *after* U.S. citizens and allies were already to safety, Biden instead made the critical mistake of giving the Islamic Republic and our terrorist enemies in ISIS a heads' up.

It's the kind of thing that would make famed war general Sun Tzu roll over in his grave.

Within weeks of Biden's announcement, Afghanistan's capital city of Kabul came under siege and fell under Taliban control. On August 14, 2021 U.S. troops faced the impossible mission: racing to get Americans and allies out of a country now controlled by terrorist forces.

With little direction from the White House and the State Department, Americans and allies were forced to beat their own paths to The Hamid Karzai International Airport in Kabul (which by the grace of God was still controlled by U.S. troops and NATO.) Evacuees reported arriving to the airport only to find mass confusion. Others reported being turned away from the airport despite having their papers in order. Families reported having to wade through sewage systems covered in filth in order to circumvent Taliban checkpoints. Another evacuee — a pregnant woman — was reportedly kicked in the stomach by Taliban forces after she arrived at the gates of the airport.[231] She finally made it home, although it was no thanks to President Biden; Congress member Darrell Issa (R-CA) worked tirelessly to ensure that she made it out of the country, even though it took nearly a month to get her to safety.[232]

It is a testament to U.S. troops that they were able to evacuate 78,000 people in just 14 days in a real race-against-the-clock effort that reportedly received little assistance from Washington. America shouldn't have had to do it in the manner in which they did, with Afghan parents tossing their babies over fences to American troops so that their children could go on to experience a better life. Yet, there they were in the midst of chaos.

By the time Biden's August 31st departure arrived, another tragedy had already struck. Thirteen U.S. troops were killed in a bomb attack on the airport.[233] Two of those troops had been pictured just days before helping those Afghan babies to safety.

In the days following the disastrous drawdown, then-White House Press Secretary Jen Psaki added insult to injury by downplaying just how many Americans had been left behind. In fact, Psaki admonished the press corps that it was "irresponsible" to suggest that Americans were "stranded" in Afghanistan.

However, just one week after the last U.S. plane departed, the U.S. government acknowledged that there were as many as one thousand American citizens, U.S. Visa holders, or Afghans with other Visas who were, indeed, stranded in Afghanistan.

Shockingly, weeks later it was confirmed by Secretary of State Tony Blinken that "several thousand" American residents and at least a hundred U.S. citizens had actually been left behind.

It was a far cry from Psaki's suggestion that everything was fine. Baghdad Bob sort of stuff.

Where those several thousand human souls are now is unknown. It's not out of the question to suggest that many of them are still in hiding today. It's also not out of the realm of likelihood that they have already been tortured, beaten, and killed at the hands of the Taliban. However, we do not know their outcome because the White House press office doesn't want their stories staining the president.

The greatest tragedy was that there was no place on earth *more* important to have success than Afghanistan. After all, the country had been the home base for the terror plot in the 9/11 attacks, the deadliest terrorist attacks on American soil. It was important we get this one right. Biden couldn't have gotten it more wrong.

Sadly, the people who suffered the most from Biden's calamitous drawdown weren't men. The people who suffered the most were women and girls.

An Early Test for Biden: Terror Attacks on All-Girls' School

In the first months of Biden's administration, the Taliban and terror-linked groups were already testing the new president's mettle.

On May 8, 2021 a terror attack on a girls' school in Afghanistan killed 95 and injured 240 people. Three bombs went off in total: a car bomb, then two separate improvised explosive devices. *The New York Times* reported that "girls" were the "target."

Just emerging from his chaotic first 100 days in office, Biden seemed unable to grapple with the seriousness of the situation, nor the damage done to the most vulnerable young girls.

However, one former president — a Republican — did.

At the request of former President George W. Bush, the George W. Bush Institute in Dallas, Texas urged President Biden to act quickly to protect the girls. The institute's executive director penned a letter to the Biden administration and Congress which warned that the attack "highlights the imminent need for action to protect the rights, agency, and well-being of Afghan women and girls and to ensure a pathway to safety for the individuals and their families who have assisted the United States in Afghanistan."

The letter went on to state:

"Since 2001, the United States has stood in solidarity with Afghan women and girls, decrying the human rights violations perpetrated by the Taliban and emphasizing that a country cannot truly be peaceful and prosperous if half of its population does not have equal access, rights, and protection.

"Our drawdown of troops in Afghanistan must not abandon vulnerable populations. As recent intelligence reports reinforce, the safety and

status of Afghan women and girls are already at serious risk should the Taliban regain national power. Their intentions are clear: The May 8 attack on a girls' school in Kabul killed nearly 100 and injured more than 150 — mostly female students.

"They have threatened women in the workforce and the organizations that employ them. We cannot ignore what these actions signal about the Taliban's intentions.

"When women and girls hold equal and active roles in societies, communities not only thrive but countries are more secure and stable. Across Afghanistan, women and girls have made substantial gains in the areas of education, health and well-being, and economic inclusion. Today, millions of girls are attending school and women have greater access to healthcare, and are voting, running for office, starting businesses, and entering the workforce and higher education.

"As research shows, peace and stability are not possible without the equitable inclusion of women across all levels of society."

Despite the letter reading like a feminist manifesto, highlighting the urgent need for the protection of equal rights for women and girls, it was from a Republican institution.

The response from the Biden administration was deeply disappointing. In fact, it was met with the sound of crickets.

All of this, of course, is a tragedy that could have been avoided. From the talent of a new generation of girls who were enjoying the promise of a brighter future, to the colossal waste of millions of dollars in American resources that went to help establish schools for girls in the country. The Biden administration was standing idly by and watching it all burn.

President Bush's doctrine for protecting women and girls in Afghanistan was much different than Biden's. In fact, it was like comparing night and day.

Fancying himself a "compassionate conservative," President Bush saw to it that women and girls were protected during his administration. He made it known that if anything happened to schoolgirls in Afghanistan on his watch, there would be hell to pay.

He established The U.S.-Afghan Women's Council with then-President Hamid Karzai. The council included a "who's-who" of leaders who agreed to focus on women's "legal, economic, political and social status throughout the country." It was a foreign concept at the time.

Bush also led the way for the 2001 Afghan Women and Children Relief Act, which provided substantial investment in education programs and health initiatives for women and their children in Afghanistan.[234]

He also leveraged a range of non-governmental organizations and every lever of the United States government — from US AID to the United Nations to the U.S. military — to ensure that policy initiatives for women and girls were supported thoroughly.

As a result, the Bush administration made significant strides in gaining more freedoms and protections for women and girls. By the time the Bush administration was finished, more than 3.5 million Afghan girls were attending school, and more than 100,000 women had enrolled in universities.

The Afghanistan Women Chamber of Commerce & Industry reports that after the Bush administration's efforts, more than 1,000 women entrepreneurs "had invested over $77 million over the span of 18 years, creating 77,000 jobs." More than 1,500 women-owned businesses were on the books.

However, that's not all.

With the encouragement of the Bush administration, women in Afghanistan ran for office and served in government. They served at nearly every level of government including rebuilding, the economy, education and security. By the time of the 2020 peace talks, four women served on the 21-member Afghanistan team which was a remarkable achievement.

Afghan girls were also finally seeing examples of women in powerful roles, thanks to a Republican from the South.

With so much talk from feminists today about "representation" and mantras such as "if you can see her, you can be her," it's a wonder that liberals didn't applaud Bush more for these trailblazing women and the young girls who had hoped to follow in their elders' footsteps.

Ultimately, following Biden's announcement that the U.S. would pull out of Afghanistan and with little response from the White House regarding what the withdrawal would mean for girls, Bush did something he had hesitated to do during previous administrations: he took to the TV airwaves to speak about current events. Speaking with a German television station Bush warned that under Biden's plan, girls would face *"unspeakable harm"* if America left the region. You could hear the pain and anguish in his voice as he said the words.

"I'm afraid Afghan women and girls are going to suffer unspeakable harm," Bush said. "They are going to be left behind to be slaughtered by these very brutal people, and it breaks my heart."[235]

On the contrary, the fact that our current president exhibited very little heart in abandoning these young girls speaks volumes about his lack of concern for their future and frankly, lack of concern for women and girls everywhere else in the world that they are vulnerable.

Arab Spring

Sadly, the Afghanistan disaster wasn't the first foreign policy blunder on the Democrat Party's watch.

In 2011, the Middle East was on the brink of a crisis during the administration of President Barack Obama, Vice President Joe Biden and Secretary of State Hillary Clinton's watch.

As tensions began to rise and protestors began to hit the streets by the hundreds of thousands, Secretary Clinton suggested that the season in that region of the world would be an "Arab Spring" — a renewal as fresh as the morning flowers at the local souk.

However, the Arab Spring turned out to be anything but joyful.

It was more like a hurricane season.

As Clinton later shared in her book, "Hard Choices," there was much internal debate within the Obama administration on just how deeply to support protestors in what were becoming weekly uprisings in the Middle East.[236]

Ultimately, Secretary Clinton and her bosses Obama/Biden ended up leveraging the full support of the United States behind the protestors, even when the uprisings violated the one golden rule of American foreign policy: not having the United States' best interests at heart.

The fact that the Obama administration and Secretary Clinton didn't put America first[237] is not terribly surprising to those who have now had the opportunity to witness what an "America first" agenda looked like under President Donald Trump — one including tough talk and placing American interests first around the globe.

With the Arab Spring simmering, what would come next would prove just how devastating the Obama/Biden/Clinton foreign policy team would turn out to be for women and girls.

Tunisia

A country that was struggling with harsh economic conditions and lack of jobs for its people, Tunisia became the first country whose leadership would fall in the contagion of Arab Spring protests.

A common street vendor selling fruits and vegetables set things into motion. The man, facing down economic prospects of no longer having a street cart after government officials seized his wares and no longer able to make a living to feed his wife and three children, Mohamed Bouazizi set himself on fire in the street in front of a provincial governor's house. It was the straw that broke Tunisia's back. Mobs of Tunisians took to the streets to protest in his name, and today that street vendor is known as "the spark that lit the Arab Spring."[238]

While Tunisians — specifically, Tunisian women — experienced better living conditions and expanded rights post-Arab Spring, it was an anomaly. Tunisa was the only country in the Middle East to experience this positive outcome. In every other Middle Eastern and North African country that would go through the Arab Spring, women ended up being worse for it.

What came next was something for which the Obama administration was not prepared.

Egypt

Egypt's citizens saw the results in Tunisia and wanted a taste of liberty for themselves after living under a strict Republican patriarch for the last half of the 20th century. Night after night, protestors gathered at Egypt's Tahrir Square to demand longtime President Hasni Mubarak step down.

Mubarak had been a loyal servant to Egypt, first serving in its Air Force then stepping up to serve as president after the assassination of Anwar Sadat.[239] He played an instrumental role in Israeli-Palestinian peace talks.

However, in the new world order under Obama where America was "leading from behind" countries were now able to riot, free of the threat of American intervention or help. Egyptians decided to make their move.

As the protests in Egypt wore on, they became increasingly violent — specifically, toward women.

Reports of women being raped and sexually assaulted in the public square began to emerge. In just one weekend, 169 rapes and sexual assaults were reported in Tahrir Square. Even after protestors had gotten their wish to topple Mubarak, another 90 rapes and sexual assaults were reported in the first 24 hours following their victory.

Lara Logan, who was a CBS News correspondent at the time, was among the women attacked. She described fearing for her life as she was raped with "hands, flagpoles and sticks" — anything that male Egyptian protestors could get their hands on to use as an instrument against women.[240]

Amnesty International called the assaults against women "circles of hell," in which violent mobs of men were encircle the women who were then to be "groped, stripped, beaten, bitten, penetrated with fingers, and raped."[241] These attacks occurred nightly as President Obama, Vice President Biden and Secretary of State Clinton sat watching from Washington, D.C.

Even the liberal think tank Center for American Progress stated that sexual assaults were the "dark side" of the Obama-era populist uprisings.[242] CNN reported the same.[243] Oddly, the world heard very little from President Obama and Secretary Clinton about the attacks against women; in fact, the United States did little to aid these women nor did the administration issue sanctions against the country nor new leadership for what clearly appeared to be a pattern of heinous acts against women in the public square upon the arrival of the new government.

Sadly, women have not fared much better in Egypt since that fateful Arab Spring.

A survey of 22 Arab nations by *Thomson Reuters Foundation* revealed that after the passage of the Obama-era Arab Spring, Egypt ended up ranking dead last in women's rights among all Arab nations.[244] Chief among the reasons were the spikes in the number of sexual assaults, sexual harassments and female genital mutilations.

By 2013 — nearly two years after the Arab Spring uprisings in Tahrir Square — a stunning 93.3% of Egyptian women had been victim to some form of sexual harassment. According to UNICEF, 91% of Egypt's females had been subjected to female genitalia mutilation.

This is hardly a success story of women's empowerment around the globe.

As women have not fared well in Egypt, neither has democracy. Although a new president Mohamed Morsi, an Islamist politician, was democratically elected within a year of Mubarak's toppling, Morsi struggled to remain in office for even one year before a coup ousted him. A new president was installed, and hasn't budged for 10 years.

So much for elections.

The cruel truth is that Egyptian citizens who sought more liberty and freedoms in 2011 ended up having fewer rights, not more, after the Arab Spring. That, my friends, is the definition of "leading from behind."

Yemen

As life in Egypt became more difficult for women, the same became true for women in the Middle Eastern country of Yemen.

As leaders were toppled in Tunisia and Egypt, Yemenis began to push for the same.

However, just as the vacuum of power in Egypt led to disastrous results, the same became true in Yemen.

After the leader of Yemen was toppled in the Arab Spring, Al-Qaddafi of the Arabian Peninsula (AQAP) and the Houthi rebels respectively began to take over towns throughout the country. They brought with them their authoritarian rule which proved far worse than the government that had just been toppled.

Just five years after the Obama- and Hillary-encouraged Arab Spring, Yemen had descended into a miserable humanitarian crisis. Nearly 80% of Yemeni citizens lacked basic access to drinking water and sanitation services, while a shocking 16 million Yemenis lacked basic food supplies by 2018 and according to the United Nations were on the brink of starvation.[245]

By 2018, terrorists in Yemen had commandeered the country's supply of Scud missiles which it had reportedly previously acquired from North Korea. According to the Brookings Institute, new missiles and equipment were also flowing into the country from Iran. (Hmm, North Korea and Iran… it appears that President Bush had been right about the axis of evil after all.) Terror groups hunkered down in Yemen, where they were bold enough to fire missiles at U.S. allies Saudi Arabia in 2018 and the United Arab Emirates after that, and the problems didn't stop there.

By 2019, Amnesty International had labeled Yemen "one of the worst places in the world to be a woman"[246] where "forced niqab (face coverings), child marriage, divorce shame, domestic violence and honor killings" had become part of everyday life.

Sadly, post-Arab Spring life turned out to be as chaotic in Yemen as it was in other Arab nations who had gone through the same metamorphosis with all of the trademarks of less stability, more terror and fewer resources for their people.

Libya

If Egypt and Yemen were no walk in the park, neither was Libya.

During the Arab Spring, the Obama administration determined it would aid the protests in the North African nation of Libya by leading a NATO air campaign along with allies Britain and France. The Obama/Biden/Clinton foreign policy machine deemed that it was time for longtime leader Mu'ammar Ghaddafi to step down from power.

What happened next shocked even the Obama administration.

After many nights of brewing uprisings, protestors stormed the U.S. Embassy in Benghazi, torching it and burning it nearly to the ground. For the first time since 1979 — when another Democrat, President Jimmy Carter was at the helm — a U.S. Embassy had been breached. Our ambassador was murdered and then dragged through the streets like a limp rag doll. (While the ambassador wasn't a woman, he was confirmed a gay man in a region of the world where that was not yet accepted. However, Clinton failed to offer him protection that both he and so many experts on the ground claimed was needed at the time.)

As if the death of U.S. Ambassador Christopher Stevens wasn't enough, it turned out that it could have all been prevented — Secretary Clinton's State Department had actually denied multiple requests for additional security at the Benghazi facility. Even the left-leaning PolitiFact verified the claim as "True" and found "that the numerous requests from officials on the ground in Libya for better security for the Benghazi compound are undeniable and well-documented."

PolitiFact went on to state, "The State Department's own Accountability Review Board concluded that the number of diplomatic security staff in Benghazi in the months leading up to the attacks was inadequate 'despite repeated requests' from the Benghazi mission and the embassy in Tripoli for additional staffing."[247]

Experts agreed.

That Clinton's State Department "didn't honor requests for additional security is established fact," said Georgetown University adjunct assistant professor Daveed Gartenstein-Ross, a senior fellow at the Foundation for Defense of Democracies and an expert on foreign policy and national security.

By the end, four additional Americans would be stranded at the besieged embassy compound where they died while awaiting help. The U.S. Embassy in Libya has remained closed since then.

Sadly, as with so many other countries touched by the Obama/Biden/Clinton foreign policy apparatus, Libya is faring terribly more than 10 years after its Arab Spring.

News outlet France 24 reported that Libya is "mired in chaos 10 years after Arab Spring"[248] with reports of "anarchy," "mass graves" and "detention camps" marking the countryside.

Like Yemen, terror groups have taken over the Libya, with a roll call of terrorists ruling the day including the Islamic State (ISIS). Whereas the country had previously been an exporter of oil, after the Arab Spring it transitioned to the business of exporting terror. Just a few years after the disastrous fall of Libya, ISIS used the North African nation to plan attacks on international tourists at Tunisian resorts in 2015 and 2016.

Once a mineral-rich self-supporting nation, many of Libya's oil production facilities were also decimated by wars that have taken place inside the country since the Obama/Biden/Clinton failure.

Just like other countries that were swept up in Democrats' "hope and change," women in Libya aren't faring well, either.

Although women were engaged in the initial revolt that ousted Ghaddafi, outlets around the globe report that women's "hopes of a more inclusive and equal treatment in the country were dashed with the eruption of civil conflict that followed."[249] At the end of the Arab Spring, Obama violated former Secretary of State Colin Powell's Pottery Barn rule of foreign relations: "If you break it, you buy it." Despite helping wreck the country, the Obama administration walked away from it, leaving those brave women to clean up the proverbial shop and fend for themselves.

More than a decade after the Arab Spring, Libya announced more bad news in 2022: that it was suspending its declaration of gender equality with the United Nations, citing concerns that its advocacy for women's equality and participation in government would offend proponents of Islamic sharia law.[250]

It is even more tragic when one considers that Libyan women were among the first feminists in the world. They were among the first women in the world to earn the right to vote, in 1920 — a full year before American women. Libyan women also spearheaded a women's rights movement in the 1950s, a full decade before the Second Wave of American feminism of the 1960s. They had clearly been ahead of the curve; that is, until the Democrat Party of America left its footprints on their necks.

Where Libyan women go from here to gain their rights back is unknown today, but one thing is certain: recorded history shows once again the Democrat Party's foreign policy apparatus failed and left behind a wake of chaos in yet another country.

Iran

During the Arab Spring uprising, the first high-profile victim of Iran's pushback on demonstrations was, sadly, female.

A young woman by the name Neda Agha-Soltan was walking down a street on a Saturday afternoon, stopping to look at protests as a shot rang out and struck her in the chest, killing her just moments later.

Within minutes, videos of her death in the streets of Iran hit the internet and social media. "Neda" became the rallying cry for the attempted revolution, just as the common-man street vendor had become the face of the revolution in Tunisia.

However, Neda's death ended up being for naught as the secret police and military worked overtime to put down the uprisings. Without any fear of intervention from Obama's United States, Iran succeeded in squelching the protests within just 10 days.

Since Neda's death, the world hasn't heard much from the women of Iran. That's because women there have already been to this dance before. They witnessed the 1979 Iranian revolution and its transition to the Islamic state.

Under sharia law, Iran slipped back into the dark ages in terms of family law, domestic violence, admonishments for women to stay out of public spaces and requiring that women be covered if they did choose to leave their homes. As other Arab nations in the region began to be taken over by Islamic forces like the forces in Iran, the Arab Spring was an all-too familiar reminder that the governments being installed across the region weren't going to be friendly to women once the news cameras left.

As this book went to print, the women of Iran were once again on the front line of protest, after a young women died in police custody over wearing her headscarf too loosely. Women are shedding their headscarves in defiance, but once again a Democrat President of United States has offered little help to back up the women who need it.

Syria

Among all of the countries who experienced the worst fallout from the Arab Spring, Syria was by far the deadliest and the most painful — especially for women and girls.

As protests in the Arab Spring of 2011 spread across the globe, Syrian youths decided as many other countries had decided that they, too, wanted a piece of the action. They lashed out at the regime of President Bashar al-Assad.

What citizens weren't counting on, however, was the harsh blowback that would come from Assad's military as well as from outside terror forces such as the Islamic State who would soon set up shop inside their country.

As the civil war heated up President Barack Obama talked tough, warning that the United States would not tolerate Syria's abuse of its citizens. In fact, in 2012 Obama went so far as to say that if President Assad dared to use chemical weapons against his own people, it would be a "red line" crossed that would result in military intervention from the United States.

A year after Obama's empty threat, Syria blew right past the red line a and never looked back, launching reported chemical weapons attacks in Aleppo, Homs and Douma, just outside of Damascus. It set off a chain of events of biblical proportions.

Global watchdogs at the Global Public Policy Institute in Berlin found that Syria launched at least 336 confirmed chemical attacks on its own citizens.[251]

Children especially suffered. The body of a young boy washed ashore and was captured by the media. The image was splashed on newspapers all across the globe and should have been a pivotal moment for Obama; yet sadly, the child's death still did not meet Obama's standard to help.

Week after week, month after month, civilians reportedly continued to be beaten, detained and killed in Syria.

Buildings were obliterated into rubble in Syria.

The treatment of women also descended into hell.

Almost immediately, armed Islamic State security forces forced women and girls to don headscarves and full-length robes called abayas. The rule quickly became if a female failed to wear the attire, they would either be beaten or would not be allowed out in public. This is a far cry from the women's rights that Democrats claim they are fighting every election year.

Human Rights Watch reported that Syria's extremists were severely limiting women's rights[252] yet liberals in America continued to be more obsessed with so-called extremists in the Republican Party. Democrats did little to help women who were actually being oppressed, daily.

With the onset of the Arab Spring and the failures of Obama's foreign policies, practices of child marriage in Syria skyrocketed, sexual assaults and violence against women spiked, and girls no longer had the expectation of attending school nor even walking down a street in safety.[253] Today, girls are told that marriage is their only option and the younger, the better. Becoming a "child bride" for an Islamic State soldier is considered success for a young girl in Syria.

As girls remained under attack, the men there couldn't help much, either because they were under attack themselves. Half of the population of Syria — 12 million people — have been chased from their homes during the 10-year conflict that began in the Spring of 2011, and those citizens now live in refugee camps or temporary housing. However, compared to those who were gassed by their own government at least they were allowed to live.

Just as all of the Arab Spring uprisings that came before Syria, the Obama-era foreign policy had once again been proven a disaster. By the time the Arab Spring ended, governments that had previously been friendly with the United States (and to freedom, for that matter) had been toppled, and far-less-friendly regimes had been installed or taken over by anarchic Islamic terrorists.

That, my friends, cannot be considered "winning the war on terror" as Obama so loved to say.

Conclusion

While it's understandable that the United States can't be the police officer to every hot spot around the globe, it has become clear in hindsight that Democrat leaders in America didn't have many solutions to protect women as they fomented the spread of chaos around the world.

If what they say is true that a picture is worth a thousand words, the now-infamous photo of Obama's cabinet members watching in horror as the violent Arab Spring unfolded is surely worth a million. They so-called "adults in the room" were as shocked as everyone else at how swiftly terror spread on their watch.

Yet you don't have to take a conservative's word for it.

The Arab Spring was a foreign policy disaster so dismal that even Hillary's longtime allies over at *The Daily Beast* admitted that "Clinton's tenure was, in hindsight, a total mess."

HOMEWORK

 ➢ The debate over which political party's foreign policy is superior for women's freedom is an easy one. You need not even take a conservative's word for it. See for yourself the numerous actions that President George W. Bush took to ensure that women were protected and empowered in Afghanistan, at the U.S. State Department's own website which still stands today: https://2001-2009.state.gov/g/wi/rls/10684.htm Once you see how women ought to be protected, it'll make your stomach churn to think of pregnant mothers being kicked in the belly as they struggled to flee Afghanistan, a country now fully under terrorist control thanks to our current President Joe Biden.

REFERENCES:

[229] U.S. State Department Employees
https://www.state.gov/about/

[230] Biden's Announcement on Troops in Afghanistan
https://www.whitehouse.gov/briefing-room/speeches-remarks/2021/07/08/remarks-by-president-biden-on-the-drawdown-of-u-s-forces-in-afghanistan/

[231] Pregnant Woman Kicked by the Taliban, Left Behind by Joe Biden
https://www.dailymail.co.uk/news/article-9943415/Taliban-kicked-pregnant-American-stomach-forced-hide-Kabul-Bidens-withdrawal.html

[232] Rep. Issa: Pregnant Woman Kicked by the Taliban Has Left the Country
https://www.foxnews.com/world/pregnant-california-woman-beaten-taliban-afghanistan-rep-darrell-issa

[233] ISIS-K Attack at Kabul Airport Kills 13 U.S. Troops, 170 Afghans
https://abcnews.go.com/Politics/single-suicide-bomber-killed-us-troops-afghans-isis/story?id=82676604

[234] How the Bush Administration Helped Afghan Women and Girls
https://2001-2009.state.gov/g/wi/rls/10684.htm

[235] President Bush: "Unspeakable Harm" Will Come to Girls Left behind in Afghanistan
https://www.thenationalnews.com/world/us-news/2021/07/14/george-bush-says-afghan-girls-will-suffer-unspeakable-harm-after-us-withdrawal/

[236] Clinton, Obama on Arab Spring
https://www.usnews.com/news/blogs/run-2016/2014/07/23/hard-choices-hillary-clinton-gets-taken-to-the-woodshed-by-obama

[237] Emails Show Hillary Clinton's Muslim Brotherhood Connections May Have Been a Conflict during the Arab Spring
https://www.israeltoday.co.il/read/american-support-for-political-islam-and-chaos-clinton-emails-exposed/

[238] Street Vendor Who Sparked the Arab Spring
https://english.alaraby.co.uk/analysis/mohamed-bouazizi-fire-lit-arab-spring

[239] Egyptian President Hosni Mubarak
https://www.bbc.com/news/world-middle-east-51630142

[240] Lara Logan's Reported Sexual Assault in Cairo's Tahrir Square
https://www.dailymail.co.uk/news/article-8216027/Former-CBS-News-reporter-Lara-Logan-recounts-Cairo-gang-rape-slams-coverage-assault.html

[241] "Circles of Hell" – Amnesty International
https://www.amnestyusa.org/files/mde_120042015.pdf

[242] Center for American Progress – "sexual violence used as" "political tool" during Obama-era Arab Spring
https://www.americanprogress.org/article/rape-and-the-arab-spring/

[243] CNN: Gang Rape, the Dark Side of Egypt's Protests
https://www.cnn.com/2013/07/03/opinion/burleigh-rapes-tahrir-square/index.html

[244]

[245] Yemen after the Arab Spring
https://www.britannica.com/place/Yemen/Transfer-of-power-to-Abd-Rabbuh-Mansur-Hadi

[246] Amnesty International: Yemen: "One of the Worst Places in the World to Be a Woman"
https://www.amnesty.org/en/latest/campaigns/2019/12/yemen-one-of-the-worst-places-in-the-world-to-be-a-woman/

[247] PolitiFact: Fact Check: True: Hillary Clinton's State Department Denied Multiple Security Requests for Benghazi
https://www.politifact.com/factchecks/2016/oct/07/paul-ryan/state-department-under-hillary-clinton-refused-sec/

[248] "Libya Mired in Chaos 10 Years after Arab Spring"
https://www.france24.com/en/live-news/20210210-libya-mired-in-chaos-10-years-after-arab-spring

[249] Women's Rights in Libya after the Arab Spring
https://newafricanmagazine.com/27180/

[250] Libya's Gender Equality Agreement with United Nations Suspended
https://www.africanews.com/2022/03/08/libya-suspends-the-implementation-of-gender-equality-agreement//

[251] NPR: Global Public Policy Institute Study Found Evidence of 336 Chemical Attacks by Syria
https://www.npr.org/2019/02/17/695545252/more-than-300-chemical-attacks-launched-during-syrian-civil-war-study-says

[252] Human Rights Watch: Syria Extremists are Restricting Women's Rights
https://www.hrw.org/news/2014/01/13/syria-extremists-restricting-womens-rights

[253] United Nations: Syria's Decade of Conflict Takes a Massive Toll on Women and Girls
https://www.unfpa.org/news/syrias-decade-conflict-takes-massive-toll-women-and-girls

VOTING RIGHTS: THE TRUTH ABOUT WHO *REALLY* SUPPRESSED WOMEN AND PEOPLE OF COLOR THROUGHOUT HISTORY

In the lead-up to the 2022 midterms and the 2024 presidential elections, Democrat Party leaders are trying to make Americans believe the false narrative that Republicans want to suppress the minority vote and that they similarly don't care about the women's vote.

History proves that nothing could be further from the truth.

Democrats – Not Republicans - Opposed Voting Rights for People of Color

It might surprise most Americans that voting records dating back more than 150 years (to the mid-1800s) prove that Republicans have voted for every civil rights act and voting rights bill for Black Americans and for women.

By sharp contrast, Democrats did the opposite by voting *against* civil liberties for Black Americans and for women.

In fact, history shows that Democrats served as fervent obstructionists to civil rights for both classes of people.

Perhaps this is why liberals of our time want to destroy or rewrite history?

The nasty truth is that Democrats as a party voted against every piece of civil rights legislation in Congress from 1866 to 1966 – a stunning 100-year period. That is a shocking record for today's Democrats who have spun the narrative that history has been against Republicans on the issue.

Far from it.

The proof is in the Congressional voting records and Presidential history records.

As a party, Democrats voted to keep Black Americans in slavery when they opposed the 13[254]th Amendment which officially freed slaves. *Only four Democrats voted for it.*

Republicans also passed the 14th Amendment which granted slaves U.S. citizenship.[255] *Democrats voted against it.*

Contrary to what Stacey Abrams and Democrats today would have you believe, Republicans also passed the 15th Amendment which gave slaves the right to vote.[256] *Not a single one of the 56 Democrats in Congress voted for it.*

Read that again: *Not a single Democrat.*

Republicans also passed all of the civil rights laws of the 1860s — including the Civil Rights Act of 1866[257] and the Reconstruction Act of 1867[258] after the Civil War.

In fact, the Republican Party itself was founded as the "anti-slavery party" in 1854. It was the party that gave us President Abraham Lincoln[259] and ultimately, the famous Emancipation Proclamation which led to the liberation of slaves.

When speaking of history, Democrats often guffaw and suggest that Republicans can only boast of supporting Black Americans way back in the old days. That's not true, either.

Republicans supported African Americans not only in the late 1800s, but in the modern era as well.

In the 1960s, Democrats were the largest single blockade to Black Americans' civil rights.

That's not an accusation, it's the truth.

The public voting record supports it. Any American can go to the Library of Congress to see the voting records dating back through history for themselves.

Long after slavery was over, the Democrat Party continued along their primrose path and continued to deny Black Americans their civil rights. Online mainstream outlets actually refer to this period as the era of "disenfranchisement" when "Democrats worked to exclude blacks" from civil liberties that the rest of society enjoyed.[260]

The Public Broadcasting Service (PBS) of America reported, "The Democrat Party identified itself as the 'white man's party' and demonized the Republican Party as being 'Negro dominated,' even though whites were in control."[261] *Pay close attention, Democrats demonized the party that was aligned with the "Negro."*

As America entered into the 1950s, it was the Democrat Party that was responsible for passing Jim Crow laws and Black Civil Codes which forced Americans to drink from separate water fountains and swim in different swimming pools, according to the historically-black Howard University.[262]

It may be tough for some Democrats and Black Americans to hear, but even beloved Democratic icons such as then-Senator John F. Kennedy voted against the 1957 Civil Rights Act.[263] Tennessee's Democrat Senator Al Gore, father of the Al Gore we know today, also opposed the landmark civil rights act.[264]

With the exception of Democrat President Lyndon B. Johnson — who seemingly had no choice in the wake of the assassination of President John F. Kennedy but to go against his party and pass the 1964 Civil Rights Act and the 1965 Voting Rights Act as American reeled in turmoil — the truth is that nearly all Democrats opposed every law advancing civil rights for blacks during the 20th Century.

Despite this, you rarely hear anyone in the public square speak of Republicans' work on behalf of Black Americans, nor the Democrat obstructionists who fought against them.

As Democrats reportedly "stood in the schoolhouse doors" and "turned fire hoses on African Americans" mid-century another Republican, President Dwight D. Eisenhower, appointed Supreme Court Justice Earl Warren. Warren would end up penning the legendary *Brown v. Board of Education* decision that ended school segregation forever.[265]

Another Republican, Sen. Everett Dirksen from Illinois, the "Land of Lincoln," wrote numerous pieces of legislation including the Civil Rights Act of 1968 which banned discrimination in housing against Black Americans.[266]

An additional Republican, President Richard M. Nixon introduced the "Philadelphia Plan" that was considered the blueprint for affirmative action today.[267]

Lastly, it was Republican President Ronald Reagan in 1984 who signed into law the holiday we now known as Martin Luther King, Jr. Day.[268]

Yet Americans today give little to no thanks to Republicans who led the way.

Republicans of those landmark events likely wouldn't want any hefty accolades; they simply would want the truth told about whom exactly championed those rights and who — unbelievably — fought so hard against them. It's the least we can do to honor these Americans' efforts on behalf of the voiceless Black Americans who have a voice today thanks to the brave Republicans who came before us. It's unfortunate that the Democrat Party now, out of their own shame for their dark past, continue to pervert history.

Women's Right to Vote: A Republican Idea, Blocked by Democrats

The fight for women's civil rights was not much different than the fight for Black civil rights in that it fell mostly along party lines.

In fact, just like the emancipation of slaves and civil rights for Black Americans, Republicans supported a woman's right to vote[269] and you guessed it, Democrats blocked it every step of the way.

Contrary to the narrative being fed to Americans today by the Democrat Party, the feminist establishment, and the mainstream media, Republicans were the greatest support network for women's voting rights — and Democrats were once again an obstacle.

With the passage of women's suffrage having surpassed its 100th anniversary, Democrats must assume because the events were so long ago, Americans forgot or never really knew who stood in the gap for women.

The truth is it was the Republican Party.

One doesn't have to take my word for it. The proof is in the National Archives, the Library of Congress and the voting records of Congress itself.

The record is very clear.

When the 19th Amendment was ratified, nearly 75% of the states that ratified the amendment granting women the right to vote had Republican-controlled legislatures.[270]

To be exact, 26 of the 36 states that granted women the right to vote were Republican-controlled states.

Among the nine (9) states that shamefully voted against a woman's right to vote, eight out of the nine were Democrat-controlled states.

For Democrats, that's not exactly a proud track record on women's rights.

But wait, there's more.

Republican support for a woman's right to vote dates back even further.

The beginning of the women's suffrage movement actually began in 1848 in Seneca Falls, New York[271] among a group of Republican women who would continue to push elected officials over the next two decades.

By 1870, the Massachusetts Republican Party had made so much progress on the involvement of women in politics, it had already seated two women suffragists as delegates: Lucy Stone and Mary Livermore. *The Democrat Party had not.*

Just two years later in 1872, the National Republican Convention passed a resolution stating that women "should have additional rights" and "should be treated with respectful consideration." The Republican Party also sanctioned that women should have additional useful roles in society. *There was no such resolution from the Democrat Party.*

Taking that message to heart, in 1878 a Republican woman named Susan B. Anthony asked a Republican U.S. Senator from California to introduce the 19th Amendment on the floor of the United States Congress. Republican Senator A.A. Sargent obliged, but the measure failed not once, not twice, not three times, but FOUR times in the *Democrat-controlled* U.S. Senate. It was only after Republicans won back control of Congress that the Equal Suffrage Amendment passed in the House, then the U.S. Senate in 1919.

Even more impressive, Republican states took matters into their own hands while Democrats fiddled and tried to swindle women out of their God-given rights to vote.

Impressively, 12 of the Republican-led states that ultimately voted to ratify the 19th Amendment had already granted women "full suffrage" (i.e., the right to vote) in their states even before the 19th Amendment was ratified nationally. This means that women were voting in Republican states in local and state elections even before they could vote in a federal election. *Women weren't allowed to vote yet in Democrat-controlled states.*

Evidence of Republican support of the women's vote dates back even further.

Decades prior to successfully winning the vote on the 19th Amendment, the Republican Party fought hard for the advancement of a woman's right to vote.

In 1892, two women were seated at the National Republican Convention for the first time after Wyoming — the first state to allow women to vote — sent two females as alternate delegates. It was the first time that women had been seated at a Republican National Convention.

At that same Republican National Convention in 1892, the first female speaker also took to the stage and vowed that her organization, the Women's Republican Association of the United States, was ready to fight for women's involvement in national politics. *This was 21 long years before Democrats finally lost their majority status with which they blocked the advancement of the women's right to vote.*

During World War I, women suffragists also protested President Woodrow Wilson — a Democrat — in an attempt to get him to reverse his opposition to a woman's right to vote. *Just like his pals in the Democrat Party, he wouldn't budge.*[272]

Luckily, the women's suffrage movement had another wonderful Republican ally — Frederick Douglass.[273] Born a slave, he came to appreciate the Republican Party for freeing the slaves. Douglass referred to himself by saying, "I am a Republican, a black, dyed in the wool Republican, and I never intend to belong to any other party than the party of freedom and progress." Progress is precisely what he pushed for when he joined the women's suffrage movement, citing "suffrage for all."[274]

Douglass must have known that the fight for the 19th Amendment was really no different than the fight for the 13th Amendment, 14th Amendment, or 15th Amendment — all of the amendments benefitted minorities in society at the time, they were all advocated for by

Republicans, and there were vehemently fought against by Democrats who stood in the way of progress.

Truly, the Republican Party's role in the advancement of the women's right to vote cannot be denied nor underrepresented. There's no excuse for Stacy Abrams, Planned Parenthood, or Nancy Pelosi to *not* be educated on the history of women's politics. Any Democrat Party leader today who tells Americans otherwise is simply lying and betraying the memory of the bold fighters who went before us to advance the voting rights of women, along with the Black Americans who joined us the all-too-familiar fight for the right to vote.

Stacey Abrams & the Democrat Party's Big Lie about Voter Suppression

The important reason for every American to be aware of the origins for both the Black right to vote and the fight for women's suffrage is the dangerous tropes being bandied about today by a Black female who doesn't seem to be aware of her own party's history on either Black or female advancement, or the lack thereof.

To understand "how we got here" to Stacey Abrams' ridiculous, deflective, false narrative that Republicans are the ones who've suppressed Black and female voters throughout history, we must first wind the clock back to the Georgia Governor's race within the 2018 midterm elections.

Liberal Stacey Abrams was the first Black female nominee for Georgia Governor and as it appeared that she was not going to win the governorship, she began to cry foul over what she said was suppression of the Black vote.

Abrams began a not-so-subtle "dog whistle" about Republicans as she claimed that her white opponent, former Secretary of State Brian Kemp, had been one of the key suppressors.

However, there was no proof that the Republican did such a thing.

The only thing Kemp did was to fulfill the duties of his job as Secretary of State, when he purged inactive voters from the voter file — people who hadn't voted in multiple election cycles — often a clear indicator that someone has either moved, or died. This is a standard operating procedure that helps elections officials clean up the voter rolls and helps to prevent voter fraud (people getting their hands on ballots not meant for them).

This was apparently a big crime in Abrams' eyes.

In the eleventh hour of vote-counting as the Abrams camp appeared to be trailing behind, Abrams reportedly had hoped to trigger a runoff by relying upon what appeared to be a flood of last-minute absentee or mail-in ballots.

What happened next helped Abrams greatly, yet set a dangerous precedent for future elections involving mail-in ballots.

As the race between Kemp and Abrams tightened, a federal judge weighed in and tipped the scales in favor of Abrams. The judge ruled that elections officials in Georgia must stop rejecting any absentee ballot which contained a signature that did not match voter's signature on the voter file. (A voter's signature is on file the moment you sign your voter registration card, and the process of matching the signatures is intended to prove that the voter is, indeed, who you claim to be.)

Devastatingly, in the case of Abrams' gubernatorial contest the judge's ruling meant that virtually no absentee ballots could be rejected — even if signatures were wildly inaccurate (meaning scribbles that look vastly different from the signature on file from when you registered to vote).

This was a huge loss for voter integrity in Georgia and mark my words, it will plague America in future elections.

So, why would a judge rule in favor of such a thing?

Well, it turns out the judge in the case favoring Stacey Abrams was none other than an appointee of former President Barack Obama.[275] If anyone should have complained about possible election fraud and interference in the 2018 Georgia Governor's race, it should have been Governor Kemp.

Shortly after the election, Abrams went on to speak at the Democratic National Convention in 2020 where she pushed her narrative that Republicans were trying to rob Black Americans of their votes, despite presenting no evidence for her claim — not even so much as a PowerPoint presentation, y'all.

Today, Abrams runs her own organizations called Fair Fight (a 501c3) and Fair Fight Action (a 501c4)[276] in which she portends (or perhaps pretends?) that Black Democrats, in particular, are being disenfranchised across America. Her claims are again without merit nor evidence, and her assertions are highly offensive.

So, why would Abrams lob such accusations?

Abrams' own website tips her hand as to what her true motives behind the scenes may be.

While her "Fight Fair" website states that its fight is against "Voter suppression, particularly of voters of color," the fine print reveals that the organization also engages "in voter mobilization and education activities and advocate[s] for progressive issues." Even further in the fine print, one can see that Fair Fight Action raises money and funds programs at Democrat Party headquarters in key states and helps "elect" "progressive leaders."

You see, it's not really about protecting the vote for "all," it's about winning elections for Democrats.

Moreover, it's about winning elections for the most radical, progressive Democrats.

If it were about protecting the vote for everyone, Abrams' party would have been in the fight for Black voters and female voters for the last 157 years instead of blocking them at every turn.

Then again, Stacey Abrams is a smart woman (she's raised $100 million to date), so of course she already knows that.

The Truth about Mail-In Ballots

I happened to have served as an Assistant Secretary of State in California, the most populous state in the nation with a whopping 40 million people. In my capacity at the Secretary of State's office, I learned extensively about voter integrity, accuracy of electronic voting machines and the numerous challenges of mail-in absentee ballots. I can tell you as an appointee who was sworn under oath to uphold the Constitution, with my right hand on a Bible, that anyone who has ever served in a Secretary of State's office or Registrar of Voters' office knows the cold, hard truth: the easiest way for bad people to cheat during an election is not through an electronic voting system — it is through *mail-in ballots.*

The reason? The completion (filling out the ballot) and delivery of the ballot (mailing it in or dropping it into a community drop box) happens almost *entirely outside the view* of trained elections officials. It is unlike using a voting machine, where elections officials are nearby and trained to look for problems.

The Heritage Foundation supports this hypothesis through its extensive examination of voter fraud over the years.[277] Through its compilation of more than 1,300 voter fraud cases, the suspicions ring true.[278]

The think tank's Manager of Election Law Reform Initiative and Senior Legal Fellow of the Meese Center for Legal and Judicial Studies, Hans von Spakovsky, asserts that because mail-in ballots are "completed and voted outside the supervision and control of elections officials" and "outside the purview of election observers" it destroys the transparency that is so critical to our democratic process.

A Florida Department of Law Enforcement investigation also found that mail-in ballots were ripe for fraud[279] mostly because no one is watching when the vote is executed. In other words, traditional voting where you have to stand in front of a trained poll worker in a room where everyone is expected to behave is still the safest, most secure way to vote.

Makes sense, doesn't it?

Mind you, this doesn't mean that voters who vote by mail are in on the fraud. To the contrary — honest voters who choose mail-in ballots may be the ones ultimately the most defrauded.

According to The Heritage Foundation, "mail-in ballots are susceptible to being stolen, altered, forged and forced."

Here's my take of how Heritage's four alleged forms of mail-in ballot fraud can happen:

"Stolen" — out of mailboxes of unsuspecting voters, who never receive their ballots; a voter might later go to a polling place on Election Day and complain of not receiving a ballot, only to be told they have already been recorded as voted. If the voter knows enough to press the issue, they might be told (depending upon whom the poll worker is) to cast a "provisional ballot," however, it will be checked only if a dispute or a close election arises at a later time;

"Altered" — a ballot may be altered by nefarious parties who wish to change information on the ballots, such as how a voter actually voted; this can happen after the ballot has been placed back into a mailbox with the voter being none the wiser that their ballot has been marked through or altered along its way to the election office;

"Forged" — a ballot can be sent in by parties casting a ballot by forging the registered voter's signature on the ballot;

"Forced" — a vote can be forced or coerced by parties, such as union leaders, caretakers for the elderly, or others who have a vested interest in ensuring that a vote gets casts for the candidate that the nefarious party prefers that the vote to go to.

While an analysis by *The Washington Post* stated that fraud only happens in 0.0025% of cases, overall error rates with mail-in ballots can be as high as 25%.[280]

On the intentional voter fraud side, the Heritage Foundation found at least two real-world examples in this neck of the woods: Paterson, New Jersey and New York City.

In a heated city election conducted entirely by mail due to the COVID-19 pandemic, multiple cases of fraud were found among mail-in ballots in New Jersey. The findings of an investigation found that allegations included "everything from voters reporting that they never received their absentee ballots (even though they are recorded as having voted) to accusations that one of the campaigns may have submitted fraudulent ballots." Ultimately, a sitting city council member and a city council member-elect were both charged with voter fraud.

In addition to the intentional fraud, inadvertent errors can also happen with mail-in ballots — at a pretty alarming rate. Elections officials in Paterson revealed that in that election alone, one out of every five mail-in ballots were rejected due to signatures not matching or voters not following instructions.

In New York City, the news wasn't any better.

In the city's primary election last June for Mayor, elections officials in the Big Apple also reported a similar rejection rate of mail-in ballots due to signature mismatches and instructions not correctly followed. That means that 25% of voters had their ballots rejected. *(Read that again. One-fourth of New Yorkers' votes didn't count.)*

In other states, Heritage reported that postal delivery in states such as Maryland and Wisconsin faltered as voters reported not receiving their ballots at all, or receiving them past their due date. I'm not suggesting foul play, but postal workers unions are often quite liberal.

I feel compelled to share that I have seen my own real-world example which falls into at least one of the Heritage Foundation categories above — "stolen ballots." It happened in the Colorado recall elections of 2013 in which a small group of us were recalling the top two Democrats in the state legislature over their unconstitutional gun control push.

The legislature had gone overboard in banning ammunition magazines in the wake of the shocking "Batman" shootings at the movie theatre in

Aurora, Colorado, and legislative leaders vowed to come after all guns eventually. Despite the horrific shooting at the hands of one unhinged man, Colorado was still very much a western hunting state and Coloradans appreciate the Second Amendment. And so the recalls began.

The recall elections just so happened to be the first elections in which Colorado would utilize mail-in ballots — a law which was conveniently passed by State Senate Democrats and State House Democrats on a party-line vote right around the time they knew their leaders were up for recall at the ballot box.

Part of the deal was that compulsory mail-in ballots would be sent to all voters — regardless of whether that was their preferred method of voting. That meant ballots would be in mailboxes even if they weren't requested by the voter, similar to how it ended up being done in many states in 2020.

Two weeks before Election Day, our worst campaign nightmare came true: our campaign team watched as young, well-known, liberal activists systematically went from apartment complex to apartment complex in Colorado Springs, fishing discarded ballots out of trash bins located next to banks of mailboxes (at apartment complexes, the mailboxes are often located all in one location onsite). Where those ballots ended up I can only guess, but I suspect the young activists weren't there on a recycling expedition. An educated guess would be that they were taken to a central location and marked for the Democrat candidate in the race before being turned in. (By the way, I'm not suggesting that the Democrat Party put them up to that; these young men could have been operating on behalf of another organization, or on their own volition. All I know is that our campaign workers witnessed ballots being fished out of trash cans, en masse.)

Since that time, voter integrity concerns have spread to other states that have considered all mail-in ballots, and the reason for alarm is rightful. Mail-in ballots are more likely to be fraudulent or even innocently error-prone than in-person voting; yet even knowing the risks, Democrats are proactively advocating for mail-in ballots across America. One has to scratch their head and ask, "Why?"

Eric Holder's Texas Showdown

No one has fought harder than Abrams to push for mail-in ballots other than former Attorney General Eric Holder.

The mainstream media didn't report on it much, if at all, but Holder was busy in Texas this past election cycle attempting to turn the state of Texas into an all-mail-in-ballot state.

Citing COVID-19, Holder argued that Texans were too scared to go to polling places in person due to fear of catching the virus. Now, I don't know if you've been down to Texas much but most of my relatives live there, I spent a great deal of time there as a child and I can share with great certainty that Texans aren't that afraid of COVID and frankly, they're not scared of much else.

However, that hasn't stopped Holder from attempting to turn the all-too-lenient voting rules enacted during the pandemic into permanent voting norms. Like his fellow Democrats, he has clearly channeled his inner Rahm Emanuel, never letting a crisis go to waste and using the crisis to radically change public policy.

In one Texas case filed by Democrat allies, plaintiffs sued to remove "guardrails" that are meant to protect voter integrity. Almost as if on cue (shock, surprise), *all* of the Democrat-allied groups such as Voto Latino, the NAACP and the Texas Alliance for Retired Americans (a liberal group) argued that Texas voting rules during COVID weren't lenient enough and needed to go even further. The group took the unusual step of suing Secretary of State Ruth Hughs to prevent her from rejecting their request.

Can you guess the party of Secretary Hughs? You guessed right, she's a Republican.

Remember, Democrats fought for mail-in ballots in the first place during the COVID-19 pandemic. Now that they were granted, Democrat Party allies claimed in their lawsuit that even more changes needed to be made. For starters, they argued that the stamps required to return a ballot was too great a burden for citizens to bear and that the $1.10 in first class postage amounted to a "poll tax." Clever.

Next they argued for more "leniency" in who can help an elderly person complete their ballot. Leniency in this particular area creates more opportunity for fraud and elder abuse, as nefarious parties could either forge an elderly person's ballot without their cognitive knowledge, or enter into an elder abuse situation where the elder is threatened to turn over their ballot and have another party deliver it to the post office *for* them. The ballot could be changed in transit once it leaves the elderly person's hands. This type of practice is illegal in most states — it is called "ballot harvesting."

Lastly, Eric Holder's Democrat-allied groups in Texas argued for two of the core tenants of their assault on voter integrity: 1) extended amounts of *time* to return mail-in ballots and 2) a waiver of the *signature-matching requirement* that would require elections officials to verify that the ballot was actually signed by the registered voter. **These are real mind-blowers in my view. It pretty much eliminates the two most important security measures for mail-in ballots.**

Mind you, Texas had already bent over backwards to give voters more time to go to polling places. Ultimately, Texas "Election Day" ended up being about 15 days long. In-person voting began on October 18, 2020 and continued through Election Day.

It doesn't take a rocket scientist to use the power of deduction to figure out that requests for days-long, sometimes weeks-long extensions which turn Election Day into "Election Month" have the real potential to disenfranchise voters. The longer the polls are open and the longer period of time that fraudsters have with mail-in ballots, the more opportunities there are for fraud which ultimately hurts honest voters.

It's undoubtedly no coincidence that Texas just so happens to be the state that Democrats have their eye on flipping to blue. Pushing for mail-in ballots which are rife with opportunities for fraud and errors just might help Democrats do that in the near future.

The Real Disenfranchisement of Women & People of Color

Of course, Democrats are always skilled at reframing the debate — just as they did when they gave away free healthcare with Obamacare; any politician who subsequently tried to cancel Obamacare was accused of "taking away our healthcare rights."

Likewise, any Republican who now suggests returning to pre-COVID rules that ensured integrity at the ballot box are voraciously accused of "stripping" voting rights, "destroying our democracy" and "suppressing the vote."

However, as they're busy accusing Republicans of disenfranchising voters, Democrats in true deflection are the ones actually pushing all of the levers that can lead to voter disenfranchisement: mail-in ballots, extended voting periods, waiving of signatures, and so forth.

Sadly, it doesn't seem to bother today's liberal feminists in the Democrat Party. As they've proven in so many other public fights — including free speech, big tech censorship, vaccine mandates, and government lockdowns — Democrats' plan for "voting rights" seems more about winning and ensuring that another Republican never gets elected again.

Conclusion

The next time someone tells you that Republicans want to suppress the votes of women and people of color, remind them of the irrefutable history: Republicans as a party pushed for every Civil Rights Act from 1866 to 1965 and were also the first to support the women's right to vote, while the Democrat Party shamefully blocked both efforts every step of the way.

HOMEWORK
- ➤ Now that you know the history of who supported a woman's right to vote, learn more about our current elections and get involved to maintain election integrity.
- ➤ Watch the movie, "2,000 Mules" about the odd patterns of ballot harvesting that appears to have taken place during the 2020

elections. Using GPS locating data, Catherine Engelbrecht and the True the Vote organization discovered that America's election integrity may be more vulnerable than ever in this film by Dinesh D'Souza and Salem Media Group. Visit them at: TrueTheVote.org

➤ Above all, the most important voting rights issue is your own participation in elections. *Are you registered to vote? When is the last time you voted?* Get engaged. Your vote can make a difference. In my career, I've personally witnessed a Congress member win by just over 400 votes, and I've seen a vicious runoff election be avoided by just 1 person's vote.

  ○ Register to Vote: https://www.usa.gov/register-to-vote This site will help connect you to your state, where you can request a voter registration form and find out your state's voter registration deadlines.

  ○ Find Your Polling Place: https://www.vote.org/polling-place-locator Moved recently? Haven't voted in a while? This site will point you to your state's Secretary of State's office, the entity in charge of elections. Scroll down on the home page for a state-by-state list to click to find your own neighborhood polling place.

REFERENCES:

[254] Library of Congress – 13th Amendment
https://guides.loc.gov/13th-amendment

[255] Library of Congress – 14th Amendment
https://guides.loc.gov/14th-amendment

[256] Library of Congress – 15th Amendment
https://guides.loc.gov/15th-amendment

[257] Civil Rights Act of 1866
https://history.house.gov/Historical-Highlights/1851-1900/The-Civil-Rights-Bill-of-1866/

[258] Reconstruction Act of 1867
https://www.britannica.com/topic/Reconstruction-Acts

[259] Abraham Lincoln
https://www.history.com/topics/us-presidents/abraham-lincoln

[260] Reconstruction Era – "Democrats Worked to Exclude Blacks"
Valelly, Richard M.; The Two Reconstructions: The Struggle for
Black Enfranchisement – University of Chicago Press, 2009, pp. 134-
139 ISBN 9780226845302

[261] Public Broadcasting Service (PBS): Democrats Were the White
Man's Party, and They Accused Republicans of Being "Negro
dominated"
https://www.thirteen.org/wnet/jimcrow/stories_org_democratic.html

[262] Democrats Enacted Racist Black Civil Codes: Howard University
https://library.law.howard.edu/civilrightshistory/blackrights/jimcrow

[263] Even Democrat Sen. John F. Kennedy Voted against the 1957 Civil
Rights Act
https://www.eisenhowerlibrary.gov/research/online_documents/civil_r
ights_act.html

[264] Democrat Sen. Al Gore, Sr. Voted against the 1957 Civil Rights
Act
https://www.encyclopedia.com/social-sciences-and-law/law/law/civil-
rights-act-1957

[265] A Republican Supreme Court Justice Ended School Segregation
Forever – Brown v. Board of Education
https://www.archives.gov/education/lessons/brown-v-board

[266] Democrats Vote against Civil Rights Act of 1968 – Fair Housing
Act
https://www.history.com/topics/black-history/fair-housing-act

[267] Republican President Richard Nixon Signs the Philadelphia Plan
https://www.presidency.ucsb.edu/ws/?pid=2382

[268] President Ronald Reagan Signs into Law Martin Luther King, Jr.
Day
https://www.politico.com/story/2017/11/02/reagan-establishes-
national-holiday-for-mlk-nov-2-1983-244328

[269] National Federation of Republican Women – Women's Suffrage
https://www.nfrw.org/women-suffrage

[270] Ratification Map of the 19th Amendment
https://www.nfrw.org/women-19thamendment

[271] The Library of Congress – 1,935 Artifacts from the Women's Suffrage Movement
https://www.loc.gov/collections/national-american-woman-suffrage-association/about-this-collection/

[272] The National Archives – Women's Suffrage Refused by Democrat President Woodrow Wilson
https://www.archives.gov/education/lessons/woman-suffrage

[273] Frederick Douglass, "Black, Dyed-in-the-Wool Republican" Helped Women's Suffrage Movement
https://www.brainyquote.com/quotes/frederick_douglass_201568

[274] The National Archives – Women's Suffrage Supported by Republican Frederick Douglass
https://www.archives.gov/education/lessons/woman-suffrage

[275] Judge in Stacey Abrams Case: An Appointee of President Barack Obama
https://www.pressreader.com/usa/sun-sentinel-broward-edition/20181024/281685435830588

[276] Stacy Abrams' Fair Fight Organizations
https://fairfight.com/about-fair-fight/

[277] Heritage Foundation: Fraud in Absentee and Mail-In Ballots
https://www.heritage.org/election-integrity/report/four-stolen-elections-the-vulnerabilities-absentee-and-mail-ballots

[278] Heritage Foundation: Voter Fraud Database of 1,300+ Examples
https://www.heritage.org/voterfraud

[279] "Voter Fraud Issues: A Florida Department of Law Enforcement Report And Observations," Florida Department of Law Enforcement (Jan. 5, 1998), p. 2, http://www.ejfi.org/Voting/Voting-9.htm

[280] Heritage Foundation on the Likelihood of Fraud, Error with Mail-In Ballots
https://www.heritage.org/election-integrity/commentary/the-risks-mail-voting

EPILOGUE

So, you've read the book and you've done your homework in each of the chapters.

This begs the question: what's next?

If you've made it this far the answer clearly is you're going to be the next woman to step up and run for office. Just kidding. Sort of.

The next step for you, dear reader, is to take your level of involvement in saving America to the next level. (Don't worry, it's not as daunting as it sounds.)

What does that look like, exactly?

It could mean running for your local school board or city council to better represent your kids. It might mean running for your state legislature because the direction things are going in your state are driving you bonkers (amirite, California?). It might mean stepping up your involvement in politics, calling your local Republican Party headquarters to volunteer or walk neighborhoods, volunteering for someone's campaign, or even googling "how to be a poll worker" (hello, election integrity! No more undated ballots or hanging chads on your watch.) Perhaps you just want to host a weekly coffee (okay, wine night) or conservative book club (also wine night) at your house to talk politics. These are all great next steps.

Whatever your path, know that you have an army of women behind you — an army that is now empowered with the facts and refuses to be called traitors to their gender or to be told "your husband told you how to vote."

The truth is, women know how exactly how they like to vote and they're not going to let the Democrat Party perpetrate this very real war on women into the next generation.

I started this series with "ladies first" (I have manners, after all). But I intend to examine the *entire* attack on the American family. I began with women because I happen to know that women are the heart of the home, the neck that turns the head, and the mama bears who will literally maul an intruder. I believe that's why Democrats chose to attack us first.

As for our gentleman counterparts? I'll be digging into that topic next as I suspect there is a *War on Men*, too. Oh, and kids? There is most definitely a *War on Kids*, and they desperately need protection from liberal madness.

Meantime, I invite you to keep in touch by visiting TheRealWarOnWomen.com where I'll post content and track stories that continue to prove that Democrats today don't have the best interests of American women at heart.

I'll see you at the next battle.

ABOUT THE AUTHOR

JENNIFER KERNS serves as one of the nation's top conservative communicators, having won more than 50 million votes in America including in tough races across blue states and swing states.

She served as a writer & researcher for the most-watched U.S. Presidential Debate in American history at the time for FOX News, the contents of which were lauded by the feminist movement.

She previously served as the spokeswoman for the California Republican Party; as the spokeswoman & communications director for Prop. 8, defeating Gavin Newsom over the landmark ballot measure on traditional marriage that went all the way to the U.S. Supreme Court. She also served as spokeswoman and communications strategist for the 2013 Colorado recall elections, which successfully protected the Second Amendment.

Kerns served as an appointee of Governor Arnold Schwarzenegger - twice - first as an Assistant Secretary of State to uphold election integrity; then as an Assistant Deputy Insurance Commissioner & Senior Press Secretary for the largest state in America.

She is the host of the nationally-syndicated "All-American Radio with Jennifer Kerns" airing on KABC Radio in Los Angeles, WGMD Radio in Delaware, and nationally on the iHeart Podcast Network.

Her writing has appeared at TheHill, The Daily Caller, Newsmax.com, The Washington Times, The Washington Examiner and USA Today.

The author lives & works in New York City.

For information about the book and daily news about the *real* war on women, visit: **TheRealWarOnWomen.com**

Early Praise for Jennifer's Book

"Our greatest news presenters are supported by researchers behind the scenes. We often don't hear their wisdom directly, but that doesn't mean they don't have a lot to say. Jennifer Kerns spent years working at the top level in the broadcast industry. 'The Real War on Women' is conservative wisdom by someone who has been there, seen it and done it."

> — **Andy Ngo, Author of *The New York Times* Bestseller "Unmasked: Inside Antifa's Radical Plan to Destroy Democracy"**

"Jen is a wealth of knowledge, an encyclopedia of politics, and one of the most knowledgeable young ladies I have ever known. I can ask her virtually anything — on-air, live — and she is ready with the answers and can back it up with polling, stats and figures, and at lightning speed."

> — **Joe Piscopo, Host of "The Joe Piscopo Show" on AM 970 The Answer in New York City and New Jersey**

"Jen is a media maven. She has worked tirelessly with media to flip the 'defund the police' narrative on its head and prove that 'defunding the police' didn't work. She has also helped raised over $100,000 for wounded law enforcement officers. She is a true blue gem."

> — **Lt. Randy Sutton (Ret.), Founder of The Wounded Blue and 33-year Police Officer, Detective and Lieutenant**

"As California goes, so goes the nation. Jennifer has been on the leading edge of the culture wars: she fought the radical feminists at Code Pink and has survived the #CancelCulture mobs. From the California recall of Gray Davis, to defeating Gavin Newsom at the ballot box as Press Secretary for Prop. 8 for traditional marriage, to serving as an appointee of Governor Arnold Schwarzenegger, Jennifer has had a VIP backstage pass to America's most newsworthy events. It is this vantage point that gives her special spidey predictive powers on where America is headed next."

> — **Lou Penrose, Host of "Slater and Lou" on News Radio KOGO 600 in San Diego & the iHeart Podcast Network**

"Jen is a media expert and a fierce defender of the First Amendment. She has helped me fight against draconian government lockdowns, church lockdowns, small business lockdowns and school closures. If you want to be in the media, you want her on your side."

> — **Harmeet K. Dhillon, Constitutional Lawyer and Founder, Center for American Liberty**